MICROSOFT OFFICE MASTERY 2026

THE ULTIMATE 10-IN-1 GUIDE FOR MASTERING WORD, EXCEL, POWERPOINT, ACCESS, OUTLOOK, DESIGNER, ONENOTE, ONEDRIVE, TEAMS AND TO DO FOR BEGINNERS TO ADVANCED USERS

TABLE OF CONTENTS

EXCEL MASTERY 2026

FROM BEGINNER TO EXPERT

THE COMPLETE GUIDE TO FORMULAS, FUNCTIONS, AND REAL-WORLD APPLICATIONS

CHAPTER 1:
GETTING STARTED WITH EXCEL

I.   INSTALLING AND LAUNCHING EXCEL

Excel is one of the most widely used tools in the Microsoft Office suite, and setting it up is the first step toward unlocking its powerful features. Whether you're new to Excel or setting it up on a new device, follow this guide to ensure a smooth installation and launch process.

1.   INSTALLING EXCEL

i.   Through Microsoft 365 Subscription:

If you have a Microsoft 365 subscription, Excel comes as part of the suite. To install:

1. Log in to your Microsoft account at www.office.com.
2. Navigate to **"Install Office"** and select the suite appropriate for your device.
3. Download the installer and follow the on-screen instructions.
4. During installation, ensure you have a stable internet connection.

ii.   Through a Standalone License:

If you have purchased Excel as a standalone product:

1. Enter the product key at www.office.com/setup.
2. Follow the instructions to download and install Excel.

2.   LAUNCHING EXCEL

Once installed, launching Excel is simple and varies slightly depending on your device.

i.   On Windows:

1. Click the **Start Menu** and type "Excel" into the search bar.
2. Select the Excel application from the results to open it.

ii.   On macOS:

1. Open the **Applications** folder and locate Microsoft Excel.
2. Double-click the Excel icon to launch the application.

3.   FIRST-TIME SETUP

When you launch Excel for the first time, you may encounter the following setup steps:

1. **Sign In:** Enter your Microsoft account credentials to activate the product.
2. **Choose Your Theme:** Select your preferred color theme for the Excel interface (default, dark, or colorful).

3. **Explore Tutorials:** Excel may offer a quick walkthrough of its features. This can be skipped or explored depending on your familiarity with the tool.

4. QUICK TIPS FOR A SMOOTH START

- **Pin Excel to Your Taskbar:** Right-click the Excel icon after launching it and select **"Pin to Taskbar"** for quick access.
- **Ensure Updates:** Regularly update Excel via the Microsoft 365 app or your device's app store to access the latest features and security enhancements.

Once installed, you're ready to dive into Excel's interface and start creating your first workbook.

II. EXPLORING THE EXCEL INTERFACE: WORKSHEETS, RIBBON, AND WORKBOOKS

When you launch Excel, the Excel Start Screen will be the first thing you see.

To begin working in Excel, locate and click "Blank Workbook" on the Start Screen. This action will take you to the main Excel interface, where you can start creating or editing your data.

WHAT IS A WORKBOOK?

A workbook is the file format used in Microsoft Excel, consisting of one or more worksheets (commonly called spreadsheets). Each workbook is assigned a default name, such as Sheet1, Sheet2, or Sheet3, depending on the number of new worksheets added.

Chapter 1 - Figure 1 illustrates a blank workbook as it appears upon opening Excel. Take a moment to familiarize yourself with the layout and tools. Note that the appearance of your screen may vary slightly depending on the version of Excel you are using.

1. KEY COMPONENTS OF THE EXCEL INTERFACE

When you open Excel, you are greeted by its default layout. Each element serves a unique purpose to help you interact with and manage data seamlessly.

i. The Ribbon

The ribbon is located at the top of the Excel window and organizes tools into tabs and groups.

TABS:

- **Home**: Includes basic formatting tools (font, alignment, number formatting) and editing options.
- **Insert**: Lets you add charts, tables, pictures, and more.
- **Page Layout**: Adjust margins, orientation, and printing settings.
- **Formulas**: Access functions, formula auditing tools, and calculation settings.
- **Data**: Tools for sorting, filtering, and importing data.
- **Review**: Includes spell check, comments, and accessibility tools.
- **View**: Adjust worksheet views, freeze panes, and show or hide gridlines.
- **Automate**: Allows you to record and run automations using TypeScript-based scripts.
- **Developer**: Access to advanced features like VBA macros, ActiveX and Form controls, and XML

commands. Some advanced Developer features in Excel for Mac may differ slightly from the Windows version.

- **Help**: Provides quick access to the Help Task Pane and allows you to contact Microsoft support, send feedback, and view training videos.

If you're using Microsoft 365, you'll see a Copilot button on the right side of the Home tab. Copilot is Microsoft's AI tool that can help explain formulas, summarize data, suggest charts, and perform other tasks.

GROUPS:

Each tab is divided into logical groups. For example, in the **Home** tab, you'll find groups like Clipboard, Font, Alignment, and Number.

ii. **Worksheets**

- **Worksheet**: Each Excel file (aka workbook) consists of individual worksheets, visible as tabs at the bottom of the screen. By default, Excel starts with one worksheet, but you can add or delete them as needed.

iii. **Rows, Columns, and Cells**

- **Rows**: Numbered sequentially along the left side (1, 2, 3…).
- **Columns**: Lettered alphabetically across the top (A, B, C…).
- **Cells**: The intersection of a row and a column (e.g., A1, B2) is called a cell, where data is entered.

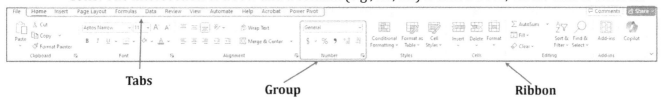

Tabs   Group   Ribbon

Figure 1.   Excel Interface New.png

iv. **Formula Bar**

- Located above the worksheet grid, the formula bar shows the content or formula of the selected cell. You use it to enter or edit data and formulas.

v. **Name Box**

- Found to the left of the formula bar, the name box displays the address of the currently selected cell (e.g., A1).
- You can also use it to navigate to specific cells or ranges.

vi. **Status Bar**

- Found at the bottom of the Excel window, it provides quick information about selected data, such as averages, sums, and counts.
- You can customize the status bar to show useful tools like Zoom Slider and View Options.

vii. **Quick Access Toolbar**

- Located above or below the ribbon, this toolbar provides shortcuts for frequently used commands like Save, Undo, and Redo. You can customize it to include other commands you use often.

viii. **Sheet Tabs and Navigation Buttons**

- The bottom left of the interface shows the sheet tabs in a workbook.
- Navigation buttons allow you to scroll through sheets when you have more tabs than can be displayed.

ix. View Options

- Located in the bottom-right corner, these options let you toggle between Normal, Page Layout, and Page Break Preview views.
- Use the Zoom Slider to adjust the magnification of the worksheet.

2. HOW TO NAVIGATE THE EXCEL INTERFACE

i. Showing the Ribbon in Excel

If the ribbon has vanished from your Excel interface, there's no need to worry. You can easily restore it using the methods below:

- Pressing **Ctrl + F1** to toggle the ribbon on or off.
- Double-clicking on any ribbon tab to expand it.
- Right-clicking any ribbon tab and deselecting **Collapse the Ribbon** (Excel 2019 - 2013) or **Minimize the Ribbon** (Excel 2010 and 2007).
- Clicking any tab temporarily to display the ribbon. In Excel 2016 and 2019, click the small **pin icon** in the lower-right corner to keep the ribbon always visible.

ii. Hiding the Ribbon in Excel

If the ribbon takes up too much space on your screen, especially on smaller laptops, you can collapse it to show only the tab names or hide it entirely.

1. Collapse the Ribbon:

- Press **Ctrl + F1**, the quickest way to hide the ribbon.
- Double-click an active tab to collapse the ribbon.
- Click the **up arrow** in the ribbon's lower-right corner.

2. Full Ribbon Disappearance:

If the entire ribbon vanishes, Excel might have switched to full-screen mode. Restore it by:

- Clicking the ▪▪▪ to temporarily display the ribbon, then clicking **Ribbon Display Options** button in the top-right corner of the Excel window.
- Selecting **Always show Ribbon** to bring back the ribbon permanently.

iii. Common Ribbon Issues and Fixes

1. Tabs Appear, but Commands Have Disappeared:

Press **Ctrl + F1** or double-click any ribbon tab to re-display commands.

2. Contextual Tabs Missing:

If object-specific tabs (e.g., for charts, images, or PivotTables) are not visible, click the object to bring the tabs back into focus.

3. Add-ins Tab Missing:

If an add-in tab (e.g., for an Excel extension) disappears, Excel might have disabled the add-in.

- Navigate to **File > Excel Options > Add-ins > Disabled Items > Go**.
- Select the add-in and click **Enable** to restore it.

iv.   **Customizing the Ribbon in Excel**

Personalizing the ribbon can make your workflow more efficient by putting frequently used commands at your fingertips.

1.   **Access the Customize Ribbon Window**:

Right-click the ribbon and choose Customize the Ribbon from the context menu. In the Customize Ribbon window, you can create custom tabs and groups, add or remove commands, show, hide, or rename tabs and rearrange tabs and groups.

2.   **Enabling Hidden Tabs**:

Some tabs, like the **Developer Tab**, are not displayed by default. To enable it:

- Right-click the ribbon and choose **Customize the Ribbon**.
- Under **Main Tabs**, check the **Developer** option and click **OK**.

Similarly, activate other hidden tabs like the **Draw Tab** using the same process.

Figure 2.   ***Enable Hidden Tabs.jpg***

v.   **Accessing Hidden Tools in Groups**

Excel organizes its tools and commands into logical groups within each tab of the ribbon. However, not all available tools in a group are immediately visible on the ribbon.

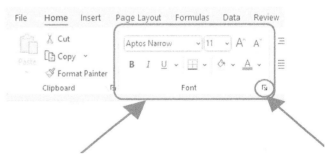

Here's how you can access hidden tools in groups.

1.   **Locate the Group**: Identify the ribbon group (e.g., Font or Alignment on the Home tab).
2.   **Find the Dialog Box Launcher**: Look for the small diagonal arrow in the group's bottom-right corner.

3.   **Open the Dialog Box**: Click the arrow to reveal advanced options and settings.

III.   UNDERSTANDING ROWS, COLUMNS, AND CELLS

Rows, columns, and cells are the fundamental building blocks of any Excel worksheet. Mastering their structure and functionality will allow you to efficiently organize, input, and analyze data.

1.   WHAT ARE ROWS, COLUMNS, AND CELLS?

i.   Rows:

- Rows are horizontal lines of data and are numbered sequentially along the left side of the worksheet (e.g., 1, 2, 3...).
- A worksheet in Excel can have up to 1,048,576 rows.

ii.   Columns:

- Columns are vertical lines of data and are labeled alphabetically across the top of the worksheet (e.g., A, B, C...).
- After column Z, Excel continues labeling columns as AA, AB, AC, and so on.

iii.   Cells:

- A cell is the intersection of a row and a column, forming a single box in the worksheet grid. Each cell is identified by its **cell reference** (e.g., A1 for the cell in column A, row 1).
- Cells are the primary units where you enter data, formulas, and functions.

2.   NAVIGATING ROWS, COLUMNS, AND CELLS

i.   Selecting Rows and Columns:

- To select a row, click on its number on the left side of the worksheet.
- To select a column, click on its letter at the top of the worksheet.

ii.   Moving Between Cells:

- Use the arrow keys on your keyboard to move up, down, left, or right.
- Press **Tab** to move to the next cell on the right, and press **Shift + Tab** to move to the cell on the left.
- Press **Enter** to move down to the next cell in a column, and **Shift + Enter** to move up.

iii.   Selecting Multiple Cells:

- Click and drag your mouse to select a range of cells.
- Use **Shift + Arrow Keys** to expand the selection.
- To select non-adjacent cells, hold **Ctrl** while clicking the cells you want.

3.   USING ROWS, COLUMNS, AND CELLS

i.   Entering Data:

- Click on a cell and start typing to enter data.
- Press **Enter** or click another cell to confirm the entry.

ii. **Adjusting Row Height and Column Width:**

- Hover over the boundary between row numbers or column letters until the cursor changes to a double arrow. Drag to resize.
- Double-click the boundary to auto-adjust to fit the content.
- In the Home tab, go to group Cells and select **Format**. From there, you can precisely enter the desired width and height of selected cells, or select AutoFit for width and height.

iii. **Inserting and Deleting Rows or Columns:**

- Right-click on a row number or column letter and select **Insert** to add a new row or column.
- Select **Delete** from the same menu to remove rows or columns.

iv. **Merging and Splitting Cells:**

- Use the **Merge & Center** option in the Home tab to combine multiple cells into one.
- To split merged cells, select the merged cell and click **Merge & Center** again to unmerge.

4. TIPS FOR WORKING WITH ROWS, COLUMNS, AND CELLS

i. **Jump to a Specific Cell:**

- Use the **Name Box** (next to the formula bar) to type a cell reference (e.g., E5) and press **Enter** to navigate directly to it.

ii. **Highlight Entire Rows or Columns:**

- Click the row number or column letter to highlight the entire row or column.

iii. **Use Shortcuts for Efficiency:**

- Select an entire row: **Shift + Space.**
- Select an entire column: **Ctrl + Space.**

IV. CREATING AND SAVING YOUR FIRST WORKBOOK

Creating and saving your first workbook is a fundamental step in using Excel. A workbook is the primary file type in Excel, and it consists of one or more worksheets where you can input, calculate, and analyze data. This section will guide you through the process of creating, naming, and saving your first workbook.

1. CREATING A NEW WORKBOOK

i. **From the Start Screen:**

1. Launch Excel. The **Excel Start Screen** will appear.
2. Click **Blank Workbook** to create a new workbook with a single blank worksheet (See Figure 1).

ii. **From Within Excel:**

1. Go to **File > New**.
2. Select **Blank Workbook** or choose a template if you need a pre-designed layout.

2. SAVING YOUR WORKBOOK

Once you've created your workbook, saving it ensures your work isn't lost and allows you to reopen it later.

    i.   **Saving for the First Time:**

    1.   Click **File > Save As**.

    2.   Choose a location to save your workbook:

- **This PC** for local storage.
- **OneDrive** for cloud storage.

    3.   Enter a file name in the **File Name** field.

    4.   Select a file format:

- **Excel Workbook (*.xlsx)**: The default file type.
- **Excel Macro-Enabled Workbook (*.xlsm)**: For workbooks containing macros.
- **CSV (Comma Delimited)**: For simple text-based data files.

    5.   Click **Save**.

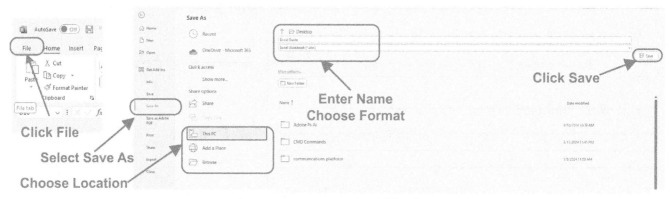

Figure 4.   *Save a Workbook.jpg*

    ii.   **Quick Saving:**

- Click the **Save** icon on the Quick Access Toolbar (floppy disk icon).
- Use the shortcut **Ctrl + S** to quickly save your work.

    iii.   **AutoSave:**

If you're using OneDrive or SharePoint, enable **AutoSave** at the top-left corner of the Excel window. This feature automatically saves changes in real-time.

3.   OPENING SAVED WORKBOOKS

To access a saved workbook:

    1.   Go to **File > Open**.

    2.   Select the location where the workbook is saved (e.g., Recent, This PC, or OneDrive).

    3.   Browse and click on the file to open it.

V.   EXCEL TERMINOLOGY

1. CELLS

A **cell** is the basic building block of an Excel worksheet, where data is entered. Each cell is identified by a unique **cell reference** based on its column and row (e.g., **A1** refers to the cell in column A, row 1).

2. RANGES

A **range** is a selection of two or more cells, identified by the references of the top-left and bottom-right cells separated by a colon (e.g., **A1:B5**). Ranges can span across rows, columns, or both.

3. FORMULAS

Formulas perform calculations or operations in Excel. They always begin with an **equals sign (=)**. A formula can include:

- **Operators**: Arithmetic symbols like +, -, *, and /.
- **Cell References**: To use data from specific cells in the calculation.
- **Functions**: Predefined formulas in Excel.

4. FUNCTIONS

Functions are built-in formulas that simplify complex calculations. Each function has a specific name and syntax.

- **AVERAGE**: Calculates the average of selected numbers.
- **IF**: Performs a logical test and returns one value for TRUE and another for FALSE.
- **VLOOKUP**: Finds values in a table based on a lookup value.
- **CONCATENATE** (or **TEXTJOIN**): Combines text from multiple cells.

5. CHARTS

Charts visually represent data in a worksheet, making it easier to analyze and interpret. Excel offers several types of charts, including:

- **Column Charts**: Display data as vertical bars.
- **Pie Charts**: Show proportions of a whole.
- **Line Charts**: Highlight trends over time.
- **Scatter Plots**: Show relationships between variables.

6. OTHERS

- Dynamic Arrays: Excel formulas that automatically spill results into multiple cells (e.g., FILTER, SORT, UNIQUE). You'll learn these in later chapters.
- Copilot Prompts: Short instructions you type into Excel Copilot to ask it to create formulas, clean data, or summarize information.

Understanding Excel terminology will make navigating the software intuitive and efficient. Whether you're performing calculations, formatting data, or creating visualizations, these concepts are the building blocks for success in Excel.

CHAPTER 2: BASIC EXCEL SKILLS

Excel's true power begins with mastering its basic skills. In this chapter, you'll learn how to enter and format data effectively, manage worksheets, and use essential formulas like SUM, AVERAGE, and COUNT. Additionally, you'll explore time-saving tools like AutoFill and Flash Fill, and gain insights into saving and printing your workbooks. These foundational skills will set you up for success as you dive deeper into Excel's capabilities.

I.   ENTERING AND FORMATTING DATA

1.   ENTERING DATA

Data entry in Excel involves typing or importing information into cells. This can include text, numbers, dates, and formulas.

Entering Text: click on the cell where you want to add text, then type your text and press **Enter** or click another cell to confirm. Excel automatically left-aligns text in cells.

Entering Numbers: numbers can be input directly into a cell. Excel aligns numbers to the right by default. Use the **Number Format** options to format numbers as currency, percentages, or dates.

Entering Dates: type the date in a recognized format (e.g., 12/31/2024). Excel stores dates as serial numbers, allowing for calculations and sorting.

Editing Data: double-click a cell to edit its contents directly or press **F2** to enter edit mode for the active cell.

2.   FORMATTING DATA

Formatting improves the visual presentation of your data, making it easier to interpret.

- **Font and Alignment:** select a cell or range of cells, then use the **Home** tab to change:
  » Font type, size, and color.
  » Bold, italic, or underline text.
  » Align text to the left, center, or right.

- **Cell Borders and Shading:**
  » Add borders by selecting cells and clicking the **Borders** icon in the **Home** tab.
  » Apply shading using the **Fill Color** tool to highlight specific cells.

- **Number Formatting:** use the **Number** group in the Home tab to apply:
  » General: Default format for numbers.
  » Number: Displays numbers with decimals.
  » Currency: Adds a currency symbol (e.g., $).
  » Percentage: Converts numbers into percentages.
  » Date: Formats data into date styles (e.g., MM/DD/YYYY).

- **Wrap Text:** use the **Wrap Text** option in the Home tab to display long text within a single cell without spilling into adjacent cells.

- **Centralize data among cells without merging:** select the cells, then:
  - » Go to **Home > Format > Format Cells** or press **Ctrl + 1**.
  - » In the **Alignment** tab, set **Horizontal** to **Center Across Selection** and click **OK**.
    The header will be centered, and you can still select individual columns (Ctrl + Space).

3. CLEARING AND DELETING DATA

- **Clearing Content:** select the cell or range and press **Delete** to remove its content.
- **Clearing Formatting:** use **Home > Clear > Clear Formats** to remove all applied formatting while keeping the data intact.
- **Deleting Cells:** right-click a cell or range and choose **Delete**, then select how to shift the surrounding cells.

4. TIPS FOR EFFECTIVE DATA ENTRY AND FORMATTING

- **Use Consistent Formatting:** consistent fonts, colors, and alignments make your worksheet easier to read.
- **Apply Cell Styles:** use pre-designed styles in **Home > Styles** for a professional look.
- **Leverage Shortcuts:**
  - » **Ctrl + 1**: Open the Format Cells dialog box.
  - » **Ctrl + Shift + $**: Apply currency format.
  - » **Ctrl + Shift + %**: Apply percentage format.

II. MANAGING WORKSHEETS: ADDING, RENAMING, AND DELETING

Worksheets are individual pages within an Excel workbook where you store and organize your data. Managing worksheets effectively is essential for organizing complex data sets or projects across multiple sheets.

1. ADDING WORKSHEETS

By default, a new workbook starts with one worksheet, but you can add as many as you need.

- **Using the New Sheet Button:** click the **"+" icon** (located next to the sheet tabs at the bottom) to add a new worksheet. The new sheet is named sequentially (e.g., Sheet2, Sheet3).
- **Using the Ribbon:** go to the **Home** tab, navigate to the **Cells** group, and click **Insert > Insert Sheet**.
- **Using Keyboard Shortcuts:** press **Shift + F11** to quickly insert a new worksheet.

Option 1
Click on "+" icon

Option 2: Home tab > Cells group > Insert > Insert Sheet

Option 3: Shift + F11

2.   RENAMING WORKSHEETS

Giving worksheets meaningful names makes your workbook easier to navigate.

- **Renaming via Double-Click:** double-click the sheet tab at the bottom of the Excel window. Type the new name and press **Enter**.
- **Renaming via Right-Click:** right-click the sheet tab you want to rename. Select **Rename** from the menu, type the new name, and press **Enter**.
- **Naming Best Practices:** use descriptive names (e.g., "Sales_Data" or "Expense_Report"). Avoid special characters and keep names short for better readability.

3.   DELETING WORKSHEETS

If you no longer need a worksheet, you can remove it from your workbook.

- **Deleting via Right-Click:** right-click the sheet tab you want to delete. Select **Delete** from the context menu.
- **Deleting via Ribbon:** go to the **Home** tab, navigate to the **Cells** group, and click **Delete > Delete Sheet**.

Precautions: Excel will prompt you to confirm the deletion if the sheet contains data. Once deleted, the action cannot be undone, so double-check before proceeding.

4.   REARRANGING WORKSHEETS

Organizing the order of your worksheets can make navigation more intuitive.

- **Reordering Tabs**: click and drag the sheet tab to a new position in the row of tabs.
- **Grouping Worksheets**: hold **Ctrl** and click on multiple sheet tabs to group them. Actions performed on one sheet (e.g., formatting) while the grouped sheets are selected will apply to all of them.

5.   HIDING AND UNHIDING WORKSHEETS

To declutter your workbook without deleting data, you can hide unnecessary worksheets.

- **Hiding a Worksheet**: right-click the sheet tab and select **Hide**.
- **Unhiding a Worksheet**: right-click any sheet tab and select **Unhide**.
  - » In the dialog box, choose the hidden sheet you want to unhide and click **OK**.

6.   TIPS FOR MANAGING WORKSHEETS

- **Use Tab Colors:** right-click a sheet tab, select **Tab Color**, and choose a color to visually organize your workbook.
- **Duplicate Worksheets:** right-click a sheet tab, select **Move or Copy**, and check **Create a Copy** to duplicate the sheet.
- **Limit Worksheet Clutter:** avoid adding unnecessary sheets and keep your workbook concise for easy navigation.

Managing worksheets effectively ensures your workbook is structured and easy to use, even when handling large datasets or complex projects. In the next section, we'll explore working with basic formulas like SUM, AVERAGE, and COUNT to perform essential calculations.

III.   WORKING WITH BASIC FORMULAS (SUM, AVERAGE, COUNT)

1.   USING THE SUM FUNCTION

The **SUM** function adds values in a range of cells.

- **Syntax**:
  =SUM(number 1, number 2,...)
- **Understand the arguments**:
  » The number1, number2, ...: These are the arguments representing the numbers you want to add. You can input up to 255 arguments.
  » The arguments can be individual numbers, cell references, ranges, or a combination of these.

- **Steps to Use SUM**:
  » Click on the cell where you want the result.
  » Type =SUM(and select the range of cells you want to add, or select the cells you want to add.
  » Press **Enter** to calculate the total.

Quick Tip: Use the **AutoSum** button in the **Home** tab or on the ribbon to quickly sum a selected range. Shortcut for this AutoSum is Alt + =.

2.   USING THE AVERAGE FUNCTION

The **AVERAGE** function calculates the mean of a range of values.

- **Syntax**:
  =AVERAGE(Number 1, Number 2,...)
- **Understand the arguments**:
  » The number1, number2, ...: These are the arguments representing the numbers you want to add. You can input up to 255 arguments.
  » The arguments can be individual numbers, cell references, ranges, or a combination of these.

- **Steps to Use AVERAGE:**
  » Select the cell where you want the result.
  » Type =AVERAGE(and highlight the range of cells or select the cells you want to calculate average of.
  » Press **Enter** to compute.

3.   USING THE COUNT FUNCTION

The **COUNT** function counts the number of numeric entries in a range of cells.

- **Syntax**:
  =COUNT(value 1, [value 2],...)
- **Understand the arguments**:

» The value1, value2, ...: These are the arguments representing the values you want to count. You can input up to 255 arguments.

» The arguments can be individual numbers, cell references, ranges, or a combination of these. COUNT only counts numeric values. Text, empty cells, and logical values (TRUE/FALSE) are ignored.

- **Steps to Use COUNT**:

» Click on the cell where you want the count.

» Type =COUNT(and select the range or select the cells you want to count.

» Press **Enter** to display the total count of numbers.

Important Note: COUNT only works with numbers. Use COUNTA to count all non-empty cells.

IV.   USING AUTOFILL

AutoFill is one of Excel's most efficient tools for quickly replicating data, creating patterns, or extending sequences in your worksheet. By mastering AutoFill, you can save time and minimize manual input when working with large datasets. This section provides a comprehensive guide to leveraging AutoFill for various scenarios.

1.   THE BASICS OF AUTOFILL

The **Fill Handle** is the small square at the bottom-right corner of a selected cell. It enables you to automatically fill adjacent cells with values, formulas, or patterns.

How to Use the Fill Handle:

» Select the cell(s) containing the data or formula you want to fill.

» Hover over the bottom-right corner of the selected cell until the cursor changes to a **plus sign (+)**.

» Click and drag the Fill Handle across rows or columns to fill adjacent cells. Release the mouse to complete the fill.

2.   AUTOFILL METHODS

i.   Filling the Same Data

To repeat the same value across multiple cells:

» Select the cell with the value.

» Drag the Fill Handle across the desired range.

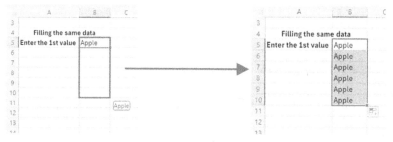

Alternatively, select all the cells (including the original), type the value in the first cell, and press Ctrl + Enter to copy the value into all selected cells.

ii. Filling Sequential Data

For sequential numbers or text patterns:
- » Enter the first few values (e.g., 1, 2).
- » Drag the Fill Handle to extend the sequence.
- » Excel will fill numbers (1, 2, 3, ...) or predefined patterns (Monday, Tuesday, ...).

iii. Filling Non-Adjacent Cells

To fill non-adjacent cells:
- » Select multiple cells while holding **Ctrl**.
- » Enter the value in one cell and press **Ctrl + Enter**. The value will populate all selected cells.

3. ADVANCED AUTOFILL SCENARIOS

i. AutoFill Dates

Excel simplifies date entry with AutoFill. The default format for dates is **MM/DD/YYYY**. Date AutoFill patterns follow your region format, so the day names or month names may differ based on system settings.

- **Sequential Dates**: enter the first date and drag the Fill Handle to fill consecutive dates.
- **Custom Intervals**: enter two consecutive dates (e.g., 01/02/2025 and 02/02/2025), select both, and drag the Fill Handle. Excel will fill based on the interval.
- **Custom Step Values**: enter the start date, drag with the **right mouse button**, and choose **Series** from the menu. Specify the interval (e.g., every 3 days) using the **Step Value**.

ii. Filling Days, Weekdays, and Months

- **Days of the Week**:
  - » Enter the first day (e.g., Monday) and drag to auto-fill consecutive days.
  - » For custom sequences (e.g., Monday, Wednesday), enter the first two days, select them, and drag the Fill Handle.
- **Weekdays Only**:
  - » Drag the Fill Handle with the **right mouse button** and select **Fill Weekdays**.

- **Months and Years**:
  - » For months, enter the first month (e.g., January) and drag the Fill Handle.
  - » For non-sequential months or years, enter the first two values and drag.

iii. AutoFill Numbers and Series

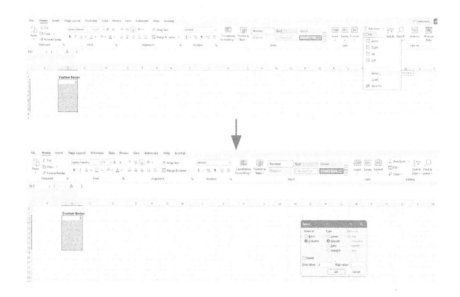

- **Linear Series**: enter the first two numbers (e.g., 2 and 4), select them, and drag. Excel will extend the sequence (e.g., 6, 8, 10).
- **Growth Series**: enter the first two values (e.g., 2 and 4), select them, drag with the **right mouse button**, and choose **Growth Trend**.
- **Custom Series**: go to **Home > Fill > Series**, choose the type (e.g., Linear or Growth), and set the **Step Value**.

iv. AutoFill Times

- **To fill sequential times (e.g., every hour)**: enter the first time and drag the Fill Handle.
- **For non-sequential times**: enter the first two times (e.g., 8:00 AM, 9:30 AM), select them, and drag to fill based on the pattern.

4. CUSTOMIZING AUTOFILL

i. Using Custom Lists

Create custom lists for frequently used patterns:
- » Go to **File > Options > Advanced**.
- » Scroll to **General** and click **Edit Custom Lists**.
- » Enter your list (e.g., Product A, Product B) and click **Add**.

ii. AutoFill Options

After dragging the Fill Handle, click the small **AutoFill Options** icon that appears to:
- » Copy cells (repeat the value).

» Fill series (extend a pattern).

» Fill formatting only (apply styles without data).

5. TIPS FOR EFFICIENT USE

- **Undo Mistakes**: use **Ctrl + Z** if the AutoFill results aren't as expected.
- **Double-Click the Fill Handle**: AutoFill will extend down a column automatically if there's data in adjacent columns.
- **Explore Patterns**: experiment with numbers, text, and dates to discover patterns Excel recognizes.

AutoFill is a versatile and time-saving tool that can simplify data entry and formatting tasks. In the next section, we'll explore Flash Fill, another powerful feature for recognizing and replicating patterns in your data.

V. USING FLASH FILL

Flash Fill is a smart and intuitive tool in Excel that automatically fills data in a column based on patterns it detects from your input. It's especially useful for repetitive tasks like combining, splitting, or reformatting data without needing complex formulas. While it's simpler than AutoFill, mastering Flash Fill can significantly enhance productivity.

Flash Fill works by recognizing patterns in your data and applying them to adjacent rows. Unlike AutoFill, it doesn't require formulas or predefined series—it learns directly from examples you provide.

1. HOW TO USE FLASH FILL

1. Enter the desired result in the first cell of a new column.
2. Start typing the second result in the cell below step 1 above. Excel will display a preview of the Flash Fill results in the remaining rows.
3. Press **Enter** to accept the suggested fill or go to **Data > Flash Fill** in the ribbon.

2. COMMON USE CASES FOR FLASH FILL

i. Combining Data

Example: Merging first and last names into a full name.

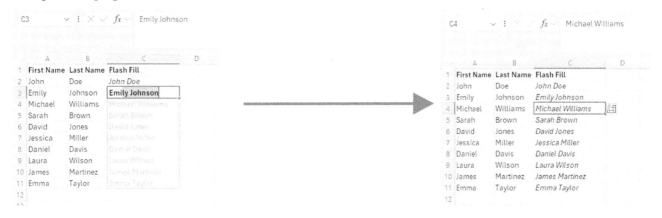

» Input: Column A: John; Column B: Doe.

» Output: Column C: John Doe

» Steps: Enter "John Doe" in C1, type the second full name in C2, and apply Flash Fill.

ii. Splitting Data

Example: Extracting first and last names from a full name.

» Input: Column A: John Doe

» Output: Column B: John; Column C: Doe.

» Steps: Enter "John" in B1, "Doe" in C1, and Flash Fill the rest.

iii. Formatting Data

Example: Adding prefixes or suffixes.

» Input: Column A: 12345

» Output: Column B: ID-12345

» Steps: Enter "ID-12345" in B1, type the second formatted value, and Flash Fill.

iv. Extracting Data

Example: Extracting initials from full names.

» Input: Column A: John Doe

» Output: Column B: J.D.

» Steps: Enter "J.D." in B1, type the second initials, and Flash Fill.

	A	B	C	D
1	First Name	Last Name	Flash Fill	
2	John	Doe	J.D.	
3	Emily	Johnson	E.J.	
4	Michael	Williams	M.W.	
5	Sarah	Brown	S.B.	
6	David	Jones	D.J.	
7	Jessica	Miller	J.M.	
8	Daniel	Davis	D.D.	
9	Laura	Wilson	L.W.	
10	James	Martinez	J.M.	
11	Emma	Taylor	E.T.	
12				

3. LIMITATIONS OF FLASH FILL

While Flash Fill is highly versatile, it has some limitations:

- **Consistency:** Flash Fill relies on clear and consistent patterns. If the input data is inconsistent, results may vary.
- **Manual Updates:** If the input data changes, Flash Fill doesn't update automatically like formulas.
- **Complex Logic:** For advanced tasks, using formulas or VBA might be more effective.

4. TIPS FOR EFFECTIVE USE OF FLASH FILL

- **Provide Clear Examples:** The clearer the pattern, the more accurate the results.
- **Review Output:** Always verify the Flash Fill results to ensure accuracy, especially with large datasets.
- **Enable Flash Fill:** If Flash Fill doesn't work, ensure it's enabled under File > Options > Advanced > Automatic Flash Fill.
- **Trigger Flash Fill Manually:** If Excel doesn't auto-detect the pattern, go to Data > Flash Fill or press Ctrl + E to apply Flash Fill manually.

VI. CONDITIONAL FORMATTING BASICS

Conditional formatting is a powerful feature in Excel that allows you to automatically apply formatting, such as colors, icons, or data bars, to cells based on their values or specific conditions. This tool is ideal for quickly identifying trends, highlighting outliers, or making your data visually intuitive.

Conditional formatting changes the appearance of cells in your worksheet based on the rules you define. For example:

» Highlighting cells greater than a certain value.

» Color-coding data to show trends or comparisons.

» Applying data bars or icons to represent data visually.

1. ACCESSING CONDITIONAL FORMATTING

1. Select the range of cells you want to format.
2. Go to the **Home** tab on the ribbon.
3. In the **Styles** group, click **Conditional Formatting**.
4. Choose a formatting rule from the dropdown menu.

2. COMMON CONDITIONAL FORMATTING OPTIONS

i. Highlight Cell Rules

These rules allow you to highlight cells that meet specific criteria.

- **Greater Than or Less Than:**
  » Example: Highlight all cells greater than 50.
  » Select the range, go to **Conditional Formatting > Highlight Cell Rules > Greater Than**, enter "50," and choose a format.

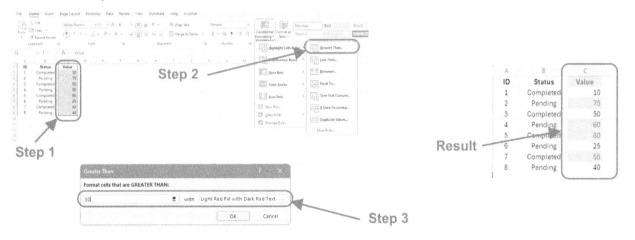

- **Equal To:**
  » Example: Highlight all cells equal to "Pending."
  » Select the range, go to **Conditional Formatting > Highlight Cell Rules > Equal To**, enter "Pending," and choose a format.

- **Between:**
  » Example: Highlight cells with values between 20 and 70.
  » Go to **Highlight Cell Rules > Between**, enter "20" and "70," and select a format.

ii. Top/Bottom Rules

Highlight cells that are at the top or bottom of a range based on value or percentage.

- **Top 10 Items:** Highlight the top 10 values in a dataset.
- **Bottom 10%:** Highlight the bottom 10% of values.

iii.   Data Bars

Add colored bars inside cells to visually represent their values relative to the dataset.

- Go to Conditional Formatting > Data Bars, and select a gradient or solid bar style.

iv.   Color Scales

Apply a range of colors to cells based on their values, creating a heatmap effect.

- Go to Conditional Formatting > Color Scales, and choose a preset.

v.   Icon Sets

Add icons (e.g., arrows, flags, or circles) to represent data trends or categories.

- Go to Conditional Formatting > Icon Sets, and select an icon set.

3.   CREATING CUSTOM RULES

For more flexibility, you can create custom formatting rules:

1. Select the range of cells.
2. Go to **Conditional Formatting > New Rule**.
3. Choose **Use a Formula to Determine Which Cells to Format**.
4. Enter a formula that defines the condition.
5. Click **Format** to select a style (e.g., color, font, or border).

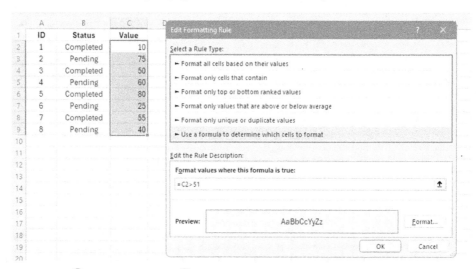

4.   MANAGING CONDITIONAL FORMATTING

You can edit, clear, or prioritize conditional formatting rules:

- **Edit Rules:**

» Go to **Conditional Formatting > Manage Rules**.

» Select a rule and click **Edit Rule** to modify it.

- **Clear Rules**:

    » To remove formatting, select the range and go to **Conditional Formatting > Clear Rules**.

- **Rule Priority**:

    » Rules are applied in the order they appear. Use **Manage Rules** to reorder or delete conflicting rules.

VII.   EXCEL TABLES

Excel tables are an essential feature that helps you organize, analyze, and visualize data more effectively. By converting a range of cells into a table, you unlock powerful tools for managing and presenting your data with ease. This section provides a detailed guide on why to use tables, their benefits, and how to create, manipulate, and filter them.

1.   WHY CREATE TABLES?

Tables in Excel offer several advantages over a standard range of cells:

- **Automatic Formatting**: tables come with built-in styles, making data easier to read.
- **Dynamic Ranges**: tables expand automatically as you add or remove data.
- **Simplified Analysis**: built-in filters and sorting options allow for quick data insights.
- **Structured References**: use column names instead of cell references in formulas for clarity.
- **Improved Integration**: tables work seamlessly with charts, PivotTables, and other Excel features.

2.   CREATING A TABLE

1.   Select the range of data you want to convert into a table (ensure your data has headers).
2.   Go to the **Insert** tab on the ribbon and click **Table**, or press **Ctrl + T**.
3.   In the **Create Table** dialog box:

    » Verify the range of cells.
    » Ensure the **My Table Has Headers** checkbox is selected.

4.   Click **OK**, and Excel will format the selected range as a table.

3.   BENEFITS OF USING TABLES

Dynamic Data Management

- Tables automatically include new rows and columns when you add data, eliminating the need to manually adjust ranges.
- Formulas and formatting applied to a table extend dynamically to new data.

Built-In Sorting and Filtering

- Each column header includes a dropdown menu for sorting and filtering data (covered in detail below).

Total Row for Quick Calculations

- Enable the Total Row by clicking **Table Design > Total Row**. Use dropdown menus in the Total Row to quickly calculate sums, averages, counts, and more.

Enhanced Visual Appeal

- Predefined table styles and banded rows make data more readable and professional-looking.

4.   INSERTING AND REMOVING ROWS/COLUMNS IN A TABLE

i.   Inserting Rows or Columns

Adding a Row:

- Place the cursor in the last cell of the table and press **Tab** to insert a new row.
- Alternatively, right-click a row number and select **Insert > Table Rows Above**.

Adding a Column:

- Right-click a column header and select **Insert > Table Columns to the Left**.

ii.   Deleting Rows or Columns

- Right-click a row or column and select **Delete > Table Rows** or **Table Columns** to remove them.
- Be cautious when deleting data to avoid losing information unintentionally.

5.   USING FORMULAS IN TABLES

Structured References

Excel tables use **structured references**, making formulas easier to write and understand. Instead of cell references (e.g., =A1 - B1), structured references use column names (e.g., =[Sales] - [Expenses]).

	D2	▾ : × ✓ fx ✓	=[@Sales]-[@Expenses]	

	A	B	C	D
1	Product ▾	Sales ▾	Expenses ▾	Sales - Expenses ▾
2	1	100	80	20
3	2	200	40	160
4	3	120	50	70
5	4	160	64	96
6	5	170	73	97
7	6	180	60	120
8	7	300	180	120
9	8	80	40	40
10				

Dynamic Formula Application

When you enter a formula in one cell of a table column, Excel automatically applies it to the entire column.

Using the Total Row

- Activate the Total Row via **Table Design > Total Row**.
- Use dropdown menus in the Total Row to calculate sums, averages, counts, and other functions without writing formulas.

6.   CREATING AND APPLYING TABLE STYLES

Applying Built-In Styles

- Select table and go to the **Table Design** tab.
- Choose a style from the **Table Styles** gallery to format your table instantly.

Customizing Styles

- Click **New Table Style** in the Table Styles gallery to create a custom style.
- Customize formatting for elements like headers, total rows, or banded rows/columns.

Banded Rows and Columns

- Enable **Banded Rows** or **Banded Columns** under the **Table Design** tab to alternate shading, improving readability.

7. CONVERTING A TABLE BACK TO A RANGE

If you no longer need the table features, you can convert it back to a normal range:

- Select the table and go to the **Table Design** tab.
- Click **Convert to Range** and confirm the action. The table will retain its formatting but lose its table-specific features.

VIII. PROTECTING WORKSHEETS AND LOCKING CELLS

1. WHY PROTECT WORKSHEETS AND LOCK CELLS?

- **Prevent Accidental Changes**: Protecting your worksheet ensures that important formulas and data aren't altered unintentionally.
- **Control Data Access**: Locking cells allows you to define which parts of the worksheet users can edit.
- **Enhance Collaboration**: Enable specific permissions for collaborators to edit only designated areas.

2. LOCKING CELLS IN EXCEL

By default, all cells in Excel are locked, but this only takes effect when you protect the worksheet.

i. Steps to Lock Cells

1. Select the cells you want to lock.
2. Right-click and choose **Format Cells**, or press **Ctrl + 1** to open the **Format Cells** dialog box.
3. Navigate to the **Protection** tab.
4. Check the **Locked** option and click **OK**.

ii. Unlocking Specific Cells

If you want to allow edits to certain cells while protecting others:

1. Select the cells you want to remain editable.
2. Open the **Format Cells** dialog box.
3. Uncheck the **Locked** option and click **OK**.

3. PROTECTING A WORKSHEET

Once you've locked the desired cells, you need to protect the worksheet for the locking feature to take effect.

Steps to Protect a Worksheet

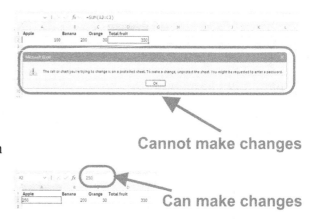

Cannot make changes

Can make changes

1. Go to the **Review** tab on the ribbon.
2. Click **Protect Sheet**.
3. In the **Protect Sheet** dialog box:
   » Enter a password (optional) to prevent unauthorized changes.
   » Select the actions users are allowed to perform (e.g., select unlocked cells, format cells, insert rows).
4. Click **OK** to apply protection.

Password Tips

- Use a strong, memorable password.
- If you forget the password, Excel doesn't provide recovery options, so keep it safe.

4. UNPROTECTING A WORKSHEET

To unprotect a worksheet:

1. Go to the **Review** tab and click **Unprotect Sheet**.
2. Enter the password if required, and the worksheet will be unlocked.

5. ADVANCED PROTECTION OPTIONS

Protecting the Workbook

Protecting the workbook prevents structural changes like adding, deleting, or renaming sheets. Go to **Review > Protect Workbook** and choose the level of protection.

Protecting Specific Ranges

Allow different permissions for specific ranges:

1. Select the range you want to protect.
2. Go to **Review > Allow Users to Edit Ranges**.
3. Add the range, set a password (optional), and define user permissions.

File-Level Protection

Protect the entire workbook with encryption: go to **File > Info > Protect Workbook > Encrypt with Password**.

CHAPTER 3: ESSENTIAL FORMULAS AND FUNCTIONS

I. MATHEMATICAL FUNCTIONS (SUMIF, COUNTIF)

Mathematical functions in Excel allow you to perform calculations and analyze numeric data efficiently. Beyond basic functions like SUM and COUNT, advanced functions like **SUMIF** and **COUNTIF** provide more precise control by applying conditions to your calculations. This section explores these powerful tools and demonstrates how to use them effectively.

1. SUMIF FUNCTION

The **SUMIF** function adds the values in a range that meet a specific condition. It is ideal for scenarios like calculating total sales for a particular region or summing expenses above a certain amount.

Syntax:
=SUMIF(range, criteria, [sum_range])

Understanding the Arguments

- **range**: this is the range of cells to evaluate against the criteria. This defines where the specified condition will be applied.
- **criteria**: this is the condition that cells must meet to be included in the sum. It can be a specific value (e.g., "Apple"), an expression (e.g., ">100"), or a cell reference (e.g., B1). The criteria must be enclosed in quotation marks if it includes symbols or text.
- **[sum_range]** (optional): This is the range containing the actual values to be summed. If omitted, Excel sums the cells in the **range** argument.

Examples of SUMIF Use Cases

- **Sales Tracking**: sum sales amounts for a specific region, a product or a certain period.
- **Expense Reports**: calculate total expenses for a specific category.
- **Gradebook Calculations**: sum scores for students scoring above 90.
- **Inventory Control**: total quantities of items in a specific category, or a certain product, or a certain zone.
- **Employee Attendance**: calculate total hours worked on a specific day.
- **Event Planning**: sum costs for specific event activities.
- **Project Management**: total hours spent on tasks assigned to a team member.
- **Customer Orders**: calculate total order amounts for a specific time period.
- **Web Analytics**: sum website visits for pages meeting specific criteria.

Tips for Using SUMIF

- **Use Wildcards**: use * to match any number of characters or ? to match a single character.
  For example: if you want to sum all the sales from products starting with "Apple", for the criteria, use "Apple*".

- **Relative and Absolute References**: use absolute references ($A$2:$A$20) for fixed ranges when copying formulas.
- **Error Handling**: if the range and sum_range sizes don't match, SUMIF will return an error.

Examples: We will use the dataset below for our examples.

	A	B	C
1	Product	Sales	Expenses
2	A	100	80
3	B	200	110
4	C	120	50
5	A	160	64
6	B	170	73
7	C	180	125
8	A	300	180
9	B	80	40

1. **Summing Sales for product A**:
   » Formula: =SUMIF(A1:A9,"A",B1:B9)
   » Result: 560.

2. **Summing Expenses Above $100**:
   » Formula: =SUMIF(C1:C9,">100") or =SUMIF(C1:C9,">100",C1:C9)
   » Result: 415.

2.   COUNTIF FUNCTION

The **COUNTIF** function counts the number of cells in a range that meet a specific condition. It's useful for counting items like the number of orders exceeding a threshold or the number of employees in a department.

Syntax:
=COUNTIF(range, criteria)

Understanding the Arguments

- **range**: This is the range of cells to evaluate against the criteria. It defines the scope of data to be analyzed.
- **criteria**: This is the condition that determines which cells to count. It can be a specific value (e.g., "Apple"), an expression (e.g., ">100"), or a cell reference (e.g., B1). The criteria must be enclosed in quotation marks if it includes symbols or text.

Examples of COUNTIF Use Cases

- **Sales Tracking**: count the number of transactions for a specific region.
- **Inventory Management**: count items in a specific category.
- **Expense Reports**: count entries for a specific type of expense.
- **Employee Attendance**: count the number of employees who worked on a specific day.
- **Gradebook Analysis**: count students who scored above 90.
- **Project Management**: count tasks assigned to a specific team member.
- **Customer Orders**: count the number of orders exceeding a certain amount.

Tips for Using COUNTIF

- **Use Wildcards for Flexibility**: use * to match any sequence of characters or use ? to match a single character.
- **Combine with Other Functions**: use **COUNTIF** with **SUMIF** to analyze both count and sum data for specific conditions.
- **Avoid Errors with Mismatched Data Types**: ensure the **criteria** matches the data type in the

range (e.g., text criteria for text ranges).

Examples: We will use the dataset below for our examples.

1. **Counting Orders Over $500**:
   » Formula: =COUNTIF(C2:C9, ">500")
   » Result: 5.

2. **Counting Employees in the HR Department**:
   » Formula: =COUNTIF(B2:B9, "HR")
   » Result: 4.

Note: SUMIF and COUNTIF are not case-sensitive. 'apple' and 'Apple' are treated the same.

	A	B	C
1	Order ID	Department	Order Amount ($)
2	101	HR	450
3	102	IT	550
4	103	HR	600
5	104	Finance	300
6	105	IT	700
7	106	HR	800
8	107	Marketing	400
9	108	HR	650

II.   EXTENDING TO SUMIFS AND COUNTIFS

While **SUMIF** and **COUNTIF** handle single conditions, **SUMIFS** and **COUNTIFS** allow you to apply multiple criteria, making them perfect for more complex scenarios.

1.   SUMIFS FUNCTION

The **SUMIFS** function adds values in a range that meet multiple conditions. It's an advanced version of **SUMIF** designed for scenarios involving multiple criteria.

Syntax:
=SUMIFS(sum_range, criteria_range1, criteria1, [criteria_range2, criteria2], …)

Understanding the Arguments

- **sum_range**: The range of cells to sum.
- **criteria_range1**: The range to evaluate for the first condition.
- **criteria1**: The first condition to meet.
- Additional **criteria_range** and **criteria** pairs can be included for multiple conditions.

Examples: We will use the dataset below for our examples.

1. **Summing Sales for Region East in January**:
   » Formula: =SUMIFS(C2:C9, A2:A9, "East", B2:B9, "Jan")
   » Result: 950.

2. **Summing Expenses Greater than 200 for Region East**:
   » Formula: =SUMIFS(D2:D9, A2:A9, "East", D2:D9, ">200")
   » Result: 650.

	A	B	C	D
1	Region	Month	Sales ($)	Expenses ($)
2	East	Jan	500	150
3	East	Feb	300	200
4	West	Jan	400	300
5	East	Mar	600	250
6	West	Feb	700	100
7	North	Jan	800	300
8	East	Jan	450	400
9	South	Mar	300	150

2.   COUNTIFS FUNCTION

The **COUNTIFS** function counts the number of cells that meet multiple conditions. It is an advanced version of **COUNTIF**.

Syntax:
=COUNTIFS(criteria_range1, criteria1, [criteria_range2, criteria2], ...)

Understanding the Arguments

- **criteria_range1**: The range to evaluate for the first condition.
- **criteria1**: The first condition to meet.
- Additional **criteria_range** and **criteria** pairs can be included for multiple conditions.

Examples: We will use the dataset below for our examples.

	A	B	C	D	E
1	Region	Category	Type	Month	Sales ($)
2	East	Electronics	Online	Jan	400
3	West	Clothing	In-Store	Feb	500
4	East	Electronics	In-Store	Jan	600
5	South	Grocery	Online	Mar	700
6	West	Clothing	Online	Jan	300
7	North	Grocery	In-Store	Feb	450
8	East	Electronics	Online	Jan	800
9	South	Grocery	Online	Mar	650
10					

1. **Counting Sales Transactions for a Specific Region and Month**:

Task: Count the number of sales transactions in the East region during January.
- » Formula: =COUNTIFS(A2:A9, "East", D2:D9, "Jan")
- » Result: 3.

2. **Counting Transactions by Category and Type:**

Task: Count the number of Electronics transactions made Online.
- » Formula: =COUNTIFS(B2:B9, "Electronics", C2:C9, "Online")
- » Result: 2.

3.   TIPS FOR USING SUMIFS AND COUNTIFS

Combine Multiple Conditions:

- Use logical operators (=, <, >, <>) in criteria for greater precision.
- Example: =SUMIFS(C2:C10, A2:A10, ">100", B2:B10, "<500") sums values between 100 and 500.

Use Wildcards for Flexible Matching:

- Use * for any number of characters or ? for a single character.
- Example: =COUNTIFS(A2:A10, "East*", B2:B10, "Jan*") counts entries starting with "East" in January.

Anchor Ranges:

- Use absolute references ($) for ranges when copying formulas.

Note: When using SUMIFS or COUNTIFS with dynamic arrays, you can reference spilled ranges using the #

symbol (for example: A2#). Excel automatically adjusts the criteria range size.

By incorporating **SUMIFS** and **COUNTIFS**, you can handle more sophisticated data analysis tasks that require multiple conditions.

III.   LOGICAL FUNCTIONS (IF, AND, OR, IFERROR)

Logical functions in Excel add decision-making capabilities to your formulas. They evaluate conditions and return results based on whether those conditions are true or false. This section introduces key logical functions—**IF**, **AND**, **OR**, and **IFERROR**—and their practical applications.

1.   IF FUNCTION

The **IF** function allows you to perform a logical test and return different values for TRUE and FALSE outcomes. It's one of Excel's most versatile functions, enabling conditional logic in your formulas.

Syntax:
=IF(logical_test, value_if_true, value_if_false)

Understanding the Arguments

- **logical_test**: this is the condition to evaluate. It can involve comparison operators like >, <, =, or combinations with other functions.
- **value_if_true**: this is the result if the condition is TRUE. It can be a number, text, formula, or even another function.
- **value_if_false**: this is the result if the condition is FALSE. It can also be a number, text, formula, or another function.

Examples of Expanded Applications

- **Grading System**: assign letter grades based on numeric scores.
- **Business Discounts**: apply discounts based on purchase amounts.
- **Attendance Tracking**: mark employees as "Late" or "On Time" based on their arrival time.
- **Inventory Status**: highlight stock levels as "Low" or "Sufficient."
- **Expense Categorization**: classify expenses as "Over Budget" or "Within Budget."
- **Project Deadlines**: determine if tasks are overdue.
- **Dynamic Pricing**: adjust prices based on quantity purchased.

Practical Applications

- **Decision Automation**: automate decisions, e.g. determining eligibility for bonuses.
- **Conditional Formatting**: combine **IF** with conditional formatting to highlight specific data points dynamically.
- **Error Handling**: handle potential errors by combining **IF** with **ISERROR** or **IFERROR**.

Tips for Using IF

- **Simplify with Nested IFs**: avoid excessively complex nested formulas. Use newer functions like **IFS** (Excel 2016+) for clarity.
- **Combine with Logical Functions**: use **AND** or **OR** within **IF** to handle multiple conditions.

- **Avoid Hardcoding Values**: reference cells or use named ranges instead of fixed numbers or text for flexibility and reusability.

Examples: We will use the dataset below for our examples.

	A	B	C
1	Student	Score	Attendance (%)
2	John	85	90
3	Emma	65	80
4	David	50	70
5	Mia	40	95
6	Liam	95	88
7	Olivia	72	60
8	Ethan	55	75
9	Sophia	30	85

1. Simple IF Statement

Task: Determine if students passed or failed based on their score. A passing score is 60 or higher.

» Formula: =IF(B2>=60, "Pass", "Fail")

» Result:

	A	B	C	D
1	Student	Score	Attendance (%)	Result
2	John	85	90	Pass
3	Emma	65	80	Pass
4	David	50	70	Fail
5	Mia	40	95	Fail
6	Liam	95	88	Pass
7	Olivia	72	60	Pass
8	Ethan	55	75	Fail
9	Sophia	30	85	Fail

2. Nested IF Statements

Task: Assign a grade based on score: A: 85 or above; B: 70-84; C: 50-69; F: Below 50.

» Formula: =IF(B2>=85, "A", IF(B2>=70, "B", IF(B2>=50, "C", "F")))

» Result:

	A	B	C	D
1	Student	Score	Attendance (%)	Result
2	John	85	90	A
3	Emma	65	80	C
4	David	50	70	C
5	Mia	40	95	F
6	Liam	95	88	A
7	Olivia	72	60	B
8	Ethan	55	75	C
9	Sophia	30	85	F

2.   AND FUNCTION

The **AND** function evaluates multiple conditions and returns TRUE only if all conditions are met. It's often used within an **IF** statement for combined logic.

Syntax:
=AND(logical1, [logical2], ...)

Understanding the Arguments

- **logical1, logical2, ...**: these are the conditions to evaluate. You can include up to 255 logical conditions in a single **AND** function. Each condition must result in either **TRUE** or **FALSE**.

Examples of Expanded Applications

- **Eligibility Check**: determine if a candidate meets multiple criteria for a loan.
- **Discount Validation**: check if a customer qualifies for a discount based on purchase quantity and total amount.
- **Inventory Restocking**: identify items that need restocking based on stock level and sales demand.
- **Project Deadlines**: check if a task is on track by evaluating completion percentage and due date.
- **Employee Attendance**: determine if an employee qualifies for a bonus based on attendance and performance rating.
- **Data Validation**: ensure entered data meets multiple criteria.

Practical Applications

- **Decision-Making**: evaluate complex conditions for business processes like approvals or eligibility.
- **Error Prevention**: validate input to ensure compliance with multiple requirements.
- **Dynamic Reporting**: highlight specific records meeting combined conditions in dashboards.

Tips for Using AND

- **Combine with IF for Decision Trees**: use **AND** inside an **IF** function to handle multiple conditions dynamically.
- **Simplify Nested Formulas**: instead of using multiple nested **IF** statements, use **AND** to simplify logic.
- **Use Cell References**: replace hardcoded values with cell references for flexibility and ease of updates.

Examples: We will use the dataset below for our examples.

	A	B	C	D
1	Employee	Department	Years of Service	Performance Rating
2	John	Sales	5	Excellent
3	Emma	IT	3	Good
4	David	HR	2	Excellent
5	Mia	IT	4	Average
6	Liam	Sales	6	Good
7	Olivia	Marketing	7	Excellent
8	Ethan	IT	1	Poor
9	Sophia	HR	8	Good

1. **Checking Multiple Conditions**:

Task: Check if employees are eligible for promotion based on these conditions: Years of Service >= 5, and Performance Rating is "Excellent."

   »   Formula: =AND(C2>=5, D2="Excellent")

   »   Result:

	A	B	C	D	E
1	Employee	Department	Years of Service	Performance Rating	Eligible for Promotion
2	John	Sales	5	Excellent	TRUE
3	Emma	IT	3	Good	FALSE
4	David	HR	2	Excellent	FALSE
5	Mia	IT	4	Average	FALSE
6	Liam	Sales	6	Good	FALSE
7	Olivia	Marketing	7	Excellent	TRUE
8	Ethan	IT	1	Poor	FALSE
9	Sophia	HR	8	Good	FALSE

2. **Using AND with IF**:

Task: Determine if employees are "Eligible" or "Not Eligible" for promotion based on the same conditions.

   »   Formula: =IF(AND(C2>=5,D2="Excellent"),"Eligible","Not Eligible")

   »   Result:

	A	B	C	D	E
1	Employee	Department	Years of Service	Performance Rating	Eligible for Promotion
2	John	Sales	5	Excellent	Eligible
3	Emma	IT	3	Good	Not Eligible
4	David	HR	2	Excellent	Not Eligible
5	Mia	IT	4	Average	Not Eligible
6	Liam	Sales	6	Good	Not Eligible
7	Olivia	Marketing	7	Excellent	Eligible
8	Ethan	IT	1	Poor	Not Eligible
9	Sophia	HR	8	Good	Not Eligible
10					

3.   OR FUNCTION

The **OR** function evaluates multiple conditions and returns TRUE if at least one condition is met. Like **AND**, it's commonly used with **IF**.

Syntax:
=OR(logical1, [logical2], ...)

Understanding the Arguments

- **logical1, logical2, ...**: these are the conditions to evaluate. You can include up to 255 conditions in a single **OR** function. Each condition must return either **TRUE** or **FALSE**.

Examples: We will use the dataset below for our examples.

	A	B	C	D
1	Student	Math Score	Science Score	Attendance (%)
2	John	85	60	92
3	Emma	45	70	88
4	David	40	35	75
5	Mia	75	80	60
6	Liam	65	50	90
7	Olivia	30	40	95
8	Ethan	90	30	85
9	Sophia	50	60	80

1. OR Function for Award Criteria

Task: Check if students are eligible for an award based on these conditions: Math Score >= 70 or Science Score >= 70.

» Formula: =OR(B2>=70, C2>=70)

» Result:

	A	B	C	D	E
1	Student	Math Score	Science Score	Attendance (%)	Award Eligibility
2	John	85	60	92	TRUE
3	Emma	45	70	88	TRUE
4	David	40	35	75	FALSE
5	Mia	75	80	60	TRUE
6	Liam	65	50	90	FALSE
7	Olivia	30	40	95	FALSE
8	Ethan	90	30	85	TRUE
9	Sophia	50	60	80	FALSE

2. Using OR with IF to Determine Eligibility

Task: Mark students as "Eligible" or "Not Eligible" based on the same criteria.

» Formula: =IF(OR(B2>=70, C2>=70), "Eligible", "Not Eligible")

» Result:

	A	B	C	D	E
1	Student	Math Score	Science Score	Attendance (%)	Award Eligibility
2	John	85	60	92	Eligible
3	Emma	45	70	88	Eligible
4	David	40	35	75	Not Eligible
5	Mia	75	80	60	Eligible
6	Liam	65	50	90	Not Eligible
7	Olivia	30	40	95	Not Eligible
8	Ethan	90	30	85	Eligible
9	Sophia	50	60	80	Not Eligible

4. IFERROR FUNCTION

The **IFERROR** function simplifies error handling by replacing error messages with custom values or text. It ensures your formulas don't break when an error occurs.

Syntax:
=IFERROR(value, value_if_error)

Understanding the Arguments

- **value**: this is the expression or formula to evaluate. This can be any calculation, such as a division, lookup, or other function.
- **value_if_error**: this is the result to return if the evaluated expression results in an error. It can be text (e.g., "Error"), a numeric value (e.g., 0), or another formula.

Common Errors Handled by IFERROR

- **#DIV/0!**: Division by zero.
- **#N/A**: Lookup functions (e.g., VLOOKUP) failing to find a match.
- **#VALUE!**: Invalid data types in formulas.
- **#REF!**: References to invalid or deleted cells.

Examples of Expanded Applications

- **Division by Zero**: handle division errors by replacing the result with a custom message.
- **Improving LOOKUPs**: avoid error messages when a value isn't found in a dataset.
- **Clean-Up Calculations**: replace errors in a dataset with default values.
- **Text Analysis**: handle errors in functions like SEARCH.
- **Dynamic Dashboards**: prevent errors from disrupting charts or summaries.
- **Data Validation**: return user-friendly messages for invalid inputs.

Examples: We will use this dataset for our example.

	A	B	C
1	Campaign	Clicks	Sales
2	Campaign A	500	50
3	Campaign B	300	-
4	Campaign C	-	-
5	Campaign D	250	25
6	Campaign E	1,000	150
7	Campaign F	-	10
8	Campaign G	800	80
9	Campaign H	200	-

Task: Calculate the Sales Conversion (%) using the formula:

Sales Conversion (%) = (Sales ÷ Clicks) × 100.

Since division by zero will cause an error, use the IFERROR function to handle it gracefully.

» Formula: =IFERROR((C2/B2)*100, "N/A")
» Result:

	A	B	C	D
1	Campaign	Clicks	Sales	Sales Conversion (%)
2	Campaign A	500	50	10
3	Campaign B	300	-	0
4	Campaign C	-	-	N/A
5	Campaign D	250	25	10
6	Campaign E	1,000	150	15
7	Campaign F	-	10	N/A
8	Campaign G	800	80	10
9	Campaign H	200	-	0

IV. TEXT FUNCTIONS (CONCAT, TEXTJOIN, LEFT, RIGHT, MID, TRIM)

Text functions in Excel help you combine, extract, and clean text stored in your cells. These tools are useful for names, codes, addresses, ID numbers, and any text-based data you need to organize. This section introduces the essential text functions you'll use in real-world workbooks.

Excel includes both older and newer text functions. You may still encounter older formulas like CONCATENATE, but modern Excel offers improved replacements that are easier to use. All the examples here use the newer versions.

1. COMBINING TEXT WITH CONCAT AND TEXTJOIN

i. CONCAT Function

The CONCAT function joins two or more text strings into one. It works like the older CONCATENATE function, but it's more flexible and recommended for new formulas.

Syntax:
=CONCAT(text1, text2, ...)

Understanding the Arguments

- **text1, text2, ...:** The text, cell references, or numbers you want to combine.

Examples of Use Cases:

- **Combine First and Last Names:**

First Name	Last Name
John	Doe

  » Formula: =CONCAT(A2, " ", B2)
  » Result: "John Doe."

ii. TEXTJOIN Function

TEXTJOIN is one of Excel's most useful text functions. It joins text with a delimiter (such as a space, comma, dash, or line break) and can ignore blank cells.

Syntax:
=TEXTJOIN(delimiter, ignore_empty, text1, text2, ...)

Arguments:

- delimiter: What you want between each piece of text (e.g., ", ", " ", "-")
- ignore_empty: TRUE ignores blank cells; FALSE includes them.
- text1, text2...: The text items to join.

Examples:

- Join names with a space:

> » =TEXTJOIN(" ", TRUE, A2, B2)
> » Result: John Doe

Why TEXTJOIN is better: If you join several fields and some are blank, TEXTJOIN skips them automatically.

2. EXTRACTING TEXT WITH LEFT, RIGHT, AND MID

    i.   **LEFT Function:** LEFT extracts a certain number of characters from the start of a text string.

Syntax:
=LEFT(text, num_chars)

    ii.   **RIGHT Function:** RIGHT extracts characters from the end of a text string.

Syntax:
=RIGHT(text, num_chars)

    iii.   **MID Function:** MID extracts text from the middle of a string, starting from a specific position.

Syntax:
=MID(text, start_num, num_chars)

3. TRIM FUNCTION

TRIM removes extra spaces from text, leaving just single spaces between words. This is especially helpful when importing data from external systems.

Syntax:
=TRIM(text)

Understanding the Arguments

- **text**: The text string or cell reference to clean.

Examples of Use Cases:

- **Clean Up Imported Data**: remove unnecessary spaces from a list of names.
  - » Formula: =TRIM(A1). Result: "John Doe" from " John Doe ."
- **Prepare Text for Analysis**: clean data for accurate counts and comparisons.
  - » Example: Convert " apple " to "apple."

Tips: You can combine with **CLEAN** to remove non-printable characters.

For example: turn "John ÆDoe" to "John Doe" by using formula =TRIM(CLEAN(A1)).

4. MORE TEXT EXTRACTION FUNCTIONS

Excel for Microsoft 365 also includes newer functions that make text extraction easier:

- TEXTBEFORE – extracts text before a specific character
- TEXTAFTER – extracts text after a specific character

- TEXTSPLIT – splits text into columns or rows based on a delimiter

These functions reduce the need for complicated combinations of LEFT, RIGHT, MID, and FIND.

V. DATE AND TIME FUNCTIONS

Excel stores dates and times as numbers behind the scenes, which allows you to sort them, compare them, and perform calculations such as adding days, finding deadlines, or tracking time. This section shows you the essential date and time functions you'll use in everyday spreadsheets.

1. TODAY FUNCTION

The **TODAY** function returns the current date based on your system clock. It's dynamic, meaning it updates automatically each day.

Syntax: =TODAY()

Examples of Use Cases:

- **Track Deadlines**: calculate days remaining until a deadline.
- **Calculate Age**: determine age based on a birthdate.
- **Dynamic Reports**: use TODAY to create daily dashboards or reports that reflect the current date.

Tips: combine with conditional formatting to highlight upcoming deadlines dynamically.

2. NOW FUNCTION

The **NOW** function returns the current date and time based on your system clock. Like **TODAY**, it updates automatically.

Syntax:
=NOW()

Examples of Use Cases:

- **Track Time-Sensitive Data**: record the time a task was completed.
  - » Formula: =NOW()
  - » Captures the exact date and time when entered.

- **Calculate Elapsed Time**: find the difference between two timestamps.
  - » Formula: =NOW() - A1
  - » Returns the elapsed time between the current moment and the timestamp in A1.

3. DATE FUNCTION

The **DATE** function creates a valid date by combining individual year, month, and day values.

Syntax:
=DATE(year, month, day)

Understanding the Arguments

- **year**: The year component of the date.
- **month**: The month component (1 for January, 12 for December).
- **day**: The day component of the date.

4.   EDATE FUNCTION

EDATE shifts a date by a specified number of months, forward or backward. This is helpful for billing cycles, subscription periods, or monthly schedules.

Syntax:
=EDATE(start_date, months)

Examples:

- Add 3 months to a date: =EDATE(A2, 3)
- Move back 1 month: =EDATE(A2, -1)
- If A2 is 1/15/2026:
  - »   =EDATE(A2, 3) → 4/15/2026
  - »   =EDATE(A2, -1) → 12/15/2025

5.   EOMONTH FUNCTION

EOMONTH returns the last day of the month, shifted by a number of months. This is great for financial reports, monthly closing dates, and end-of-month reminders.

Syntax:

=EOMONTH(start_date, months)

Examples: If A2 is 1/10/2026:

- End of this month: =EOMONTH(A2, 0)
  - »   Result: 1/31/2026
- End of next month: =EOMONTH(A2, 1)
  - »   Result: 2/28/2026 (or Feb 29 in a leap year)

Notes:

- Date display is based on your system's regional format (MM/DD/YYYY or DD/MM/YYYY).
- Dates are stored as sequential numbers, so you can add or subtract days easily. Example: =A2 + 7 adds one week.
- If you see a date value as ##### (hash symbols), the column is simply too narrow — widen it to view the date.

VI.   LOOKUP FUNCTIONS (VLOOKUP, XLOOKUP)

Lookup functions help you find information in a table or data range based on a value you're searching for.

These formulas are useful when you need to match product codes, pull in customer details, combine lists, or search through large datasets.

The most flexible lookup function today — XLOOKUP — which replaces most older lookup formulas. However, since many existing spreadsheets still use VLOOKUP, we'll cover both so you can work confidently with both modern and legacy workbooks.

1. VLOOKUP FUNCTION (LEGACY)

The **VLOOKUP** function searches for a value in the first column of a range and returns a value in the same row from another column.

Syntax:
=VLOOKUP(lookup_value, table_array, col_index_num, [range_lookup])

Understanding the Arguments

- **lookup_value**: the value to search for in the first column of the table array. It can be a text string, number, or cell reference.
- **table_array**: the range of cells containing the data. The first column of this range is where the lookup value will be searched.
- **col_index_num**: the column number in the table array from which to return the result.
- **[range_lookup]**: this argument is optional, it specifies whether to find an exact or approximate match. Use TRUE or omit for an approximate match (table must be sorted). Use FALSE for an exact match (most common).

Examples: We will use the dataset below for our example.

	A	B	C	D
1	Product ID	Product Name	Category	Price
2	101	Widget A	Electronics	50
3	102	Widget B	Electronics	75
4	103	Widget C	Home Appliances	100
5	104	Widget D	Home Appliances	125

Task: Find the price of "Widget C" using the vertical dataset.
- » Formula: =VLOOKUP("Widget C", A2:D5, 4, FALSE)
- » Result: 100.

2. XLOOKUP FUNCTION

The **XLOOKUP** function is a more powerful and flexible alternative to **VLOOKUP** and **HLOOKUP**. It can search both vertically and horizontally and doesn't require the lookup column to be the first column.

Syntax:
=XLOOKUP(lookup_value, lookup_array, return_array, [if_not_found], [match_mode], [search_mode])

Understanding the Arguments

- **lookup_value**: this is the value to search for in the lookup array. It can be a text string, number, or cell reference.
- **lookup_array**: the range to search for the lookup value. It can be a single column or row.
- **return_array**: this is the range to return the corresponding value from. It can be in the same row or column as the lookup array.
- **[if_not_found]**: optional; the value to return if no match is found.
- **[match_mode]**: optional; determines the type of match to perform.
  - » 0 (default): Exact match.
  - » -1: Exact match or next smaller item.
  - » 1: Exact match or next larger item.
  - » 2: Wildcard match (* for any characters, ? for a single character).
- **[search_mode]**: optional; specifies the search order.
  - » 1: Search from first to last (default).
  - » -1: Search from last to first.
  - » 2: Binary search (table must be sorted in ascending order).

Examples of Use Cases:

- **Dynamic Data Retrieval**: search for a product name and return its price.
- **Horizontal Lookup**: find sales data for a specific region.
- **Error Handling**: include a custom message when no match is found.
- **Range Lookup**: retrieve data based on approximate matches.

Examples: We will use the same dataset as VLOOKUP for our example.

Task: Find the product category for "Widget D" using the vertical dataset.
  - » Formula: =XLOOKUP("Widget D", B2:B5, C2:C5)
  - » Result: Home Appliances.

3. HLOOKUP FUNCTION

HLOOKUP works like VLOOKUP, but searches across rows instead of down columns. It is rarely needed in modern Excel because XLOOKUP and INDEX/MATCH handle horizontal lookups more easily and reliably.

Syntax:
=HLOOKUP(lookup_value, table_array, row_index_num, [range_lookup])

Understanding the Arguments

- **lookup_value**: the value to search for in the first row of the table array. It can be a text string, number, or cell reference.
- **table_array**: the range of cells containing the data. The first row of this range is where the lookup value will be searched.
- **row_index_num**: the row number in the table array from which to return the result.
- **[range_lookup]**: this argument is optional; it specifies whether to find an exact or approximate match.

4.   COMPARISON OF LOOKUP FUNCTIONS

Feature	VLOOKUP	HLOOKUP	XLOOKUP
Lookup Direction	Vertical	Horizontal	Both
Requires First Column/Row	Yes	Yes	No
Multiple Search Modes	No	No	Yes
Custom Error Message	No	No	Yes

5.   TIPS FOR USING LOOKUP FUNCTIONS

- **Use XLOOKUP When Possible:** it's more versatile and eliminates the limitations of **VLOOKUP** and **HLOOKUP**.
- **Sort Data for Approximate Matches:** ensure the lookup array is sorted in ascending order when using approximate match (TRUE or 1).
- **Error Handling:** for older versions of Excel, pair **VLOOKUP** or **HLOOKUP** with **IFERROR** for cleaner outputs.

VII.   A QUICK PREVIEW OF DYNAMIC ARRAY FUNCTIONS

Excel includes a set of powerful formulas called dynamic array functions. These formulas can return multiple results at once, and Excel automatically "spills" those results into neighboring cells. This means you don't need to copy formulas down or across, Excel generates all the output for you.

1.   WHAT IS A DYNAMIC ARRAY?

When a formula returns more than one value, Excel places the extra results into the cells below or beside the formula. This is called a spill range.
For example, if a formula produces five results, Excel fills five cells automatically.

If you reference a spilled range in another formula, use the # symbol: =SUM(C2#)
This tells Excel to use the entire spilled range created by the formula in C2.

2.   WHY DYNAMIC ARRAYS MATTER

Dynamic array formulas are easier to build, easier to read, easier to update and more flexible than older formulas. They also work beautifully with Tables, XLOOKUP, data cleanup steps, dashboard formulas and pivot table preparation.

You'll start using these dynamic array functions in later chapters, especially when we work with data cleaning and advanced formulas.

CHAPTER 4: WORKING WITH DATA

I. SORTING AND FILTERING DATA

Sorting and filtering data in Excel are essential tools for organizing and analyzing large datasets. They help you quickly locate information, rank values, and focus on specific subsets of data.

1. SORTING DATA

Sorting allows you to arrange data in a specific order, either ascending or descending, based on one or more columns.

i. Types of Sorting:

- **Single-Column Sorting**: sort a single column in ascending or descending order.
- **Multi-Level Sorting**: sort by one column and then by another for hierarchical organization.

ii. Steps to Sort Data:

Sort a Single Column:

1. Select the column to sort.
2. Go to the **Data** tab and click **Sort A to Z** (ascending) or **Sort Z to A** (descending).

Sort by Multiple Columns:

3. Select the data range (including headers).
4. Click **Sort** under the **Data** tab.
5. In the **Sort** dialog box: choose the first column to sort by, and add additional levels to sort by secondary criteria.

	A	B	C
1	**Employee Name**	**Department**	**Years of Service**
2	John Smith	IT	5
3	Emma Johnson	HR	3
4	David Brown	IT	2
5	Mia Davis	Sales	4
6	Liam Wilson	IT	5
7	Olivia Miller	HR	6

Example:

» **Task:** sort above data by department, then by years of service.

» **Steps:**

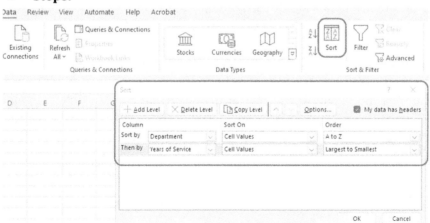

» **Result:**

	A	B	C
1	Employee Name	Department	Years of Service
2	Olivia Miller	HR	6
3	Emma Johnson	HR	3
4	John Smith	IT	5
5	Liam Wilson	IT	5
6	David Brown	IT	2
7	Mia Davis	Sales	4

2. FILTERING DATA

Filtering helps you display only the rows that meet specific criteria while hiding the rest. It's a powerful tool for focusing on relevant data in large datasets.

i. Types of Filters:

- **Text Filters**: filter text-based columns by specific values, partial matches, or custom conditions.
- **Number Filters**: filter numeric data using conditions like greater than, less than, or between.
- **Date Filters**: filter date-based columns by time periods, such as today, last month, or custom ranges.

ii. Steps to Apply Filters:

1. Select the data range or place the cursor in the dataset.
2. Go to the **Data** tab and click **Filter**.
3. Dropdown arrows appear in the header row.
4. Use the dropdown menu to apply filters:
   » For text columns, choose specific values or use options like **Contains** or **Does Not Contain**.
   » For numeric columns, use options like **Greater Than** or **Less Than**.
   » For date columns, select ranges like **Last Week** or **Next Month**.

3. CUSTOM SORT AND FILTER OPTIONS

- **Custom Lists for Sorting**: define a custom order (e.g., sort days as Monday, Tuesday, Wednesday).
  » Go to **File > Options > Advanced > General > Edit Custom Lists**.
- **Advanced Filter**: use complex criteria for filtering.
  » Go to **Data > Advanced** and define a criteria range.

II. DATA VALIDATION: DROPDOWN LISTS AND RULES

1. WHAT IS DATA VALIDATION?

Data validation is a feature that restricts the type, range, or format of data that can be entered into cells. It can be used to define specific criteria for valid inputs, create dropdown menus for selecting predefined options or display warnings or messages when invalid data is entered.

2. CREATING DROPDOWN LISTS

Dropdown lists simplify data entry by allowing users to select from a predefined set of values.

i. Steps to Create a Dropdown List

1. Prepare the List:
- » Enter the list of valid values in a separate range (e.g., A2:A8).

2. Apply Data Validation:
- » Select the cell or range where the dropdown will appear.
- » Go to the **Data** tab and click **Data Validation**.
- » In the **Data Validation** dialog box: set **Allow** to **List**.
- » Set the **Source** to the range containing your list (A2:A8).

3. Optional Enhancements:
- » **Error Alert**: Display a warning if invalid data is entered.
- » **Input Message**: Add a tooltip to guide users.

ii. Practical Use Cases:

- **Order Forms**: Allow users to select product names from a dropdown.
- **Project Management**: Create status dropdowns with options like "In Progress," "Completed," and "Pending."

3. DEFINING VALIDATION RULES

Validation rules restrict data based on numeric, text, date, or custom criteria.

Common Validation Rules:

1. Whole Numbers: restrict inputs to integers within a range.
- » Set **Allow** to **Whole Number** and specify the **Minimum** and **Maximum** values.

2. Decimal Numbers: allow decimal values within a specific range.

3. Dates: restrict inputs to specific date ranges.
- » Set **Allow** to **Date** and define the start and end dates.

4. **Text Length**: limit the number of characters.
5. **Custom Formulas**: use formulas for complex rules.

4. HANDLING INVALID DATA

When invalid data is entered, Excel can display:

- **Stop Message**: Prevents entry and shows an error message.
- **Warning Message**: Warns the user but allows invalid entry.
- **Information Message**: Notifies the user but permits the entry.

Steps to Configure Error Alerts:

1. In the **Data Validation** dialog box, go to the **Error Alert** tab.
2. Choose the style (Stop, Warning, or Information).
3. Enter a custom title and message for the alert.

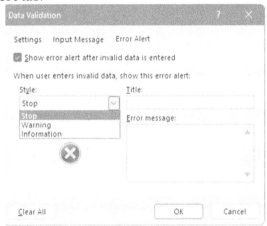

5. EDITING AND REMOVING VALIDATION

Edit Validation Rules:

» Select the cell or range with validation.
» Go to **Data > Data Validation** and modify the criteria.

Remove Validation:

» Select the cells.
» Open the **Data Validation** dialog box and click **Clear All**.

6. USING LAMBDA IN DATA VALIDATION

i. Introducing the LAMBDA Function

The LAMBDA function lets you create your own custom functions in Excel. A LAMBDA function takes inputs, performs a calculation, and returns a result. Once created, you can reuse it throughout your workbook just by calling its name, which makes your formulas cleaner and easier to maintain.

Syntax:
=LAMBDA(parameter1, parameter2, ..., calculation)

- Parameters are placeholder names you assign (like x, y, range).
- Calculation is the formula Excel should run using those parameters.

You can store a LAMBDA function in the Name Manager so it behaves like a normal Excel function.

Key features:

- Create reusable custom functions without VBA.
- Simplify long or repeated formulas.
- Combine with newer functions like IF, FILTER or REGEXTEST (see page .

- Make data validation and cleaning rules more powerful.
- Share logic across multiple sheets consistently.

LAMBDA is an advanced feature, but once you learn it, it lets you build your own toolkit of custom Excel functions tailored to your work.

ii.   Using LAMBDA in Data Validation

Example: you need to send a template to HR department to fill in all employees' names. You'll create a named LAMBDA function called LettersOnly, then use it in Data Validation so a column only accepts A–Z letters (no numbers or symbols).

Create the LAMBDA function

1.   Go to the Formulas tab. Click Name Manager (or Define Name), then click New….

2.   In Name, type: LettersOnly.

3.   In Refers to, type this formula: =LAMBDA(x, REGEXTEST(x, "^[A-Za-z]+$"))

4.   Select the range where names go, for example: A2:A100 (start at the first data row).

5.   Go to Data → Data Validation. On the Setting tab, set Allow to Custom, then set Formula to =IFERROR(LettersOnly(A2)=TRUE, FALSE).

6.   On the Error Alert tab: select "Show error alert after invalid data is entered", select Style as Stop and input Error Message. Then click OK.

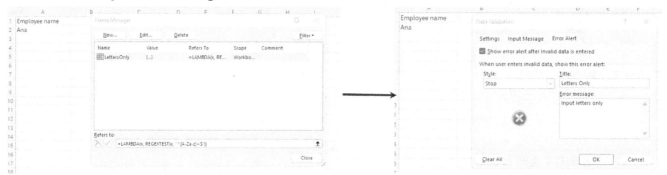

Result:

When users type in characters that are not letters, it will trigger the error message.

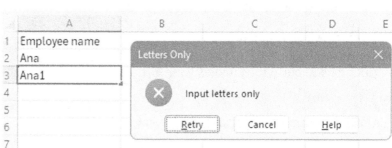

7.   PRACTICAL TIPS FOR DATA VALIDATION

- **Dynamic Dropdown Lists**:
  use a named range or **OFFSET**
  formula to create dynamic lists that update automatically when new items are added.

- **Combining with Conditional Formatting**: highlight invalid entries by applying conditional formatting to cells that don't meet the validation rules.

- **Use Custom Messages for Clarity**: guide users by adding input messages that explain the criteria.

III.   CLEANING DATA USING FIND & REPLACE, AND REMOVE DUPLICATES

1. CLEANING DATA WITH FIND & REPLACE

The **Find & Replace** tool allows you to locate specific values in your dataset and replace them with new values. It's versatile and can handle a wide range of data-cleaning tasks.

i. Steps to Use Find & Replace:

1. **Access the Tool**:
   - » Go to **Home > Find & Select > Replace** or press Ctrl + H.

2. **Find Specific Values**:
   - » In the **Find what** box, enter the value to search for.
   - » In the **Replace with** box, enter the replacement value.

3. **Replace Options**:
   - » Click **Replace All** to update all instances in the worksheet.
   - » Click **Replace** to update one instance at a time.

ii. Common Use Cases:

- **Standardizing Text**: replace inconsistent text entries (e.g., "NYC" with "New York").
- **Correcting Errors**: fix typos or formatting errors in large datasets (e.g., find "janury", replace with "January").
- **Cleaning Special Characters**: remove unwanted characters like underscores (_) or hashtags (#).
- **Updating Data**: replace outdated information with current data.

2. CLEANING DATA WITH REMOVE DUPLICATES

Duplicate values can skew your analysis and result in inaccurate insights. The **Remove Duplicates** tool eliminates these redundancies efficiently.

i. Steps to Remove Duplicates:

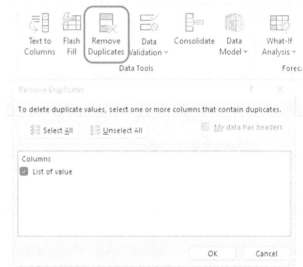

1. **Select the Data**:
   - » Highlight the range of data to clean.

2. **Access the Tool**:
   - » Go to **Data > Remove Duplicates**.

3. **Configure Columns**:
   - » In the dialog box, select the columns to check for duplicates.
   - » Deselect columns that should not affect the duplication criteria.

4. **Remove Duplicates**:
   - » Click **OK** to remove duplicates. Excel will display a summary of duplicates removed and unique values retained.

ii. Common Use Cases:

- **Cleaning Customer Data**: eliminate duplicate customer entries based on names, emails, or phone numbers. Example: Remove duplicates from a "Customer ID" column.

- **Inventory Management**: identify unique products by SKU or item name. Example: Remove duplicates from a "Product SKU" column.
- **Survey Responses**: ensure only unique responses are retained for analysis. Example: Remove duplicates from an "Email" column in a survey dataset.

3.   COMBINING FIND & REPLACE WITH REMOVE DUPLICATES

These tools can be used together for comprehensive data cleaning:

- **Standardize Data**: use **Find & Replace** to correct inconsistencies, then remove duplicates to ensure unique entries.
- **Fix Formatting**: replace special characters or extra spaces, then remove duplicate values caused by minor variations.

IV.   SPLITTING DATA (TEXT TO COLUMNS)

Splitting data is key operations for cleaning and organizing information in Excel. Splitting data allows you to separate text into multiple columns. The **Text to Columns** tool splits data in a single column into multiple columns based on a delimiter or fixed width.

1.   STEPS TO USE TEXT TO COLUMNS:

1. **Select the Data**:
   » Highlight the column containing the data you want to split.

2. **Access the Tool**:
   » Go to **Data > Text to Columns**.

3. **Choose the Data Type**:
   » Select **Delimited** if the data is separated by specific characters (e.g., commas, spaces).
   » Select **Fixed Width** if the data is split at specific character positions.

4. **Configure Delimiters or Widths**:
   » For **Delimited**, choose the delimiter (e.g., comma, tab, space).
   » For **Fixed Width**, set break lines to indicate column divisions.

5. **Select Destination**:
   » Choose where the split data will appear. The default is to overwrite the original column.

6. **Complete the Process**:
   » Click **Finish** to split the data.

Example: split below dataset to 2 columns for first name and last name.

Employee Name
Olivia Miller
Emma Johnson
John Smith
Liam Wilson
David Brown
Mia Davis

» Steps:

» Result:

Employee Name	
Olivia	Miller
Emma	Johnson
John	Smith
Liam	Wilson
David	Brown
Mia	Davis

2. USING POWER QUERY TO SPLIT COLUMNS

Text to Columns is perfect for quick, one-time splits. However, if you need to repeat the same split on new data or handle more complex patterns, Power Query is a better choice. Power Query lets you define the split once and then refresh it whenever the data changes.

1. Loading Data into Power Query
   » Select any cell inside your data range. Go to the Data tab.
   » In the Get & Transform Data group, click From Table/Range.
   » Check the range and tick My table has headers if your data includes headers. Click OK.
   » Excel opens the Power Query Editor with your data.

2. Select the column you want to split
   » Click the header of the column that contains the text you want to split.
   » On the Ribbon, go to Home → Split Column (or Transform → Split Column). Pick the method: delimiter, number, positions, etc.
   » Configure the split according to your split method.

3. Rename the new columns
   » Power Query will create new column names (such as Column1.1, Column1.2).
   » Double-click the headers and rename them to something meaningful.

4. Load the results back to Excel
   » Go to Home → Close & Load.
   » Excel creates a new table with the split columns.
   » When the original data changes, use Data → Refresh to reapply all steps automatically.

Example:

Split the Department Code below into 2 columns: Department and Number.

Step-by-step instruction:

1. Select a cell in the data and go to Data → From Table/Range, then click OK.
2. In Power Query, click the Code column header.
3. Go to Home → Split Column → By Delimiter...
4. In Delimiter, choose Custom and type a dash: -.
5. Under Split at, keep Each occurrence of the delimiter.
6. Under Advanced options, keep Split into Columns selected and click OK.
7. Rename the new columns: First column → Department, Second column → Number
8. Click Home → Close & Load.

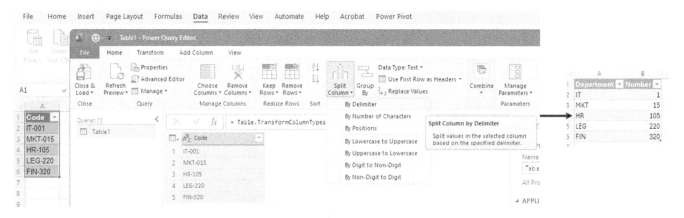

V.   USING REGEX FUNCTIONS TO CLEAN AND EXTRACT TEXT

Modern Excel includes three REGEX functions that make it easier to clean data, validate text, extract certain patterns, and standardize formatting.

1.   THE THREE REGEX FUNCTIONS IN EXCEL

Excel provides three REGEX functions:

- REGEXTEST – checks if text matches a pattern (returns TRUE/FALSE).
- REGEXEXTRACT – extracts text that matches a pattern.
- REGEXREPLACE – replaces matching text with something else.

You don't need to memorize regex rules, you only need a few simple patterns to clean most real-world data.

2.   STEPS FOR USING REGEX FUNCTIONS

1. Identify the text you want to fix or extract
   » Common examples: product codes, employee IDs, phone numbers, numbers inside text.

2. Choose the right regex function
   » Use REGEXTEST when you want Excel to answer yes/no.

- » Use REGEXEXTRACT when you want Excel to pull out part of the text.
- » Use REGEXREPLACE when you want to remove or fix certain characters.

3. Pick a regex pattern
- » \d+ → any digits
- » [A-Za-z]+ → letters only
- » [^A-Za-z0-9] → anything that is not a letter or number
- » @(.+)$ → everything after the @ symbol
- » ^\d{3} → first three digits

4. Write the formula in the next column
- » Enter the REGEX formula (examples below).
- » Fill it down as needed.

5. (Optional) Convert results to values
- » If you want to replace your original data, copy the results and choose Paste → Values.

Example for using regrex

Suppose you have a dataset as below and you need to extract the numeric part only. The dataset is inconsistent in terms of formatting.

Item
A-5001 : Available
B-223 :   Not Available
C-9999: Low

Instruction:

6. In an empty column, enter this formula: =REGEXEXTRACT(A2, "\d+")
7. Fill the formula down the column. You will receive the numeric part only

3.   WHEN TO USE REGEX INSTEAD OF STANDARD TEXT FUNCTIONS

Regex functions are especially helpful when:

- The pattern varies in length
- You need to extract text buried inside messy strings
- You want to clean imported data quickly
- Standard functions (LEFT, RIGHT, MID) would require many nested formulas

If your data has structure, even if the structure is messy, regex can usually extract or clean it in one formula.

VI.   USING COPILOT

Excel includes two AI helpers: Copilot Chat and the full Microsoft 365 Copilot version.

- Copilot Chat is already rolling out to most Microsoft 365 users. You can open it from the ribbon and ask questions, get help writing formulas, and learn steps without a separate subscription.

- Microsoft 365 Copilot is the paid add-on that unlocks full editing and automation features (such as sorting, filtering, cleaning, modifying workbook content) inside Excel and other apps. A subscription is required.

If you don't have the full version, you can still use Copilot Chat to support your work — you'll just perform the actions yourself instead of having AI apply them automatically.

Examples you can use:

- "Sort this table by Department, then by Years of Service."
- "Filter to show only rows where Sales are greater than 10,000."
- "Show only the people in the Marketing department."
- "Clear all filters."

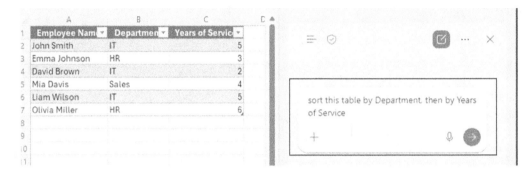

Copilot will apply the steps or guide you through them. This is especially helpful when working with large datasets.

CHAPTER 5: DATA VISUALIZATION

I. CREATING BASIC CHARTS: BAR, LINE, AND PIE CHARTS

Charts are powerful tools for visualizing data and gaining insights. In this section, we'll explore the most commonly used charts — bar, line, and pie charts — including their use cases, examples, steps to create them, and additional tips for effective visualization.

1. BAR CHARTS

Use Cases: bar charts are ideal for comparing data across categories.

- **Sales Analysis**: Compare revenue across different regions.
- **Project Management**: Visualize tasks completed by team members.
- **Survey Results**: Display responses by category.

Steps to Create a Bar Chart:

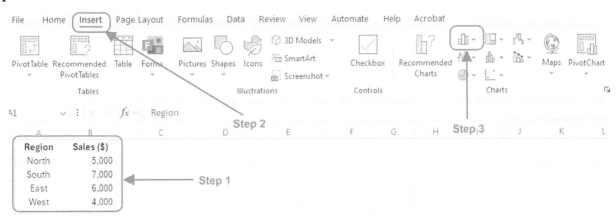

1. Select the data range (e.g., A1:B5).
2. Go to the **Insert** tab.
3. In the **Charts** group, click **Insert Column or Bar Chart** and choose a bar chart type.
4. Customize the chart using the **Chart Tools** ribbon:
   » Add axis titles, labels, and a chart title;
   » Format bars with custom colors.

Example result:

Notes:

- Use horizontal bars for clearer comparisons when category names are long.
- Combine with a secondary axis if needed for multi-variable comparisons.

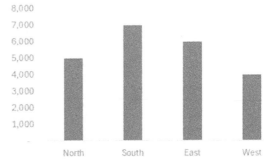

2. LINE CHARTS

Use Cases: line charts are excellent for showing trends over time.

- **Sales Growth**: Track revenue over months or years.
- **Website Analytics**: Visualize traffic trends.
- **Temperature Data**: Show daily temperature changes.

Steps to Create a Line Chart:

1. Select the data range (e.g., A1:B5).
2. Go to the **Insert** tab.
3. In the **Charts** group, click **Insert Line or Area Chart** and select a line chart.
4. Customize the chart by:
   » Adding a title, data labels, and gridlines.
   » Formatting the line style and color.

	A	B
1	Month	Sales ($)
2	January	4,000
3	February	3,800
4	March	6,000
5	April	5,200

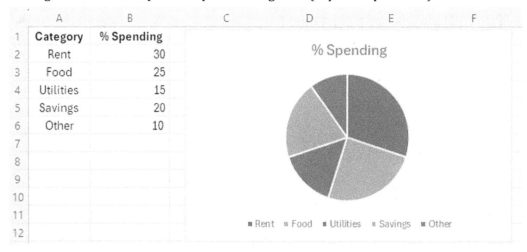

3. PIE CHARTS

Use Cases: pie charts are great for showing proportions or parts of a whole.

- **Budget Allocation**: Display spending by category.
- **Market Share**: Show the distribution of market share among competitors.
- **Survey Analysis**: Visualize response percentages.

Steps to Create a Pie Chart:

1. Select the data range (e.g., A1:B5).
2. Go to the **Insert** tab.
3. In the **Charts** group, click **Insert Pie or Doughnut Chart** and choose a pie chart.
4. Customize the chart by:
   » Adding data labels to show percentages.
   » Pulling out slices to emphasize specific categories (exploded pie chart).

	A	B
1	Category	% Spending
2	Rent	30
3	Food	25
4	Utilities	15
5	Savings	20
6	Other	10

Notes:

- Avoid using too many slices; stick to 5–7 categories for clarity.
- Combine with legends or data labels to enhance readability.

II. CUSTOMIZING CHART STYLES AND LAYOUTS

Customizing chart styles and layouts allows you to enhance the visual appeal and clarity of your charts, making them more effective for communicating insights. Excel offers various customization options to ensure your charts align with your data story.

1. WHY CUSTOMIZE CHARTS?

Improve Readability: Highlight key data points and make the chart easier to interpret.

Enhance Visual Appeal: Use colors, fonts, and layouts to make charts more engaging.

Focus Attention: Draw attention to critical insights with annotations or specific styles.

2. KEY CUSTOMIZATION OPTIONS

i. Chart Styles

Excel provides predefined chart styles that you can apply to your charts for a professional look.

Steps to Apply a Chart Style:

1. Click on the chart to activate it.
2. Go to the **Chart Tools > Design** tab.
3. In the **Chart Styles** group, hover over a style to preview it and click to apply.

ii. Chart Layouts

Chart layouts define the arrangement of elements like titles, legends, and labels.

Steps to Change Chart Layout:

1. Select the chart.
2. Go to the **Chart Tools > Design** tab.
3. In the **Chart Layouts** group, choose a predefined layout or customize manually.

iii. Manual Customization Options:

Add or Edit Chart Titles:

- » Go to **Chart Tools > Layout > Chart Title**.
- » Select **Above Chart** or **Centered Overlay Title**.
- » Click on the title to edit the text.

Add Data Labels:

- » Select the chart and go to **Chart Tools > Layout > Data Labels**.

> » Choose from options like **Center**, **Inside End**, or **Outside End** to display values on the chart.

Modify Legend Position:
> » Go to **Chart Tools > Layout > Legend**.
> » Move the legend to the **Top**, **Right**, **Left**, or **Bottom**, or hide it if unnecessary.

Gridlines:
> » Enable or disable gridlines to simplify the chart view.
> » Go to **Chart Tools > Layout > Gridlines** and select **Primary Major Gridlines** or **Primary Minor Gridlines**.

Axis Customization:
> » Format the axis to display data more effectively.
> » Right-click the axis and choose **Format Axis** to adjust scaling, intervals, or display options.

3. FORMATTING CHARTS

Beyond styles and layouts, Excel allows granular formatting to enhance chart appearance.

Change Chart Colors:
> » Select the chart.
> » Go to **Chart Tools > Format > Shape Fill** or **Shape Outline**.
> » Choose custom colors to match your theme or emphasize specific data.

Use Custom Fonts:
> » Click on any chart text element (title, labels, or legend).
> » Go to the Home tab and select a font style, size, or color.

Apply Effects:
> » Select the chart element to apply effects.
> » Go to **Chart Tools > Format > Shape Effects**.
> » Add shadows, glow, or 3D effects to enhance the visual appeal.

4. EXAMPLE: CUSTOMIZING A BAR CHART

We will use below dataset for our example:

Steps to Create the Chart:
> » Highlight the data range (A1:B5).
> » Go to **Insert > Bar Chart > Clustered Bar**.
> » A bar chart appears with default styling.

	A	B
1	Region	Sales ($)
2	North	5,000
3	South	7,000
4	East	6,000
5	West	4,000

Customization tasks:

» **Add a Chart Title**: Replace the default title with "Regional Sales."

» **Change Bar Colors**: Select bars and apply a gradient from blue to green.

» **Move the Legend**: Place the legend at the top for better visibility.

» **Display Data Labels**: Add labels to show exact sales figures on each bar.

Result:

III. USING SPARKLINES FOR QUICK INSIGHTS

Sparklines are mini-charts embedded within a single cell in Excel. They provide a quick and compact way to visualize trends and patterns in your data without taking up much space.

1. WHAT ARE SPARKLINES?

Sparklines are small, lightweight charts that fit into individual cells. They allow you to see trends, variations, and highlights in data at a glance. Unlike traditional charts, sparklines are tied to the data in their corresponding rows or columns.

Types of Sparklines:

- Line Sparklines: Display trends over time.
- Column Sparklines: Highlight variations in values.
- Win/Loss Sparklines: Show positive and negative trends.

Use Cases of Sparklines

- **Sales Performance**: track monthly sales trends for each product in a compact view.
- **Stock Prices**: visualize daily or weekly fluctuations in stock prices.
- **Employee Attendance**: highlight patterns of absences or irregular attendance across weeks.
- **Budget Analysis**: compare spending trends across categories or months.

2. CREATING SPARKLINES

1. Select the Data:
- » Highlight the data range you want to visualize (e.g., B2:E2).

2. Insert Sparklines:
- » Go to the **Insert** tab.
- » In the **Sparklines** group, choose the type of sparkline: **Line**, **Column**, or **Win/Loss**.

3. Choose Location:
- » In the **Create Sparklines** dialog box, specify the cell where the sparkline will appear (e.g., F2).

4. Customize the Sparkline:
- » Select the cell containing the sparkline.
- » Use the **Sparkline Tools > Design** tab to customize:
  - » **Style**: Change the color or design.
  - » **Markers**: Highlight specific points (e.g., high and low values).
  - » **Axis**: Adjust the vertical axis to normalize comparisons across rows.

3. CUSTOMIZING SPARKLINES

Add Markers: highlight important points like the highest and lowest values. Go to **Sparkline Tools > Design > Show > High Point/Low Point**.

Adjust Sparkline Color: select the sparkline cell, then go to **Sparkline Tools > Design > Sparkline Color**.

Group Sparklines: group similar sparklines to apply changes uniformly. Use **Sparkline Tools > Group**.

Clear Sparklines: to remove sparklines, go to **Sparkline Tools > Clear**.

4. EXAMPLE: USING SPARKLINES TO TRACK MONTHLY SALES TRENDS

Dataset:

	A	B	C	D	E	F
1	Product	Jan	Feb	Mar	Apr	Trend
2	Product A	50	60	55	70	
3	Product B	40	45	50	55	

Steps to Add Sparklines:
- » Select the range B2:E2 for Product A. Go to **Insert > Sparklines > Line**.
- » In the **Location Range**, enter F2 and click **OK**.
- » Repeat for Product B with B3:E3 and location F3.

Result:

	A	B	C	D	E	F
1	Product	Jan	Feb	Mar	Apr	Trend
2	Product A	50	60	55	70	⌇
3	Product B	40	45	50	55	⌇

Customizations:

> » Highlight **High Points** and **Low Points** using markers.
> » Apply a contrasting sparkline color for each row.

Formatted result:

The sparklines in column F provide a clear visual of monthly sales trends, showing steady growth for Product B and a spike in sales for Product A in April.

	A	B	C	D	E	F
1	Product	Jan	Feb	Mar	Apr	Trend
2	Product A	50	60	55	70	
3	Product B	40	45	50	55	

IV. INSERTING IMAGES AND SHAPES IN YOUR WORKSHEETS

Inserting images and shapes in Excel enhances the visual appeal and functionality of your worksheets. These elements can help explain data better, create interactive dashboards, and improve overall presentation.

1. BENEFITS OF USING IMAGES AND SHAPES IN EXCEL

Visual Explanation: Use images to clarify data points or concepts.

Highlight Important Areas: Shapes like arrows and callouts can direct attention to critical parts of the worksheet.

Interactive Dashboards: Combine shapes with hyperlinks to create navigation buttons.

Branding: Insert company logos to maintain a consistent brand identity in reports.

2. HOW TO INSERT IMAGES

Excel supports the insertion of images from various sources, including your computer and online.
Steps to Insert an Image:

1. **Insert from File**:
   > » Go to **Insert > Pictures > Place in Cell/ Place over Cells > This Device**.
   > » Browse to select the image and click **Insert**.

2. **Insert from Online**:
   > » Go to **Insert > Pictures > Place in Cell/ Place over Cells > Online Pictures**.
   > » Search for the desired image and insert it into the worksheet.

3. **Resize and Position**:
   > » Drag the image corners to resize while maintaining aspect ratio.
   > » Click and drag the image to position it within the worksheet.

3. HOW TO INSERT SHAPES

Shapes are versatile tools for annotating, highlighting, or enhancing worksheet design.

   i. **Types of Shapes:**

- **Arrows**: Indicate trends or point to key data.
- **Rectangles and Circles**: Highlight data sections.
- **Callouts**: Add notes or explanations.
- **Lines**: Separate sections or guide the viewer.

ii. **Steps to Insert Shapes:**

1. **Go to the Insert Tab**:
   » Click **Insert > Shapes** and select the desired shape.

2. **Draw the Shape**:
   » Click and drag on the worksheet to draw the shape.

3. **Format the Shape**:
   » Use the **Shape Format** tab to:
      » Change the fill color and outline.
      » Apply effects like shadows or 3D formatting.
      » Add text inside the shape.

V. ADVANCED VISUALIZATION TOOLS: COMBO CHARTS AND DATA BARS

Advanced visualization tools like combo charts and data bars enable you to represent complex datasets effectively. They are ideal for showing relationships between multiple variables or visualizing data directly within cells.

1. COMBO CHARTS

Combo charts combine two or more chart types (e.g., bar and line charts) in a single visualization, making it easier to analyze datasets with varying types of data.

Use Cases of Combo Charts:

- **Sales and Profit Analysis**: Display total sales as bars and profit margins as a line.
- **Website Analytics**: Show page views as columns and bounce rate as a line.
- **Weather Trends**: Combine temperature data as columns and rainfall as a line.

Example:

Steps to Create a Combo Chart:

	A	B	C
1	Month	Sales ($)	Profit Margin
2	January	5,000	20%
3	February	7,000	25%
4	March	6,000	18%
5	April	8,000	30%

1. **Select the Data**:
   » Highlight the dataset, including headers (e.g. A1:C5).

2. **Insert a Combo Chart**:
   » Go to **Insert > Charts > Insert Combo Chart**. Select **Create Custom Combo Chart**.

3. **Configure Chart Types**:
   » Assign "Sales" to a clustered column chart.
   » Assign "Profit Margin" to a line chart.
   » Check **Secondary Axis** for the line chart.

4. **Customize the Chart**:
   » Add a title.
   » Format the secondary axis to display percentages.
   » Adjust colors to differentiate the bars and line.

Result:

Sales and Profit Trends

Tips for Combo Charts:

- Use a secondary axis for clarity when combining metrics with different scales.
- Limit to two or three data series to avoid clutter.

2.   DATA BARS

Data bars are a form of conditional formatting that visually represent values directly within cells. They provide an intuitive way to compare data without creating separate charts.

Use Cases of Data Bars:

- **Sales Targets**: Highlight performance levels across regions.
- **Project Progress**: Display completion percentages for tasks.
- **Inventory Levels**: Visualize stock quantities.

Example:

	A	B
1	Region	Sales ($)
2	North	5,000
3	South	7,000
4	East	6,000
5	West	4,000

Steps to Add Data Bars:

1. **Select the Data**: Highlight the range with numeric data.
2. **Apply Conditional Formatting**:
   » Go to **Home > Conditional Formatting > Data Bars**.
   » Choose a gradient or solid fill style.
3. **Customize Data Bars**:
   » Open the **Manage Rules** dialog box under **Conditional Formatting**.
   » Adjust the minimum and maximum values if needed (e.g., set specific thresholds).

Result:

	A	B
1	Region	Sales ($)
2	North	5,000
3	South	7,000
4	East	6,000
5	West	4,000

Tips for Data Bars:

- Use solid fills for better visibility in dense datasets.
- Combine data bars with numerical values in adjacent columns for added context.

VI.   USING COPILOT TO SUPPORT VISUALIZATIONS

Copilot can assist you while creating charts and visuals, even if you only have the built-in Copilot Chat version. Copilot Chat appears in a panel on the right side of Excel and helps you understand chart types, choose the right visual, and walk through steps when you're unsure where to click.

If you have the full Microsoft 365 Copilot subscription (paid add-on), Copilot can also apply formatting, suggest visual layouts, and make changes directly to your workbook.

i.   How Copilot Chat Can Help With Visualizations

Copilot Chat is especially helpful when you're deciding which chart to create or when you need instructions. You can ask it questions at any time, and it will guide you using your current data.

Example prompts:

- "What is the best chart type to compare monthly sales?"
- "Explain the difference between a bar chart and a column chart."
- "Which chart should I use to show a trend over time?"
- "How do I add data labels to this chart?"

Copilot Chat can't click the buttons for you, but it will tell you exactly how to perform the steps.

ii.   What the Full Microsoft 365 Copilot Can Do

If you have the full Copilot license, you can also ask Copilot to:

- Suggest the most appropriate chart for a selected range.
- Apply chart formatting automatically.
- Create summaries or insights from the visual.
- Highlight key points or trends.
- Build a chart based on what you describe ("Create a column chart showing total sales by region").

These features streamline your workflow and help you produce clearer visuals more quickly.

iii.   When Copilot Is Most Useful

Copilot is most helpful when:

- You're unsure which chart type fits your data
- You want to adjust chart formatting but don't know where to find the settings
- Your data needs a summary before charting
- You want an explanation of why a trend or outlier appears
- You need quick guidance without leaving your worksheet

Even with Copilot Chat alone, having an AI assistant inside Excel makes visualization tasks easier to learn and understand.

CHAPTER 6: INTERMEDIATE EXCEL SKILLS

I.   WORKING WITH NAMED RANGES

Named ranges in Excel simplify formulas, enhance readability, and make managing large datasets more efficient. A named range is a custom label assigned to a cell or group of cells, allowing you to reference it easily in formulas or other operations.

1.   BENEFITS OF USING NAMED RANGES

- **Improved Formula Clarity**: Instead of referencing cells like A1:A10, you can use a descriptive name like SalesData.
- **Easier Data Management**: Named ranges simplify navigating and maintaining large datasets.
- **Dynamic Updates**: Named ranges can adapt dynamically to changes in data when defined as dynamic ranges.

2.   HOW TO CREATE NAMED RANGES

1.   **Select the Cells**:
   » Highlight the cells you want to name (e.g., A1:A10).

2.   **Name the Range**:
   » Go to the **Formulas** tab and click **Define Name** in the **Defined Names** group.
   » Enter a descriptive name (e.g., SalesData) in the **New Name** dialog box and click **OK**.

3.   **Verify the Range**:
   » Use the **Name Manager** under the **Formulas** tab to view, edit, or delete named ranges.

3.   USING NAMED RANGES IN FORMULAS

Named ranges can replace cell references in formulas, making them easier to understand.

Example: We have the dataset as below:

Create a Named Range:
   » Select the range B2:B4 and name it MonthlySales.

	A	B
1	Month	Sales ($)
2	January	5,000
3	February	7,000
4	March	6,000

1.   **Use the Named Range in a Formula**:
   » Calculate the total sales:
   =SUM(MonthlySales)
   » Returns: 18,000

2.   **Dynamic Named Range**:
   » Use formulas to define a range that expands automatically as data is added.
   » Example:
   Go to **Formulas > Define Name**, and for the range, enter:
   =OFFSET(Sheet1!$B$2, 0, 0, COUNTA(Sheet1!$B$2:$B$100), 1)

» This dynamic range adjusts as new data is entered in column B.

4. MANAGING NAMED RANGES

View or Edit Named Ranges:
- » Go to **Formulas > Name Manager** to see all named ranges.
- » Select a name and click **Edit** to modify it or **Delete** to remove it.

Use Named Ranges Across Sheets:
- » Named ranges are workbook-wide, meaning they can be used in formulas across different sheets.

Apply Scope to Named Ranges:
- » When creating a named range, set the scope to a specific sheet or the entire workbook.

II. CREATING AND MANAGING PIVOT TABLES

Pivot tables are one of Excel's most powerful features, enabling you to summarize, analyze, and extract insights from large datasets efficiently. They allow you to rearrange, group, and filter data dynamically without altering the original dataset.

1. WHAT ARE PIVOT TABLES?

A pivot table is an interactive table that summarizes data by aggregating values (e.g., sum, average, count) and grouping them into categories. It helps users analyze trends, patterns, and relationships within the data.

Use Cases:
- **Sales Analysis**: Summarize revenue by product, region, or salesperson.
- **Inventory Management**: Track stock levels by category and supplier.
- **Survey Analysis**: Count responses for different questions by demographic.

2. STEPS TO CREATE A PIVOT TABLE (WITH EXAMPLE)

Example Dataset

	A	B	C	D	E
1	Region	Product	Salesperson	Sales ($)	Date
2	North	Widget A	Alice	500	01-Jan-24
3	South	Widget B	Bob	700	02-Jan-24
4	East	Widget A	Alice	600	03-Jan-24
5	West	Widget C	Charlie	400	04-Jan-24
6	North	Widget B	Alice	800	05-Jan-24

1. **Select the Data**
   - » Highlight the dataset (A1:E6), including headers.
   - » Go to **Insert > PivotTable**.
2. **Configure the Pivot Table**

» In the **Create PivotTable** dialog box:
  » Select **New Worksheet** or **Existing Worksheet** for the table location. Click **OK**.
» In the **PivotTable Field List** pane: drag fields to different areas:
  » **Rows**: Region
  » **Columns**: Product
  » **Values**: Sales ($) (set to Sum by default)
  » **Filters**: Salesperson

3. **Analyze the Results**

	A	B	C	D	E	F	G	H	I	J	K
1	Region	Product	Salesperson	Sales ($)	Date		Salesperson	(All)			
2	North	Widget A	Alice	500	01-Jan-24						
3	South	Widget B	Bob	700	02-Jan-24		Sum of Sales ($)	Column Labels			
4	East	Widget A	Alice	600	03-Jan-24		Row Labels	Widget A	Widget B	Widget C	Grand Total
5	West	Widget C	Charlie	400	04-Jan-24		East	600			600
6	North	Widget B	Alice	800	05-Jan-24		North	500	800		1,300
7							South		700		700
8							West			400	400
9			Filter to view				Grand Total	1,100	1,500	400	3,000
10			each salesperson								

The pivot table summarizes sales by region and product. Use the filter dropdown to view data for specific salespeople.

3. MANAGING PIVOT TABLES

Updating the Data:
» If the source data changes, click the pivot table.
» Go to **PivotTable Analyze > Refresh** to update.

Grouping Data:
» Right-click on a field (e.g., Date) and select **Group**.
» Choose how to group (e.g., by months, quarters, or years).

Adding Calculated Fields:
» Go to **PivotTable Analyze > Fields, Items & Sets > Calculated Field**.
» Define a formula using existing fields. Example: Add a "Profit" field with the formula =Sales * 0.2.

Sorting and Filtering:
» Use the dropdown arrows in the row or column headers to sort or filter data.
» Apply filters in the **Filters** area to analyze subsets of data.

4. TIPS FOR USING PIVOT TABLES

Use Slicers for Dynamic Filtering:
» Add slicers to filter data visually.
» Go to **PivotTable Analyze > Insert Slicer**.

Apply Conditional Formatting:

> » Highlight key values in the pivot table for better visualization.

> » Select data, then go to **Home > Conditional Formatting**.

Summarize with Different Functions:

> » Change the aggregation type (e.g., Average, Max, Count).

> » Right-click a value field, select **Summarize Values By**, and choose the function.

Use Multiple Tables:

> » Combine data from multiple sheets using Power Pivot for advanced analysis.

III.   USING SLICERS FOR DYNAMIC DATA ANALYSIS

Slicers are an advanced filtering tool in Excel that provide a user-friendly way to dynamically analyze data in pivot tables and tables. They allow you to filter datasets visually by clicking buttons, making them ideal for creating interactive dashboards and reports.

1.   WHAT ARE SLICERS?

Slicers are graphical filters that display clickable buttons to filter data dynamically. Unlike traditional dropdown filters, slicers are more intuitive and visually appealing, especially when analyzing large datasets or sharing reports with others.

Benefits of Using Slicers

- **Interactive Filtering**: Quickly filter pivot tables and tables by clicking buttons.
- **Ease of Use**: No need to open dropdown menus; filters are applied instantly.
- **Multiple Filters**: Apply filters to multiple pivot tables or tables simultaneously.
- **Professional Dashboards**: Enhance the interactivity and visual appeal of dashboards.

2.   STEPS TO CREATE AND USE SLICERS (WITH EXAMPLE)

Example Dataset

1.   **Create a Pivot Table**

> » Highlight the dataset and go to **Insert > PivotTable**.

> » Configure the pivot table:

>> » **Rows**: Add Region.

>> » **Columns**: Add Product.

>> » **Values**: Add Sales ($).

	A	B	C	D	E
1	Region	Product	Salesperson	Sales ($)	Date
2	North	Widget A	Alice	500	01-Jan-24
3	South	Widget B	Bob	700	02-Jan-24
4	East	Widget A	Alice	600	03-Jan-24
5	West	Widget C	Charlie	400	04-Jan-24
6	North	Widget B	Alice	800	05-Jan-24

2.   **Insert a Slicer**

> » Select the pivot table.

> » Go to **PivotTable Analyze > Insert Slicer**.

> » Choose fields to filter by (e.g., Region, Product, or Salesperson).

> » Click **OK** to insert the slicer.

3. Use the Slicer
   » Click buttons on the slicer to filter data dynamically.
   » To select multiple items, hold Ctrl while clicking the buttons.
   » Use the clear filter icon in the slicer to remove all filters.

Sum of Sales ($)	Column Labels				Region
Row Labels	Widget A	Widget B	Widget C	Grand Total	
East	600			600	East
North	500	800		1,300	North
South		700		700	South
West			400	400	West
Grand Total	1,100	1,500	400	3,000	

3.   CUSTOMIZING SLICERS

Resize and Move Slicers:
   » Drag the slicer to reposition it on the worksheet. Resize it by dragging the edges.

Change Slicer Style:
   » Go to **Slicer Tools > Options > Slicer Styles** and choose a preformatted style.

Adjust Button Layout:
   » Under **Slicer Tools > Options > Buttons**, adjust the number of columns and button size.

Connect to Multiple Pivot Tables:
   » Select the slicer, go to **Slicer Tools > Options > Report Connections**, and link it to multiple pivot tables.

4.   TIPS FOR USING SLICERS

Group Related Filters: Place slicers close to related pivot tables for easy access.

Use Descriptive Titles: Rename slicers to clarify their purpose (e.g., "Filter by Region").

Combine with Conditional Formatting: Highlight filtered data in pivot tables for better visualization.

Limit Overlapping Filters: Avoid applying too many slicers that could conflict or confuse users.

IV.   INTRODUCTION TO POWER QUERY

Power Query is a data transformation and automation tool built into Excel. It allows you to connect, clean, and transform data from various sources without manual intervention. By mastering Power Query, you can streamline data preparation and improve efficiency in your workflows.

1.   WHAT IS POWER QUERY?

Power Query simplifies importing and transforming data. It works through an intuitive interface where you can clean, reshape, and combine data from various sources like text files, databases, or web pages, all without needing advanced coding skills.

Key Features:

- Connects to multiple data sources (Excel files, databases, web, APIs).
- Automates repetitive data-cleaning tasks.
- Supports advanced transformations like merging, unpivoting, and splitting columns.

Benefits of Using Power Query

- **Automation**: save time by automating repetitive data-cleaning steps.
- **Integration**: combine data from multiple sources into a unified format.
- **Consistency**: apply the same transformation logic to ensure data accuracy.
- **Ease of Use**: no coding required; use an intuitive point-and-click interface.

2. EXAMPLE CLEANING AND COMBINING DATA WITH POWER QUERY

Scenario: You have monthly sales data stored in separate files, and you want to combine them into a single table while removing duplicates and formatting columns.

Files: 2 files named January Sales and February Sales with data as below:

Steps to Combine Data:

	A	B	C
1	Month	Region	Sales ($)
2	January	North	500
3	January	South	700

	A	B	C
1	Month	Region	Sales ($)
2	January	North	500
3	January	South	700
4	February	North	600
5	February	South	800

1. **Connect to Data Sources**:
   » Go to **Data > Get Data > From Folder**.
   » Select the folder where you store January and February sales files.

2. **Combine Data:**
   » Select Combine & Load
   » In the Combine Files dialog box, select Sheet1. Click OK.

Result:

	A	B	C	D
1	Source.Name	Month	Region	Sales ($)
2	February Sales.xlsx	January	North	500
3	February Sales.xlsx	January	South	700
4	February Sales.xlsx	February	North	600
5	February Sales.xlsx	February	South	800
6	January Sales.xlsx	January	North	500
7	January Sales.xlsx	January	South	700

Steps to Clean Data:

> » Select a cell in the combined data, then go to **Query > Edit** to open Power Query Editor.

> » Remove duplicate rows: select the column you want to remove duplicates from, then go to **Home > Remove Duplicates**.

> » Group By: for more complicated data, Group By function works better to remove duplicates.

> » Remove unnecessary columns: select the column, then go to **Home > Remove Columns.**

> » Rename columns: Double-click column headers to rename them for clarity.

> » Result:

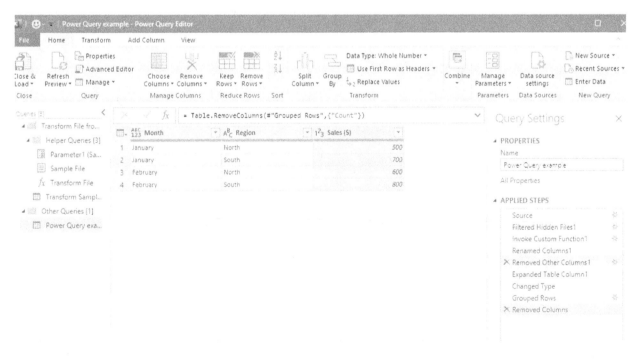

3. **Load Data into Excel**:
   » Once cleaned, click **Close & Load**. The previous table will be updated with duplicates removed.

Result:

	A	B	C
1	Month ▼	Region ▼	Sales ($) ▼
2	January	North	500
3	January	South	700
4	February	North	600
5	February	South	800

3. COMMON TRANSFORMATIONS IN POWER QUERY

Filtering Rows: remove unnecessary rows by applying filters, such as excluding blanks or values outside a range.

Splitting Columns: divide data in one column into multiple columns based on delimiters (e.g., commas or spaces).

Merging Queries: combine data from two tables using a common key (e.g., Region or Product ID).

Unpivoting Columns: transform wide datasets into long-format tables for easier analysis.

Grouping Data: aggregate data by categories, such as summing sales by region.

4. PRACTICAL APPLICATIONS

- **Sales Reporting**: import monthly sales data from multiple CSV files and clean it for analysis.
- **Inventory Management**: merge inventory lists from suppliers into a single table and filter out discontinued items.
- **Survey Analysis**: combine survey responses from various sources and pivot data for analysis.
- **Data Preparation for Dashboards**: create a clean and dynamic dataset that automatically updates when source files change.

5. TIPS FOR USING POWER QUERY

- **Save Queries**: save your queries for reuse, especially when working with frequently updated data.
- **Use Parameters**: create parameters for dynamic filtering or paths, like selecting a specific year or file location.
- **Preview Changes**: use the preview pane in Power Query Editor to verify transformations before loading data.
- **Document Steps**: Power Query keeps a step-by-step log of all transformations, ensuring transparency and repeatability.

V. BASIC MACROS: AUTOMATING REPETITIVE TASKS

Macros in Excel allow you to automate repetitive tasks by recording a sequence of actions and replaying them with a single click or shortcut. Learning to use macros is a significant step toward improving productivity and mastering Excel's advanced capabilities.

1. WHAT ARE MACROS?

A macro is a set of recorded instructions that automates routine tasks in Excel. Macros are written in VBA

(Visual Basic for Applications), but Excel provides a user-friendly recorder for those unfamiliar with coding.

Common Use Cases:

- Automating formatting across multiple sheets.
- Performing repetitive calculations or updates.
- Generating reports with standardized layouts.
- Consolidating data from multiple files.

2. ENABLING MACROS IN EXCEL

By default, Excel disables macros for security reasons. To use them:

1. Go to **File > Options > Trust Center > Trust Center Settings**.
2. Select **Macro Settings** and enable **Enable all macros** or **Disable all macros with notification**.
3. Click **OK** to save changes.

3. RECORDING A MACRO

Excel's Macro Recorder simplifies automation by recording actions without requiring you to write code.

Steps to Record a Macro:

1. **Start Recording**:
   » Go to **View > Macros > Record Macro**.
   » Name the macro (e.g., FormatReport) and assign a shortcut key (optional).
   » Choose where to store the macro:
      » **This Workbook**: Macro is saved only in the current workbook.
      » **Personal Macro Workbook**: Macro is available in all workbooks.
2. **Perform the Actions**: carry out the tasks you want to automate (e.g., formatting a table, applying formulas).
3. **Stop Recording**: go to **View > Macros > Stop Recording**.

4. RUNNING A MACRO

To run a recorded macro:

1. Go to **View > Macros > View Macros**.
2. Select the macro from the list and click **Run**.

Alternatively, use the assigned shortcut key to execute the macro instantly.

5. EDITING AND MANAGING MACROS

Viewing Macro Code:

   » Go to **View > Macros > View Macros**.

» Select a macro and click **Edit** to view the VBA code in the editor.

Deleting a Macro:
» Open **View > Macros > View Macros**.
» Select the macro and click **Delete**.

Saving a Workbook with Macros:
» Save the workbook as a **Macro-Enabled Workbook** (.xlsm) to retain macros.
» Go to **File > Save As** and choose **Excel Macro-Enabled Workbook** from the file type dropdown.

6. EXAMPLE: FORMATTING A SALES REPORT

We will use dataset below for our example (Table 1):

	A	B
1	Region	Sales ($)
2	North	5,000
3	South	7,000
4	East	6,000
5	West	4,000

Formatting tasks:
» Bold the headers.
» Apply currency formatting to the Sales column.
» Add a total row using =SUM(B2:B5).

Steps to format:
» Go to **View > Macros > Record Macro**.
» Name the macro as FormatReport and store the macro in current workbook.
» Select A1: B1 and bold it. Use arrow down key to select B2: B5 and press Ctrl+1 to format currency.
» Use arrow keys to go to cell A5, click on **Macros > Use Relative References** to go to cell A6, type in Total.
» Use arrow right key to go to cell B6, type in =SUM($B$2:B5)
» To stop recording, go to **Macros > Stop Recording.**

To repeat the same steps for other sales reports (Table 2), we can now run our Recorded Macros.

Run the macros::
» Go to **View > Macros > View Macros**.
» Select FormatReport and click Run.

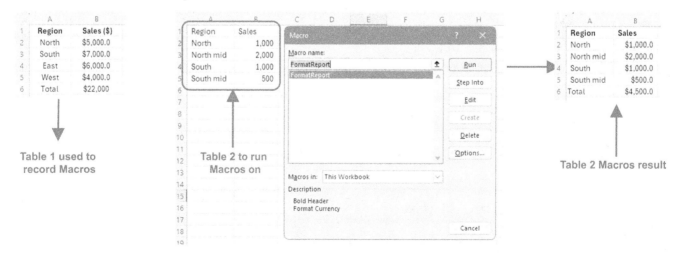

Table 1 used to record Macros

Table 2 to run Macros on

Table 2 Macros result

CHAPTER 7: ADVANCED TECHNIQUES

I.   ADVANCED FORMULAS: INDEX, MATCH, INDIRECT

Advanced Excel formulas like **INDEX**, **MATCH**, and **INDIRECT**, when combined with nested functions, allow you to perform powerful, efficient, and dynamic calculations. These formulas excel in scenarios requiring flexibility, dynamic range references, and advanced lookups, providing solutions that surpass basic functions like **VLOOKUP** or **SUMIFS**.

1.   INDEX FUNCTION

The **INDEX** function retrieves the value of a cell within a specified range based on its row and column position. It is highly versatile and can handle both two-dimensional arrays (tables) and one-dimensional arrays (rows or columns). The function supports two syntaxes: array form and reference form.

i.   Array form

Syntax: =INDEX(array, row_num, [column_num])

Understanding the Arguments

- **array**: the range of cells or array from which to retrieve data.
- **row_num**: the row number in the array to retrieve data from.
- **column_num**: (Optional) the column number in the array to retrieve data from.

ii.   Reference form

Syntax: =INDEX(reference, row_num, [column_num], [area_num])

Understanding the Arguments

- **reference**: Multiple ranges or areas separated by commas. Example: (A1:A3, B1:B3).
- **row_num**: The row number in the selected range.
- **[column_num]** (optional): The column number in the selected range. Defaults to the first column if omitted.
- **[area_num]** (optional): Specifies which range (or area) to use when multiple areas are provided.

iii.   Differences between Array form and Reference form

Feature	Array Form	Reference Form
Range	Single range or array	Multiple ranges (non-contiguous areas)
Flexibility	Simplified lookup	Supports dynamic selection of ranges
Complexity	Less complex, easier to use	Slightly more advanced, requires area_num
Primary Use Case	Row and column lookups within a table	Dynamic range selection for larger datasets

When to Use Each Syntax

- **Array Form:** When working with a single, contiguous dataset. Ideal for straightforward lookups and simple formulas.
- **Reference Form:** When dealing with multiple datasets or ranges, or when you need dynamic flexibility in selecting a range.

iv.   Examples

We will use below dataset for our examples.

	A	B	C	D
1	Product ID	Product Name	Category	Price ($)
2	101	Widget A	Electronics	50
3	102	Widget B	Electronics	75
4	103	Widget C	Home Appliances	100
5	104	Widget D	Home Appliances	125
6				
7	Store	Region	Manager	
8	Downtown	North	Alice	
9	Uptown	South	Bob	
10	Suburb	East	Carol	
11	City Center	West	David	

Task: Find the price of the second product.
- » Formula: =INDEX(A2:D5, 2, 4)
- » The formula asks Excel to find the value in range A2:D5, second row and fourth column.
- » Result: 75

Task: Find the store manager of the second store.
- » Formula: =INDEX((A2:D5, A8:C11), 2, 3, 2)
- » The formula asks Excel to find value in 2 ranges A2:D5 (range 1) and A8:C11 (range 2), second row and third column of range 2.
- » Result: Bob

2.   MATCH FUNCTION

The **MATCH** function finds the relative position of a value within a range. It is often used in combination with **INDEX** for flexible and dynamic lookups.

Syntax:
=MATCH(lookup_value, lookup_array, [match_type])

Understanding the Arguments

- **lookup_value**: The value to search for.
- **lookup_array**: The range to search in.
- **match_type**: 0 for an exact match, 1 for the largest value less than or equal to the lookup value, -1 for the smallest value greater than or equal to the lookup value.

Use Cases:

- **Find Position in a List**: Identify the position of a specific product or value.
- **Dynamic Row or Column Reference**: Use the result of **MATCH** to dynamically locate rows or columns in other formulas.

Example:

Task: Find the position of Widget C in column B.
- » Formula: =MATCH("Widget C",B1:B5,0). Result: 4.

	A	B	C	D
1	Product ID	Product Name	Category	Price ($)
2	101	Widget A	Electronics	50
3	102	Widget B	Electronics	75
4	103	Widget C	Home Appliances	100
5	104	Widget D	Home Appliances	125
6				

Task: Find the position of Widget C in row 4.

>   Formula: =MATCH("Widget C", A4:D4,0). Result: 2.

3.   COMBINING INDEX AND MATCH

The combination of **INDEX** and **MATCH** provides a more robust solution than **VLOOKUP**, allowing for dynamic lookups in both rows and columns.

Advantages Over VLOOKUP:

-   **Flexible Column Selection**: Unlike **VLOOKUP**, which requires the lookup column to be the first column, **INDEX** and **MATCH** can work with data in any order.
-   **Error Resilience**: They are not affected by column insertions or deletions.
-   **Performance**: Faster in large datasets.

Use Cases:

-   **Two-Dimensional Lookup**: Retrieve data based on both row and column criteria.
-   **Dynamic Dashboards**: Build interactive dashboards where users can select lookup criteria.

Example:

Task: Find the price for Widget C.

	A	B	C	D
1	Product ID	Product Name	Category	Price ($)
2	101	Widget A	Electronics	50
3	102	Widget B	Electronics	75
4	103	Widget C	Home Appliances	100
5	104	Widget D	Home Appliances	125
6				

>   Formula: =INDEX(D1:D5,MATCH("Widget C",B1:B5,0))

>   The formula asks Excel to find the value in range D1:D5, row number is whichever position Widget C is in range B1:B5.

>   Result: 100.

4.   INDIRECT FUNCTION

The **INDIRECT** function dynamically references ranges based on a text string. It is particularly useful for creating dynamic, flexible formulas.

Syntax:
=INDIRECT(ref_text, [a1])

Understanding the Arguments

-   **ref_text**: A text string representing a cell or range reference.
-   **a1**: (Optional) TRUE for A1-style references, FALSE for R1C1-style references.

Use Cases:

-   **Dynamic Range References**: Switch ranges based on user inputs or dropdown selections.
-   **Flexible Consolidation**: Combine data from multiple sheets without manually updating formulas.
-   **Shortening Complex Formulas**: Simplify long **VLOOKUP** or **SUMIFS** formulas with dynamic ranges.

Examples: We will use dataset below for our examples.

Simple Use Case: Referencing a Cell Address

	A	B	C	D	E
1	Salesperson	Region	Jan Sales ($)	Feb Sales ($)	Mar Sales ($)
2	Alice	North	500	600	550
3	Bob	South	450	700	800
4	Carol	East	700	750	720
5	David	West	600	500	650
6					
7	Region	Target ($)			
8	North	1,500			
9	South	2,000			
10	East	2,000			
11	West	1,800			

Task: Retrieve the sales for Alice in January.

 » Formula: =INDIRECT("C2")
 » "C2" references the cell where Alice's January sales data is stored.
 » Result: 500.

Dynamic Range Reference

Task: Retrieve total sales for Bob using a dynamically constructed range.

 » Formula: =SUM(INDIRECT("C3:E3"))
 » "C3:E3" dynamically constructs the range covering Bob's sales for January to March.
 » Result: 1,950.

Combining INDIRECT with SUM and IF

Task: Compare a region's total sales to its target dynamically.

 » Formula: =IF(SUM(INDIRECT("C"&MATCH('North',B1:B5,0)&" E"&MATCH("North",B1:B5,0))) >= INDIRECT("B"&MATCH("North",A8:A11,0)+7), "Met Target", "Below Target")
 » MATCH("North",B1:B5,0): Finds the row number for "North" in the first table (row 2).
 » INDIRECT("C"&MATCH("North",B1:B5,0)&":E"&MATCH("North",B1:B5,0)): Dynamically references the sales data range for the "North" region (C2:E2).
 » INDIRECT("B"&MATCH("North",A8:A11,0)+7): Dynamically references the sales target for the "North" region from the second table.
 » Result: Met Target.

II.   GOAL SEEK

1.   WHAT IS GOAL SEEK?

Goal Seek is part of Excel's **What-If Analysis** tools. It works by adjusting a single input value in a formula to achieve a desired output.

Use Cases:

- **Financial Modeling**: Determine the required sales to meet a profit target.
- **Loan Calculations**: Find the interest rate or term to meet a specific monthly payment.
- **Break-Even Analysis**: Calculate the required units to break even.
- **Pricing Strategy**: Identify the optimal price to hit revenue goals.

2.   HOW GOAL SEEK WORKS

Goal Seek requires three inputs:

- **Set Cell**: The cell containing the formula or value you want to achieve.
- **To Value**: The target value you want the set cell to achieve.
- **By Changing Cell**: The input cell that Excel will adjust to achieve the target.

3. EXAMPLE

Scenario: Determine the Required Sales to Meet a Profit Target

	A	B	C	D	E	F
1	Product	Price ($)	Units Sold	Total Revenue ($)	Costs ($)	Profit ($)
2	Widget A	50	100	5,000	3,000	2,000

Goal: Adjust **Units Sold** to achieve a profit of **$3,000**.

Steps:

1. **Set Up the Formula**:
   » Calculate **Total Revenue**: =Price * Units Sold
   » Calculate **Costs**: = Unit Cost * Units Sold. From the data given, we know the Unit Cost is $30 per unit.
   » Calculate **Profit**: =Total Revenue - Costs

2. **Access Goal Seek**:
   » Go to **Data > What-If Analysis > Goal Seek**.

3. **Enter Goal Seek Parameters**:
   » **Set Cell**: Select the Profit cell (F2).
   » **To Value**: Enter 3000.
   » **By Changing Cell**: Select the Units Sold cell (C2).

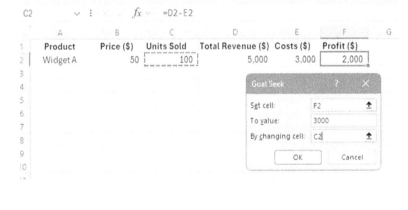

4. **Run Goal Seek**:
   » Excel adjusts the **Units Sold** value to 150 to meet the profit target.

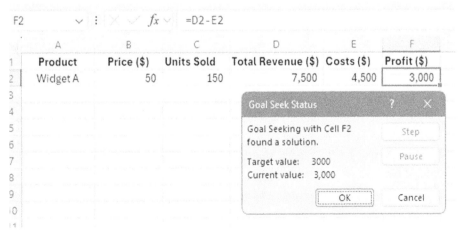

III. USING ARRAY FORMULAS

Array formulas in Excel are powerful tools that enable calculations on multiple values simultaneously. They can process data arrays (a single column, row, or a combination of both) to return either a single result or multiple results. With the introduction of dynamic arrays in Excel (Microsoft 365 and Excel 2021), array formulas have become easier to use and more versatile, offering a wide range of practical applications.

1. WHAT ARE ARRAY FORMULAS?

Array formulas operate on arrays rather than individual values. They allow you to perform multiple calculations in a single formula, simplifying complex tasks like conditional aggregations, generating dynamic ranges, or creating multi-dimensional datasets. There are two types of array formulas:

- **Single-Cell Array Formula**: Performs calculations and returns a single result.
  Example: Summing sales based on conditions.
- **Multi-Cell Array Formula**: Performs calculations and outputs multiple results across a range of cells.
  Example: Calculating totals for each row in a dataset.

Advantages of Array Formulas

- Consistency: A single array formula applies the same logic across all calculations.
- Efficiency: Reduces the need for intermediate formulas, leading to smaller file sizes.
- Flexibility: Handles complex tasks like dynamic ranges, multi-criteria lookups, or condition-based calculations.
- Updates: Automatically adjusts when the source data changes (with dynamic arrays).

2. EXAMPLE USE CASES

Scenario 1: Multi-Cell Array Formula: Total Sales per Item

	A	B	C
1	Product	Units Sold	Unit Price ($)
2	Widget A	10	5
3	Widget B	15	7
4	Widget C	20	9

Goal: Calculate the total sales for each product.

- » Formula: =B2:B4*C2:C4
- » Enter the formula and press **Ctrl + Shift + Enter** (if using traditional arrays).
- » Result: Spills the results into adjacent cells:
  - » Widget A: 50.
  - » Widget B: 105.
  - » Widget C: 180.

D2   ∨ : × ✓ fx ∨   =B2:B4*C2:C4

	A	B	C	D
1	Product	Units Sold	Unit Price ($)	Total Sales ($)
2	Widget A	10	5	50
3	Widget B	15	7	105
4	Widget C	20	9	180
5				

Scenario 2: Single-Cell Array Formula: Grand Total Sales

We use the same dataset in scenario 1.

- » Formula (Dynamic Array): =SUM(B2:B4*C2:C4)
- » Result: 335.

D5   ∨ : × ✓ fx ∨   =SUM(B2:B4*C2:C4)

	A	B	C	D
1	Product	Units Sold	Unit Price ($)	Total Sales ($)
2	Widget A	10	5	50
3	Widget B	15	7	105
4	Widget C	20	9	180
5		Grand Total		335

Scenario 3: Extracting Unique Values (Dynamic Arrays)

Goal: Extract unique regions from the dataset.

> » Formula: =UNIQUE(A1:A4)
> » Result: Spills the unique values: North, South, East.

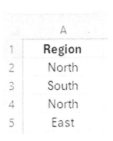

Scenario 4: Dynamic Ranges with SEQUENCE

Goal: Generate a list of numbers from 1 to 10 in a single step.

> » Formula: =SEQUENCE(10)
> » Enter the formula in one cell. Excel spills numbers 1–10 into adjacent cells automatically.

Array formulas, particularly with the advent of dynamic arrays, have transformed how Excel handles calculations. They allow for powerful, efficient, and flexible data analysis, enabling both novice and advanced users to solve complex problems with ease. While they come with a learning curve, mastering array formulas opens up a world of possibilities in Excel.

IV. ADVANCED PIVOT TABLE TECHNIQUES: GROUPING, CALCULATED FIELDS

Pivot tables are a versatile tool for summarizing and analyzing large datasets. Advanced techniques like grouping and calculated fields can enhance their power, allowing for more detailed analysis.

1. GROUPING DATA IN PIVOT TABLES

Grouping data helps you organize and analyze large datasets by clustering values into meaningful categories, such as grouping dates into months or years, or numerical data into ranges.

Use Cases:

- **Date Grouping**: Summarize sales data by specific periods.
- **Numeric Grouping**: Group income ranges into categories (e.g., $0–$10,000, $10,001–$20,000).
- **Custom Grouping**: Combine specific items into custom groups (e.g., grouping regions into larger territories).

Example Dataset:

Steps for Grouping Data:

1. **Create a Pivot Table**:
   > » Highlight the dataset and go to **Insert > PivotTable**.

Date	Region	Sales ($)
1/1/2024	North	500
1/2/2024	South	700
2/15/2024	East	600
2/20/2024	West	400
3/10/2024	North	800

» Place **Sales** in Rows and **Region** in Values.

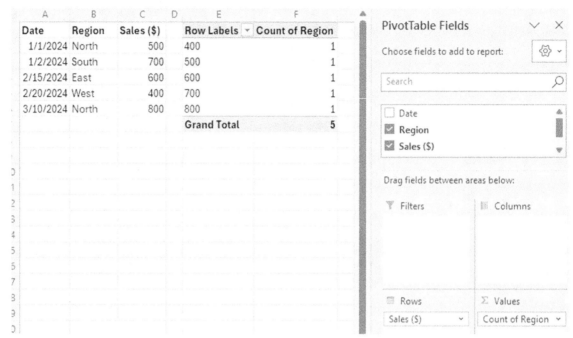

2. **Group Numeric Data:**
   » Right-click a value and choose **Group**.
   » Enter range intervals (e.g., Start: 0, End: 1000, By: 500).

Result:
   » The data is now grouped into 2 groups.

	A	B	C	D	E	F
1	Date	Region	Sales ($)		Row Labels	Count of Region
2	1/1/2024	North	500		0-499	1
3	1/2/2024	South	700		500-1000	4
4	2/15/2024	East	600		Grand Total	5
5	2/20/2024	West	400			
6	3/10/2024	North	800			

2. USING CALCULATED FIELDS

A **calculated field** is a custom formula you define within the pivot table that is based on existing data. It allows you to add new metrics without altering the original dataset. **Use Cases:**

- **Profit Calculation**: Add a calculated field for profit (e.g., Sales - Costs).
- **Profit Margin**: Calculate profit as a percentage of sales.
- **Custom Ratios**: Create metrics like sales per region o

Example Dataset:

Steps to Add a Calculated Field:

1. **Create a Pivot Table**:

	A	B	C	D
1	Product	Region	Sales ($)	Costs ($)
2	Widget A	North	500	300
3	Widget B	South	700	400
4	Widget C	East	600	350

» Place Region in Rows and Sales and Costs in Values.

2. **Add a Calculated Field**:
   » Go to PivotTable Analyze > Fields, Items & Sets > Calculated Field.
   » Name the field (e.g., "Profit") and enter the formula: ='Sales ($)'- 'Costs ($)'. Note that you have to double-click into the field name in the listed Fields to enter formula.

3. **Customize Calculated Field**:
   » Add the new field to the pivot table.
   » Change the number format for better readability (if needed).

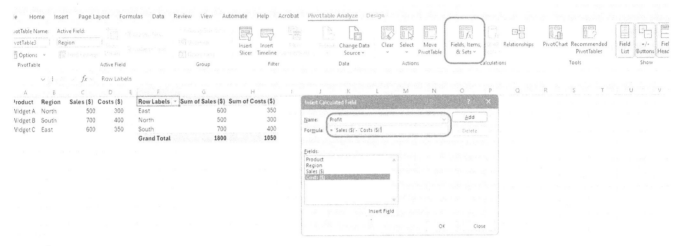

Result:

	A	B	C	D	E	F	G	H	I
1	Product	Region	Sales ($)	Costs ($)		Row Labels	Sum of Sales ($)	Sum of Costs ($)	Sum of Profit
2	Widget A	North	500	300		East	600	350	250
3	Widget B	South	700	400		North	500	300	200
4	Widget C	East	600	350		South	700	400	300
5						Grand Total	1800	1050	750

V.   AUTOMATING TASKS WITH VBA

1.   WHAT IS VBA?

VBA is a programming language integrated into Microsoft Office applications. It allows users to write macros and scripts that automate tasks or add functionality. While macros can be recorded, VBA provides full control to customize and extend Excel's behavior.

Benefits of Using VBA

- **Automation**: Streamline repetitive tasks like formatting, data processing, and report generation.
- **Custom Solutions**: Create tailored tools and features not natively available in Excel.
- **Improved Accuracy**: Reduce manual errors by automating complex workflows.
- **Scalability**: Handle large datasets and advanced tasks with minimal effort.

Key VBA Concepts

- **Variables**: Store data for use in scripts. Example: Dim salesTotal As Double
- **Loops**: Automate repetitive actions. Example: For Each cell In Range("A1:A10")
- **Conditions**: Perform tasks based on criteria. Example: If cell.Value > 250 Then
- **Objects and Methods**: Work with Excel elements like worksheets, ranges, and charts. Example: Worksheets("Sheet1").Range("A1")

2. EXAMPLE: AUTOMATING A SIMPLE TASK

Scenario: Automate the formatting of a sales report.

We have below data in Sheet1 of our workbook.

	A	B	C	D
1	Region	Sales ($)	Costs ($)	Profit ($)
2	North	500	300	200
3	South	700	400	300
4	East	600	350	250
5				

Goal:

- Bold headers.
- Apply currency formatting to numerical values.
- Highlight profits greater than $250.

VBA Code:

```
Sub FormatDataset()

    Dim ws As Worksheet

    Dim dataRange As Range

    Dim headerRange As Range

    Dim profitColumn As Range

    Dim cell As Range

    ' Set the worksheet and data range

    Set ws = ThisWorkbook.Sheets(1) ' Adjust sheet index if necessary

    Set dataRange = ws.Range("A1:D4") ' Adjust range based on your dataset

    Set headerRange = ws.Range("A1:D1") ' Adjust header range

    Set profitColumn = ws.Range("D2:D4") ' Adjust profit column range


    ' Bold headers

    headerRange.Font.Bold = True


    ' Apply currency formatting to numerical values

    dataRange.Columns("B:D").NumberFormat = "$#,##0"


    ' Highlight profits greater than $250

    For Each cell In profitColumn
```

If cell.Value > 250 Then

    cell.Interior.Color = RGB(144, 238, 144) 'Light green color

End If

Next cell

MsgBox "Formatting applied successfully!", vbInformation

End Sub

Explanation of the code:

» **Worksheet and Data Range Setup**: The worksheet is defined as *ws*, and the range containing the dataset is *dataRange*.

» **Bold Headers**: The *headerRange.Font.Bold = True* line applies bold formatting to the headers.

» **Currency Formatting**: The *dataRange.Columns("B:D").NumberFormat = "$#,##0"* line applies currency formatting to the Sales, Costs, and Profit columns.

» **Highlight Profits**:
The *For Each cell In profitColumn* loop checks each value in the Profit column. If the value is greater than $250, the cell is highlighted with a light green color using RGB(144, 238, 144).

» **Success Message**:
A confirmation message (MsgBox) is displayed after the macro is executed.

Steps to Run the Code:

1. Open the **VBA Editor**: Press Alt + F11.
2. Insert a new module: **Insert > Module**.
3. Paste the code into the module.
4. Close the editor and return to Excel.
5. Run the macro: Press Alt + F8, select FormatDataset, and click **Run**.

Result:

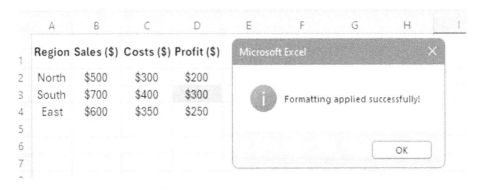

VI.   INTRODUCTION TO POWER PIVOT FOR LARGE DATASETS

Power Pivot is an advanced data modeling and analysis tool in Excel that enables you to work with large datasets, create relationships between data tables, and perform complex calculations efficiently. It extends Excel's capabilities by leveraging the power of a built-in database engine and the DAX (Data Analysis Expressions) language.

1. WHAT IS POWER PIVOT?

Power Pivot is an Excel add-in designed for advanced data analysis. It allows you to create data models, establish relationships, and create calculations. With Power Pivot you can work with large data sets, build extensive relationships, and create complex (or simple) calculations, all in a high-performance environment, and all within the familiar experience of Excel.

Key Features:

- Handle large datasets beyond Excel's row limit.
- Create relationships between tables without using **VLOOKUP**.
- Use DAX formulas for complex calculations.
- Build efficient, memory-optimized data models.

Use Cases for Power Pivot

- **Combining Data from Multiple Sources**: import data from SQL databases, Excel files, and web services into a single model.
- **Complex Relationships**: build relationships between tables without flattening data into one worksheet.
- **Advanced Reporting**: create interactive dashboards with calculated fields and advanced metrics.
- **Handling Large Data**: analyze millions of rows without performance issues.

2. ENABLING POWER PIVOT

Power Pivot is available in Excel for Microsoft 365, Excel 2024, Excel 2021, Excel 2019, and Excel 2016. To enable it:

1. Go to **File > Options > Add-Ins**.
2. Under **Manage**, select **COM Add-ins** and click **Go**.
3. Check **Microsoft Power Pivot for Excel** and click **OK**.

3. STEPS TO USE POWER PIVOT

Step 1: Import Data

- Open Power Pivot: Go to **Power Pivot > Manage**.
- Import data from multiple sources: Excel files, databases, web data, etc.

Step 2: Create Relationships

- In the Power Pivot window, go to **Diagram View**.
- Drag and drop fields to establish relationships between tables (e.g., link ProductID in the Sales table to ProductID in the Product table).

Step 3: Add Calculations Using DAX

- Use DAX formulas to create calculated fields, columns, and measures.

Step 4: Build Pivot Tables and Charts

- Close the Power Pivot window. Then insert a PivotTable in Excel using **Insert > PivotTable > From Data Model**; or
- Within the Power Pivot window, select PivotTable > New Worksheet.

4. EXAMPLE: ANALYZING SALES DATA WITH POWER PIVOT

Scenario: Combine sales data from multiple tables to analyze total sales by region and product.

We have Sales table and Products table in 2 sheets in our workbook.

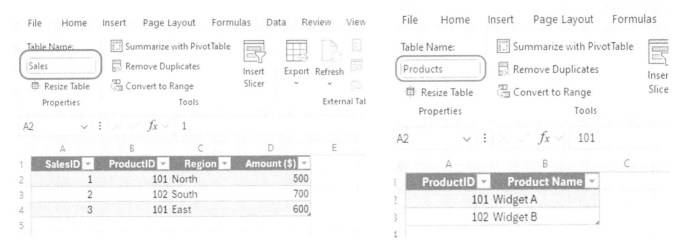

Steps:

1. Go to the Power Pivot tab in Excel and click Manage to open the Power Pivot window

2. In the Power Pivot window:
   - » Click Home → From Other Sources → Excel File.
   - » Browse to the current workbook and select it.
   - » Check both Sales and Products tables for import and click Next.
   - » Rename tables if needed and click Finish. The data from both tables will now be loaded into Power Pivot.

3. In the Power Pivot window, go to the Diagram View (button on the top-right).
   Drag the ProductID column from the Sales table to the ProductID column in the Products table.

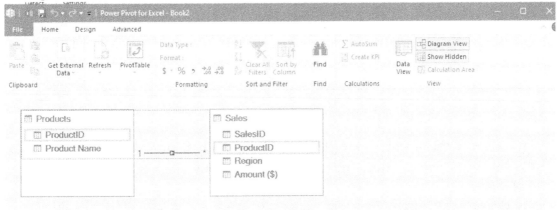

4. Add a calculated field for total sales and rename the header of that column as Total Sales.

5. In the Power Pivot window, click on PivotTable to build a PivotTable to display sales by region and product.

6. In the PivotTable Field List:

» Drag Region (from the Sales table) to the Rows area.

» Drag Product Name (from the Products table) to the Columns area.

» Drag Amount ($) (from the Sales table) to the Values area.

» This will display the total sales amount for each region and product.

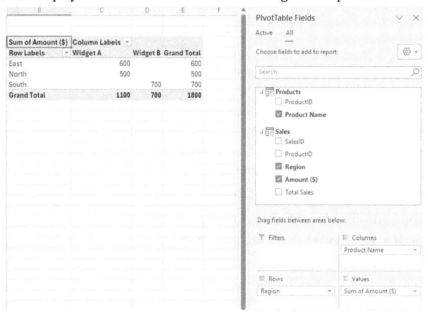

Result:

Sum of Amount ($)	Column Labels		
Row Labels	Widget A	Widget B	Grand Total
East	600		600
North	500		500
South		700	700
Grand Total	1100	700	1800

5. ADVANCED FEATURES IN POWER PIVOT

- **Hierarchies**: create hierarchies (e.g., Year > Quarter > Month) for intuitive reporting.
- **KPI (Key Performance Indicators)**: define KPIs using measures and thresholds to track performance.
- **Data Views**: use **Diagram View** to visualize relationships and **Data View** for editing tables.
- **Time Intelligence**: use DAX functions like TOTALYTD, SAMEPERIODLASTYEAR, or DATEADD for time-based analysis.

CHAPTER 8: COLLABORATION AND CLOUD INTEGRATION

I.   SHARING WORKBOOKS WITH ONEDRIVE

Sharing workbooks via OneDrive simplifies collaboration by enabling access from anywhere, ensuring all users work on the most up-to-date version of the file.

1.   WHY USE ONEDRIVE FOR SHARING?

- **Accessibility**: Access files from any device connected to the internet.
- **Real-Time Updates**: Changes are saved and synced instantly, reducing version conflicts.
- **Security**: Manage permissions to control who can view or edit your workbooks.

2.   STEPS TO SHARE WORKBOOKS WITH ONEDRIVE

Save Workbook to OneDrive:
   » Go to **File > Save As** and select **OneDrive** as the location.

Share the Workbook:
   » Click **Share** in the top-right corner of Excel.
   » Enter email addresses of collaborators or copy the link to share.
   » Set permissions: Choose **Can Edit** or **Can View** based on the collaborator's role.

Access Sharing Settings:
   » Click **Manage Access** to update permissions or stop sharing.

II.   CO-EDITING IN REAL-TIME

Real-time co-editing allows multiple users to work simultaneously on the same workbook, enhancing productivity and reducing delays in collaborative tasks.

1.   BENEFITS OF REAL-TIME CO-EDITING

- **Increased Efficiency**: No need to wait for others to complete their changes.
- **Instant Updates**: Changes appear in real-time for all collaborators.
- **Version Control**: One shared file eliminates the need for multiple versions.

2.   STEPS TO ENABLE REAL-TIME CO-EDITING

1. **Save Workbook to OneDrive or SharePoint**: ensure the workbook is stored in a shared cloud location.
2. **Share the Workbook**:
   » Click **Share** in the top-right corner.

» Set permissions to **Can Edit** for collaborators.

3. **Collaborate in Real-Time**: when collaborators open the shared workbook, their presence is indicated by colored flags or initials on the cells they are editing.

3. ADDING AND MANAGING COMMENTS

- **Add a Comment**: right-click a cell and select **New Comment** to open the comment thread.
- **Reply to Comments**: collaborators can reply directly in the comment thread for easy discussion.
- **Resolve or Delete Comments**: once a discussion is completed, mark the comment as resolved or delete it.

III. LINKING EXCEL WITH WORD, POWERPOINT, AND TEAMS

Integrating Excel with other Microsoft tools like Word, PowerPoint, and Teams enhances productivity by streamlining workflows and enabling seamless sharing of data across platforms.

1. LINKING EXCEL WITH WORD

Linking Excel to Word allows you to embed or link data for reports or documents that require dynamic updates.

Use Cases:

- Creating reports with live Excel tables and charts.
- Embedding financial summaries or data snapshots.

Steps:

- **Copy and Paste as a Linked Object:**
  » In Excel, copy the desired range (e.g., a table or chart).
  » In Word, use **Paste Special > Paste Link** to link the data dynamically.
  » Updates in the Excel file reflect automatically in Word.

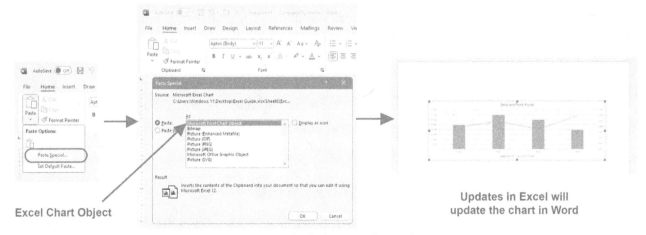

Excel Chart Object

Updates in Excel will
update the chart in Word

Figure 6.   Linked Object with Word.png

- **Embed as a Static Object:**
  » Copy the range from Excel and paste it into Word as a static table or image.

» Use this for documents that don't require updates.

- **Insert Excel Workbook as an Object:**
  » In Word, go to **Insert > Object > Create from File**, and select your Excel workbook.
  » Choose **Link to file** for dynamic updates or leave it unchecked for a static version.

2. LINKING EXCEL WITH POWERPOINT

Excel's integration with PowerPoint is ideal for presentations requiring live or formatted data visualizations.

Use Cases:

- Displaying charts and graphs in presentations.
- Updating tables in PowerPoint automatically when Excel data changes.

Steps:

- **Copy and Paste as a Linked Object:**
  » Copy an Excel chart or table.
  » In PowerPoint, use **Paste Special > Paste Link**.
  » Updates in the Excel file are reflected in PowerPoint.

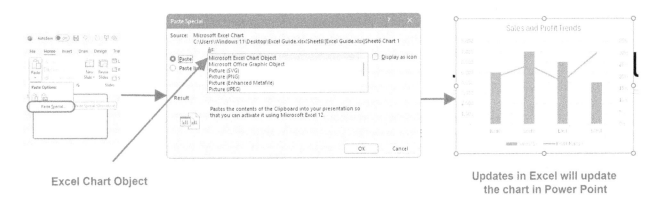

Excel Chart Object

Updates in Excel will update
the chart in Power Point

Figure 7.   Linked Object with PowerPoint.png

- **Embed Excel Data:**
  » Insert the Excel file as an object using **Insert > Object > Create from File**.
  » Double-clicking the embedded file opens it for editing.

- **Use Export Options:**
  » In Excel, format your data and export it directly to PowerPoint using **File > Export > Create Handouts**.

3. LINKING EXCEL WITH TEAMS

Microsoft Teams integrates seamlessly with Excel for collaborative editing and sharing of workbooks in real-time.

Use Cases:

- » Collaborating on shared workbooks during Teams meetings.
- » Sharing dynamic dashboards or reports.

Steps:

- **Share an Excel Workbook in Teams:**
  - » Upload your workbook to a Teams channel or chat using **Files > Upload**.
  - » Click the uploaded file to open it directly in Teams for editing.

- **Collaborate in Real-Time:**
  - » Multiple users can edit the workbook simultaneously in Teams or open it in Excel Online.

- **Pin Excel Files for Quick Access:**
  - » Pin important workbooks to the channel tab for easy access by team members.

- **Use Excel During Meetings:**
  - » Share the Excel workbook live in a Teams meeting using **Share Screen** or by opening it in the meeting chat.

BONUS CONTENT

Thank you for purchasing the paperback edition! As a special token of our appreciation, we're excited to offer you a free eBook version of this guide. Simply scan the QR code below to access the eBook on any device and unlock exclusive bonus content:

Your Exclusive Bonuses:

1. 20+ Ready-to-Use Templates — budgets, dashboards, project planners, invoice trackers & more (instant download)
2. Exclusive ChatGPT & Copilot Guide — supercharge formulas, cleaning, analysis & automation with simple prompts
3. Excel Shortcuts Cheatsheet — time-saving keys pros rely on every day
4. Video Tips Library — bite-sized walkthroughs for every skill level
5. Practice Exercises + Solutions — learn by doing and self-check instantly
6. New! Monthly Template Drops — join our readers' club for fresh resources all year

Take your Excel skills to the next level with these additional resources. Enjoy exploring!

WORD MASTERY 2026

FROM BEGINNER TO EXPERT

THE ULTIMATE GUIDE TO FEATURES, FUNCTIONS, AND PRODUCTIVITY TIPS

CHAPTER 1: GETTING STARTED

I.   INSTALLING AND LAUNCHING WORD

Installing and launching Microsoft Word as part of Microsoft 365 is straightforward. This section will guide you through the process to ensure you have Word set up and ready to use on your device.

1.   INSTALLING MICROSOFT WORD

i.   Microsoft 365 Subscription:

1. Visit the Microsoft 365 website (www.microsoft.com/en/microsoft-365) to purchase a subscription or sign in if you already have one.
2. Choose the plan that best suits your needs (e.g., Personal, Family, or Business).

ii.   Download and Installation:

1. After purchasing a subscription, sign in with your Microsoft account.
2. Go to the **Services & Subscriptions** section, and select **Install Office**.
3. Download the Office installer and run it on your device.
4. Follow the on-screen instructions to complete the installation process.

2.   LAUNCHING MICROSOFT WORD

i.   On Desktop:

1. Open the **Start Menu** (Windows) or **Applications Folder** (Mac).
2. Search for "Microsoft Word" and click to launch.
3. Alternatively, pin Word to your Taskbar or Dock for quick access.

ii.   On Mobile:

1. Tap the Word app icon on your smartphone or tablet.
2. Sign in with your Microsoft 365 credentials to access your documents.

iii.   Cloud Integration:

1. When launching Word, connect it to OneDrive for seamless access to your cloud-saved files.
2. Use the **Recent Documents** list to quickly open previously edited files.

II.   THE WORD ENVIRONMENT: RIBBON, TOOLBAR, AND NAVIGATION PANE

Microsoft Word introduces a modernized and user-friendly interface designed to streamline your document creation process. This section will guide you through the essential components of the Word environment to ensure you are comfortable navigating and using its features effectively.

1.   THE RIBBON

The Ribbon is the central hub for all commands and tools in Word. It is organized into tabs, each focusing on a specific aspect of document creation and editing. Key tabs include:

- **Home**: Basic text formatting, paragraph alignment, and clipboard functions.
- **Insert**: Tools for adding tables, pictures, shapes, charts, and more.
- **Layout**: Adjust page setup, margins, and spacing.
- **References**: Add citations, tables of contents, and footnotes.
- **Review**: Check spelling, track changes, and collaborate with others.

2. QUICK ACCESS TOOLBAR

The toolbar houses frequently used tools and can be customized for your workflow. By default, the Quick Access Toolbar includes shortcuts like Save, Undo, and Redo. You can add or remove commands to match your preferences.

3. THE NAVIGATION PANE

This powerful feature simplifies navigating large documents.

- **View the Navigation Pane**: Go to the **View** tab and check the **Navigation Pane** box.
- **Browse by Headings**: Jump between sections easily using your document's headings.
- **Search**: Quickly find specific text or phrases in your document.

4. STATUS BAR

Located at the bottom of the Word window, the status bar provides quick insights about your document:

- Page and word count.
- View options (e.g., Print Layout, Web Layout). You can right-click the status bar to customize what information is displayed.

5. CUSTOMIZING THE WORD ENVIRONMENT

Tailor Word to suit your needs: you can personalize your theme Word environment to show commands and tabs you use frequently and hide the ones you use less often.

Under the **File** menu, select **Options > General.** From there, you can customize Theme, Ribbon, Language, Display settings, Quick Access Toolbar, etc.

III. WORKING ON THE WORD START SCREEN

1. NAVIGATING THE WORD START SCREEN

The Start Screen appears when you open Word, providing several options to begin your work.

- **Recent Documents**: Quickly access files you've worked on recently.
- **Templates**: Choose a pre-designed template for common document types like resumes or reports.
- **New Blank Document**: Click on the **Blank Document** icon to start fresh.
- **Search for Templates**: Use the search bar to find templates that match your needs (e.g., "Invoice" or "Newsletter").

2.   CREATING YOUR FIRST DOCUMENT

Starting from Scratch:

1. Select **Blank Document** from the Start Screen.
2. Begin typing in the main workspace, also known as the canvas.

Using a Template:

1. Select a template that fits your needs.

2. Customize the text, formatting, and design elements as needed.

Open a document:

1. Double-click on the document to open it.
2. Press Ctrl + O to open the options. From here, you can quickly open the recent documents or browse the locations of the documents you need.

3.   SAVING YOUR WORK

Saving for the First Time:

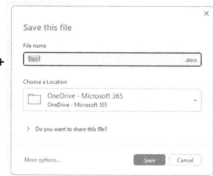

1. Go to **File > Save As** or click **Save** or press **Ctrl + S** (Windows) or **Command+S** (Mac).
2. Choose a location (e.g., your computer or OneDrive) and name your file.
3. Select a file format (default: **DOCX**).

AutoSave: Ensure AutoSave is enabled for files saved on OneDrive or SharePoint to avoid losing progress.

4.   CLOSING AND EXITING WORD

- **Close the Document**: Click the **X** in the top-right corner of the document window or select **File > Close**.
- **Exit Word**: Close all open documents and click the **X** in the application window.

IV. WORD TERMINOLOGY: PARAGRAPHS, STYLES, SECTIONS, AND HEADERS

Before diving deeper into using Microsoft Word, it's essential to understand some of its core terminology. These terms will frequently appear throughout the guide and help you navigate Word with ease.

1. PARAGRAPHS

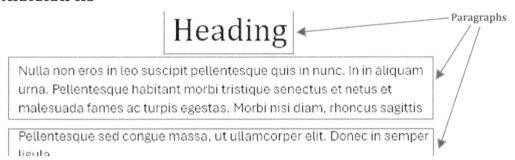

In Word, a paragraph is defined as any text followed by a hard return (pressing the Enter key). Paragraphs are the building blocks of documents and can be formatted individually.

- **Formatting Options**: Line spacing, indentation, and alignment.
- **Uses**: Create headings, body text, bullet points, or numbered lists.

2. STYLES

Styles are pre-defined sets of formatting options you can apply to text, paragraphs, or tables.

- **Types**: Heading styles, normal styles, and custom styles.
- **Benefits**: Ensures consistency throughout the document and speeds up formatting.
- **How to Apply**: Go to the **Home** tab and select from the **Styles Gallery**.

3. HEADERS AND FOOTERS

Headers appear at the top of each page, and footers appear at the bottom. They are used for consistent elements like page numbers, document titles, or dates.

4. SECTIONS

Sections divide your document into parts, allowing for different formatting settings (e.g., margins, headers, or footers) in each section.

5. FILE FORMATS

Microsoft Word supports a variety of file formats for saving and sharing documents. Common formats include:

- **DOCX**: The default format for Word documents.
- **PDF**: Ideal for sharing documents while preserving formatting.
- **RTF**: A basic text format compatible with most text editors.
- **Plain Text (TXT)**: A format without any formatting, ideal for plain text storage.

V. SETTING WORD ASIDE: USING WORD ON CLOUD PLATFORMS

Microsoft Word isn't just for desktops; it's designed to work seamlessly across devices with Cloud integration. This flexibility allows you to create, edit, and collaborate on documents anytime, anywhere.

1. USING WORD WITH CLOUD INTEGRATION

i. OneDrive Integration:

- Save your documents to **OneDrive** to ensure they are accessible across devices.
- Real-time syncing means changes are updated instantly, whether on desktop, mobile, or the web.

ii. Accessing Word Online:

- Open a browser and go to Office.com.
- Log in with your Microsoft 365 credentials.
- Use the web version of Word to edit documents directly without downloading the software.

iii. Benefits of Cloud-Based Word:

- **Real-Time Collaboration**: Work with teammates on the same document simultaneously.
- **Autosave**: Never lose progress as Word automatically saves your changes to the cloud.
- **Version History**: Access and restore previous versions of your document as needed.

2. SWITCHING BETWEEN PLATFORMS

Word ensures a smooth transition across devices. You can start drafting a document on your desktop, then continue editing on your smartphone during your commute, and present or finalize the document using a tablet or web browser.

3. MAXIMIZING MOBILITY AND FLEXIBILITY

To make the most of Word's mobile and cloud capabilities:

- Keep your devices synced with the same Microsoft 365 account.
- Use the **Share** button to send links or collaborate on cloud-stored documents.

CHAPTER 2: TYPING & EDITING

Mastering the basics of typing and formatting in Microsoft Word is fundamental to creating professional and visually appealing documents. This section will guide you through the essentials, helping you type efficiently and apply basic formatting to enhance your content.

I.   BASIC WORD TYPING

1.   TYPING TEXT

Start Typing:

- Click anywhere on the document canvas and begin typing.
- Press **Enter** to start a new paragraph and **Tab** to indent text.

Navigating Text:

- Use the arrow keys to move the cursor within your text.
- Hold **Ctrl** (Windows) or **Command** (Mac) while using the arrow keys to jump between words or lines.

2.   FORMATTING TEXT: FONTS, COLORS, AND SIZES

Basic formatting options are available in the **Home** tab under the **Font** group.

Font Style and Size:

1. Select your text and choose a font and size from the dropdown menus.
2. Use the **Increase Font Size** or **Decrease Font Size** buttons for quick adjustments.

Bold, Italic, Underline:

1. Highlight the text and click **B** (Bold), **I** (Italic), or **U** (Underline) in the toolbar.
2. Keyboard Shortcuts:
   - » **Bold: Ctrl+B** (Windows) or **Command+B** (Mac).
   - » **Italic: Ctrl+I** (Windows) or **Command+I** (Mac).
   - » **Underline: Ctrl+U** (Windows) or **Command+U** (Mac).

Text Color: select your text, click the **Font Color** icon (a colored "A"), and choose a color from the palette.

Highlighting: use the **Text Highlight Color** tool to draw attention to specific words or sentences.

3.   PARAGRAPH ALIGNMENT, INDENTATION, AND SPACING

Properly aligning and spacing paragraphs ensures your document is easy to read and visually appealing.

Paragraph Alignment

You can align text in different ways to suit the purpose of your content:

- **Left Alignment** (default): Aligns text to the left margin. Shortcut: **Ctrl+L** (Windows) or **Command+L** (Mac).
- **Center Alignment**: Aligns text to the center of the page. Shortcut: **Ctrl+E** (Windows) or **Command+E** (Mac).
- **Right Alignment**: Aligns text to the right margin. Shortcut: **Ctrl+R** (Windows) or **Command+R** (Mac).
- **Justify**: Aligns text evenly across the left and right margins for a polished look. Shortcut: **Ctrl+J** (Windows) or **Command+J** (Mac).

Indentation

Control how far text is indented from the margins:

- **None:** Indents the entire paragraph.
- **First Line Indent**: Indents only the first line of a paragraph. Use the ruler or go to **Home > Paragraph > Indentation**.
- **Hanging Indent**: Indents all lines except the first line of a paragraph. Commonly used for bibliographies and citations.

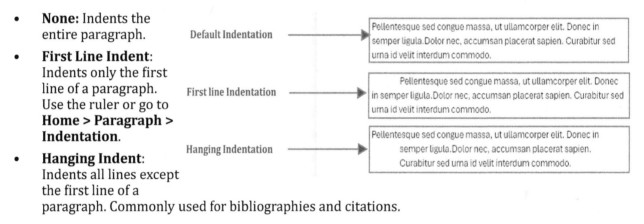

Line Spacing

Adjust the amount of space between lines for better readability:

1. Go to **Home > Paragraph > Line and Paragraph Spacing**.
2. Choose options like **1.0 (Single)**, **1.5**, or **2.0 (Double)**.
3. For custom spacing, select **Line Spacing Options**.

4. BULLETED AND NUMBERED LISTS

Organizing information into lists makes your document easier to read and understand.

Bulleted Lists

Use bullet points to create an unordered list:

1. Go to the **Home** tab and click the **Bullets** icon.

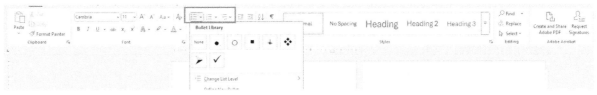

2. Type your items, pressing **Enter** after each one.
3. Customize bullets by clicking the dropdown menu next to the **Bullets** icon.

Numbered Lists

Use numbers for ordered lists, such as steps or priorities:

1. Click the **Numbering** icon in the **Home** tab.
2. Start typing your list, pressing **Enter** after each item.
3. Customize numbering styles (e.g., Roman numerals or letters) using the dropdown menu.

Nested Lists

Create sub-levels within a list:

1. Press **Tab** to indent and create a sub-item under a list.
2. Use **Shift+Tab** to move the item back to the main level.

Bullet list items:

- Item 1
- Item 2
- Item 3

Numbered list items:

1. Item 1
2. Item 2
3. Item 3

Nested list items:

1. Item 1
   a. Item 1a
   b. Item 1b
   c. Item 1c
2. Item 2
   a. Item 2a
   b. Item 2b
   c. Item 2c

5. SAVING TIME WITH FORMAT PAINTER

The **Format Painter** is a powerful tool for quickly applying consistent formatting to your text.

How to Use Format Painter

1. Select the text with the formatting you want to copy.
2. Click the Format Painter icon in the Home tab (a paintbrush icon). For multiple uses, double-click the icon to lock it.
3. Highlight the text or object you want to apply the formatting to.

When to Use Format Painter

- Copy formatting for headings, titles, or specific text styles.
- Apply consistent styles to bullet points, numbered lists, or table elements.
- Save time when working on large documents with repeated formatting needs.

6. INSERTING PAGE BREAKS MANUALLY AND REMOVING PAGE BREAKS

Page breaks allow you to start a new page without filling the current one, giving you control over your document's layout.

Inserting Page Breaks Manually

1. Place your cursor where you want to start a new page.
2. Go to the **Insert** tab and select **Page Break**, or use the shortcut **Ctrl+Enter** (Windows) or **Command+Enter** (Mac).
3. Word will immediately start a new page from the cursor's position.

Why Use Page Breaks?

- To start a new chapter or section on a fresh page.
- To separate content like tables or images from text.

Removing Page Breaks

1. Switch to **Print Layout** view to see where the breaks are.
    - » **Tip**: Enable **Show/Hide** in the **Home** tab to view page break indicators.

2. Place your cursor directly before the page break line.
3. Press **Delete** (Windows) or **Backspace** (Mac).
4. The page break will be removed, merging the content into the previous page.

7. DELETING TEXT

Deleting Words

- Hold down **Ctrl** (Windows) or **Option** (Mac) and press **Backspace** or **Delete** to remove one word at a time.

Deleting Sentences or Paragraphs

1. Select the sentence or paragraph you want to delete by dragging your mouse over it.
2. Press **Delete** or **Backspace** to remove the selection.

Deleting a Page

1. Go to the page you want to delete.
2. Highlight all the content on the page (use **Ctrl+A** or **Command+A** to select everything if needed).
3. Press **Delete** or **Backspace**.
    - » **Tip**: Ensure there are no manual page breaks causing the empty page to remain.

II. BASIC FORMATTING

1. SPLIT AND JOIN PARAGRAPHS: MERGING AND SEPARATING IDEAS

Paragraphs in Word can be easily split or joined to help structure your content effectively, whether you're breaking ideas into smaller chunks or merging them for better flow.

Splitting Paragraphs

To separate a single paragraph into two:

1. Place your cursor where you want to create the split.
2. Press **Enter** to start a new paragraph from that point.
    » The text following the cursor will move to a new paragraph.

Joining Paragraphs

To combine two paragraphs into one:

1. Place your cursor at the end of the first paragraph.
2. Press **Backspace** or **Delete** to remove the paragraph break.
3. The second paragraph will merge with the first, continuing on the same line.

2. SOFT AND HARD RETURNS: WHEN TO USE EACH

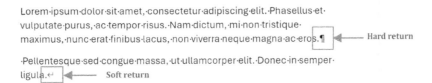

Returns determine how lines and paragraphs are spaced and structured in Word. Understanding the difference between soft and hard returns is key to creating a well-formatted document.

Hard Returns

- Created by pressing **Enter**.
- Signals the end of a paragraph and starts a new one.
- Use hard returns when you want a clear separation between paragraphs or sections.

Soft Returns

- Created by pressing **Shift+Enter**.
- Moves the cursor to the next line without starting a new paragraph.
- Use soft returns for breaking lines within the same paragraph, such as in an address or a poem.

Tip: Use the **Show/Hide Formatting Marks** (icon in the Home tab) to identify soft and hard returns in your document. Soft returns appear as arrows, and hard returns as paragraph symbols.

3. UNDO, REDO, AND REPEAT COMMANDS

Mistakes happen, and changes are sometimes necessary. Microsoft Word makes it easy to reverse, redo, or repeat actions with simple commands.

Undo: The Undo command reverses your last action:

- Use the keyboard shortcut **Ctrl+Z** (Windows) or **Command+Z** (Mac).
- Alternatively, click the **Undo** button (a curved arrow) on the Quick Access Toolbar.
- To undo multiple actions, click the Undo button repeatedly or click the dropdown arrow next to it to select specific actions to undo.

Redo: The Redo command reinstates the action you made before the Undo command:

- Use the keyboard shortcut **Ctrl+Y** (Windows) or **Command+Y** (Mac).
- Alternatively, click the **Redo** button (a curved arrow pointing in the opposite direction of Undo) on the Quick Access Toolbar.

Repeat: The Repeat command re-applies the last action you performed:

- Use the keyboard shortcut **F4** or **Ctrl+Y** (Windows) or **Command+Y** (Mac).

4. COPYING, CUTTING, AND PASTING CONTENT EFFICIENTLY

Moving or duplicating content is a frequent task in Word. These commands help you streamline the process.

Copying Content: The Copy command duplicates selected text or objects:

- Highlight the text or object you want to copy. Use the keyboard shortcut **Ctrl+C** (Windows) or **Command+C** (Mac).
- Alternatively, right-click the selection and choose **Copy** from the context menu.

Cutting Content: The Cut command removes selected content from its original location and places it on the clipboard:

- Highlight the text or object you want to cut. Use the keyboard shortcut **Ctrl+X** (Windows) or **Command+X** (Mac).
- Alternatively, right-click the selection and choose **Cut** from the context menu.

Pasting Content: The Paste command places the copied or cut content in a new location:

- Position the cursor where you want the content to appear. Use the keyboard shortcut **Ctrl+V** (Windows) or **Command+V** (Mac).
- Alternatively, right-click and choose **Paste** from the context menu.

Paste Options: Word offers additional options for how the content is inserted:

- **Keep Source Formatting**: Maintains the original font, size, and style.
- **Merge Formatting**: Adjusts the formatting to match the destination content.
- **Keep Text Only**: Strips all formatting and inserts plain text.

To access the paste option, right-click and choose Paste Options from the dialog.

Clipboard Manager: For multiple items, use the Clipboard Manager:

1. Go to the **Home** tab and click the small arrow in the Clipboard group.
2. Copy or cut multiple items, and the Clipboard will store them.
3. Select an item from the Clipboard pane to paste it into your document.

CHAPTER 3: DOCUMENT FORMATTING

I. FORMATTING WITH STYLES AND THEMES

Styles and themes are essential tools in Microsoft Word for creating documents that look polished and professional. By applying consistent formatting, you save time and ensure a cohesive design across your document.

1. WHAT ARE STYLES?

Styles are predefined sets of formatting instructions that can be applied to text, paragraphs, or tables. They include font type, size, color, spacing, and alignment.

Using Built-in Styles

1. Select the text or paragraph you want to format.
2. Go to the **Home** tab and locate the **Styles** group.
3. Click a style from the gallery, such as **Heading 1**, **Title**, or **Normal**.

Modifying Styles

1. Right-click a style in the **Styles** gallery.
2. Select **Modify** to adjust font, size, alignment, or other attributes.
3. Click **OK** to save changes and apply the modified style.

Creating a Custom Style

1. Highlight text formatted with the attributes you want to save as a style.
2. In the **Styles** group, click the dropdown arrow and select **Create a Style**.
3. Name your style and click **OK**. The custom style will now appear in the **Styles** gallery.

2. WHAT ARE THEMES?

Themes are collections of fonts, colors, and effects that can be applied to an entire document for a unified look.

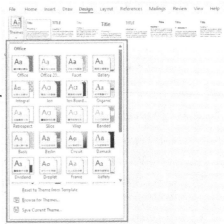

Applying a Theme

1. Go to the **Design** tab and locate the **Themes** group.
2. Select a theme from the dropdown menu. The theme will adjust fonts, colors, and graphical effects throughout your document.

Customizing a Theme

1. In the **Design** tab, select **Colors** or **Fonts** to modify specific elements of the theme.
2. Choose **Set as Default** if you want the custom theme to be used for new documents.

3. BEST PRACTICES FOR USING STYLES AND THEMES

- **Combine Styles with Themes**: Use styles for individual formatting and themes for overall design consistency.

- **Plan Ahead**: Decide on styles and themes before starting your document to avoid repetitive adjustments.

- **Keep It Simple**: Avoid overloading your document with many styles and themes, which creates a cluttered look.

II. SETTING PAPER SIZE, MARGINS, AND ORIENTATION

Properly setting the paper size, margins, and orientation is crucial for ensuring your document meets professional or personal requirements. Microsoft Word makes it easy to customize these settings for any project.

1. SETTING PAPER SIZE

The paper size determines the dimensions of your document. Standard sizes inc and A4 (8.27 x 11.69 inches).

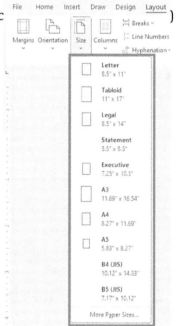

Accessing Paper Size Settings:

1. Go to the **Layout** tab and click **Size** in the **Page Setup** group.

2. Select a preset size from the dropdown menu (e.g., Letter, A4, Legal).

Customizing Paper Size:

1. Click **More Paper Sizes** at the bottom of the **Size** dropdown.

2. In the dialog box, input custom width and height dimensions.

3. Click **OK** to apply.

2. ADJUSTING MARGINS

Margins are the blank spaces between your content and the edges of the page. Adjusting them can optimize your document's layout and readability.

Using Preset Margins:

1. Go to the **Layout** tab, click **Margins** in the **Page Setup** group.

2. Choose from presets like **Normal**, **Narrow**, **Wide**, or **Custom Margins**.

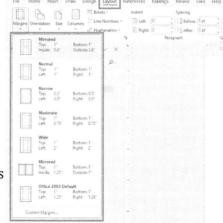

Customizing Margins:

1. Select **Custom Margins** from the **Margins** dropdown.

2. In the **Page Setup** dialog box, input specific values for top, bottom, left, and right margins.

3. Click **OK** to save changes.

3. CHOOSING PAGE ORIENTATION

Orientation determines whether your document is displayed vertically (Portrait) or horizontally (Landscape).

Changing Orientation:

1. Go to the **Layout** tab and click **Orientation** in the **Page Setup** group.
2. Select either **Portrait** or **Landscape**.

When to Use Each Orientation:

- **Portrait**: Best for text-heavy documents like letters, essays, or reports.
- **Landscape**: Ideal for charts, graphs, or wide tables.

4. TIPS FOR SETTING UP YOUR DOCUMENT LAYOUT

- **Check Printing Requirements**: Ensure your paper size and margins match the specifications of your printer.
- **Preview Your Layout**: Use **File > Print** to view how your document will appear when printed.
- **Use Consistent Settings**: For multi-section documents, ensure the layout settings are consistent throughout.

III. USING SECTION BREAKS FOR ADVANCED LAYOUT

Section breaks allow you to organize and structure your document effectively. They help you manage complex layouts, control content flow, and apply different formatting to specific parts of your document.

Types of Section Breaks

- **Next Page**: Starts a new section on the next page.
- **Continuous**: Starts a new section on the same page.
- **Even Page**: Begins a new section on the next even-numbered page.
- **Odd Page**: Begins a new section on the next odd-numbered page.

Inserting Section Breaks

1. Place your cursor where you want to insert the break.
2. Go to the **Layout** tab, click **Breaks**, and choose the desired section break.

Removing Section Breaks

1. Enable **Show/Hide Formatting Marks** in the **Home** tab to see section breaks.
2. Highlight the section break and press **Delete** or **Backspace**.

IV. ADDING HEADERS, FOOTERS, AND PAGE NUMBERS

Headers, footers, and page numbers are essential elements in creating well-organized and professional documents. They provide context and navigation for readers while maintaining a consistent layout.

1. ADDING HEADERS AND FOOTERS

Headers appear at the top of each page, while footers are placed at the bottom. Both can include text, graphics, or dynamic elements like page numbers and dates.

Inserting a Header or Footer

1. Go to the **Insert** tab and click **Header** or **Footer** in the **Header & Footer** group.
2. Choose a style from the dropdown menu or select **Edit Header/Edit Footer** to create a custom design.
3. Type your content in the header or footer area, such as a title, date, or company logo.

Customizing Headers and Footers

1. Use the **Header & Footer Tools** tab to:
   » Align content left, center, or right.
   » Insert images, text, or additional elements like dates.
   » Format text using font styles and sizes.
2. To apply different headers or footers to specific sections:
   » Insert a section break (see previous section).
   » Uncheck **Link to Previous** in the **Header & Footer Tools** tab.

2. ADDING PAGE NUMBERS

Page numbers make it easier to navigate long documents and reference specific sections.

Inserting Page Numbers

1. Go to the **Insert** tab and click **Page Number** in the **Header & Footer** group.
2. Choose a location (Top of Page, Bottom of Page, or Page Margins) and select a style.
3. The page numbers will appear automatically in the chosen position.

Customizing Page Numbers

1. To start numbering from a specific page:
   » Insert a section break before the desired page.
   » Go to **Insert > Page Number > Format Page Numbers**, and set the starting number.
2. To format page numbers:
   » Select **Format Page Numbers** from the **Page Number** dropdown.
   » Choose a number format (e.g., Roman numerals or alphabetical).

3. To remove page numbers from specific sections:
   » Use a section break to isolate the section.
   » Uncheck **Link to Previous** in the header or footer area and delete the page number.

3. TIPS FOR HEADERS, FOOTERS, AND PAGE NUMBERS

- **Preview Your Changes**: Use the **Print Layout** view to see how headers, footers, and page numbers appear.
- **Avoid Clutter**: Keep headers and footers simple for readability and professionalism.
- **Use Dynamic Fields**: Add dynamic elements like the document title or current date by clicking **Quick Parts > Field** in the **Header & Footer Tools** tab.

V. INSERTING AUTOMATIC TABLE OF CONTENTS

A table of contents (TOC) provides a structured overview of your document, making it easier for readers to navigate. Word allows you to generate a TOC automatically based on the headings in your document.

1. INSERTING A TABLE OF CONTENTS

Preparing Your Document for a Table of Contents

Before inserting a TOC, ensure your document is properly structured:

1. Use **Heading Styles** for section titles:
   » Highlight the section title.
   » Go to the **Home** tab and select a heading style (e.g., **Heading 1**, **Heading 2**) from the **Styles** group.
2. Apply consistent heading levels throughout your document for clear organization.

Inserting a Table of Contents

1. Place your cursor where you want the TOC to appear (typically at the beginning of the document).
2. Go to the **References** tab and click **Table of Contents** in the **Table of Contents** group.
3. Choose a built-in TOC style from the dropdown menu (e.g., Classic, Modern, or Formal).
4. Word will automatically generate a TOC based on your headings.

2. UPDATING AND CUSTOMIZING TABLE OF CONTENTS

Updating the Table of Contents

As you make changes to your document, the TOC does not update automatically. Here's how to refresh it:

1. Click anywhere inside the TOC.
2. Select **Update Table** in the upper-left corner of the TOC.

3. Choose either:

- **Update page numbers only**: If you've made no structural changes but content has shifted.
- **Update entire table**: If you've added, removed, or renamed headings.

Customizing the Table of Contents

1. Go to **References > Table of Contents > Custom Table of Contents**.
2. In the dialog box, adjust the following:
   - » **Show Levels**: Choose how many heading levels to include.
   - » **Tab Leader**: Select dots, dashes, or no leader for the TOC.
   - » **Formats**: Choose from pre-defined TOC designs or create a custom style.
3. Click **OK** to apply the changes.

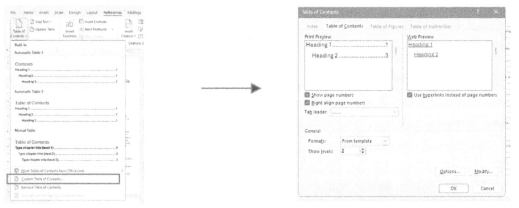

Removing the Table of Contents

If you need to remove the TOC:

1. Click inside the TOC.
2. Go to **References > Table of Contents > Remove Table of Contents**.

3. TIPS FOR A CLEAR TABLE OF CONTENTS

- **Use Descriptive Headings**: Ensure each section title clearly represents the content it covers.
- **Keep It Simple**: Avoid overloading the TOC with too many levels to maintain readability.
- **Preview Before Printing**: Check the TOC in **Print Layout** view to ensure accuracy and proper alignment.

VI. ADDING CAPTIONS AND INSERTING AUTOMATIC TABLE OF FIGURES

Captions and an automatic Table of Figures are essential for organizing and referencing visual elements like images, charts, and tables in your document. They make your content more accessible and professional.

1. ADDING CAPTIONS TO FIGURES

Captions provide a short description for visual elements, helping readers understand their context.

Steps to Add a Caption

1. Select the figure (image, chart, or table) you want to caption.
2. Go to the **References** tab and click **Insert Caption** in the **Captions** group.
3. In the dialog box:
    »   Enter the caption text (e.g., "Figure 1: Sales Trends for 2025").
    »   Choose the label type (e.g., **Figure**, **Table**, or **Equation**).
    »   Select the position (**Above Selected Item** or **Below Selected Item**).
4. Click **OK** to insert the caption.

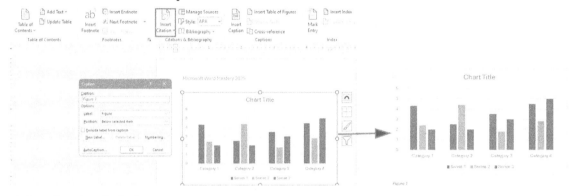

Customizing Caption Labels

1. In the **Insert Caption** dialog box, click **New Label** to create a custom label. Example: Replace "Figure" with "Image" or "Chart."
2. Use consistent labels throughout your document for clarity.

2.   CREATING AN AUTOMATIC TABLE OF FIGURES

A Table of Figures is a list of all the captions in your document, similar to a Table of Contents.

Steps to Insert a Table of Figures

1. Place your cursor where you want the Table of Figures to appear (typically after the Table of Contents).
2. Go to the **References** tab and click **Insert Table of Figures** in the **Captions** group.

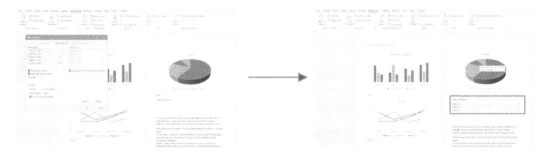

3. In the dialog box:
    »   Choose the caption label to include (e.g., **Figure**, **Table**).
    »   Customize the tab leader (dots, dashes, or none).
    »   Adjust formatting options as needed.
4. Click **OK** to generate the Table of Figures.

Updating the Table of Figures

1. After adding or modifying captions, click inside the Table of Figures.
2. Click **Update Table** in the upper-left corner of the table.
3. Choose **Update page numbers only** or **Update entire table**, depending on your changes.

3. BEST PRACTICES FOR CAPTIONS AND TABLES OF FIGURES

- **Be Consistent**: Use the same label style and formatting for all captions.
- **Keep Captions Concise**: Provide just enough detail to describe the visual element.
- **Preview Layout**: Check the Table of Figures in **Print Layout** view to ensure proper alignment and readability.

VII. DESIGNING A COVER PAGE

A well-designed cover page sets the tone for your document and provides essential information such as the title, author, and date. Microsoft Word offers built-in tools and templates to create professional and visually appealing cover pages with ease.

1. USING BUILT-IN COVER PAGE TEMPLATES

Word includes a variety of pre-designed cover page templates that you can customize to suit your document's needs.

Steps to Insert a Cover Page

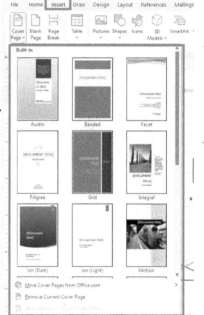

1. Go to the **Insert** tab and click **Cover Page**.
2. Select a template from the dropdown menu. Templates include placeholders for text, images, and other elements.
3. Click on the placeholders and replace the sample text with your own content (e.g., document title, author name, and date).

2. CUSTOMIZING A COVER PAGE

To make the cover page unique and tailored to your needs, you can modify or create your own design.

Modify a Template

After inserting a template, customize it by:

- Changing fonts, colors, and sizes using the **Home** tab.
- Adding your company logo or other images using the **Insert > Pictures** option.
- Adjusting layout elements by dragging and resizing text boxes or images.

Creating a Custom Cover Page

1. Start with a blank page by inserting a **Blank Page** from the **Insert** tab.
2. Use the following tools to design your cover page:

- » **Text Boxes**: Go to **Insert > Text Box** to add titles, subtitles, or author names.
- » **Shapes**: Use **Insert > Shapes** to add decorative elements like lines or rectangles.
- » **Pictures**: Insert images or logos to enhance the visual appeal.
- » **Themes**: Apply a theme from the **Design** tab for consistent formatting.

3. Once the design is complete, save it as a template:
- » Highlight all elements on the cover page.
- » Go to **File > Save As** and choose **Word Template** as the file format.

3. TIPS FOR AN EFFECTIVE COVER PAGE

- • **Keep It Simple**: Avoid clutter by including only essential information.
- • **Align with Your Document's Purpose**: Use fonts, colors, and images that match the tone of your document (e.g., professional for reports, creative for event programs).
- • **Maintain Consistency**: Ensure the cover page design aligns with the rest of your document's theme and style.

VIII. WORKING WITH CITATIONS AND REFERENCES

Citations and references are essential for academic, professional, and research-based documents. Microsoft Word simplifies the process of managing sources and creating bibliographies.

1. ADDING CITATIONS

Steps to Add a Citation

1. Go to the **References** tab and click **Insert Citation** in the **Citations & Bibliography** group.
2. Select **Add New Source** from the dropdown.
3. In the **Create Source** dialog box:
   - » Choose the source type (e.g., book, journal, website).
   - » Fill in the required details (author, title, year, etc.).
   - » Click OK to save the source.

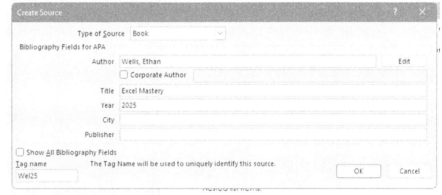

4. The citation will be inserted in the selected format (e.g., APA, MLA).

2. MANAGING SOURCES

The **Source Manager** allows you to organize and reuse citations across documents.

1. Click **Manage Sources** in the **Citations & Bibliography** group.
2. In the dialog box:
   - » View all sources in the **Current List** or **Master List**. Edit or delete existing sources as needed.

» Copy sources between the lists for use in different documents.

3. CREATING A BIBLIOGRAPHY OR WORKS CITED PAGE

A bibliography or works cited page is a list of all the sources cited in your document.

Steps to Insert a Bibliography

1. Place your cursor where you want the bibliography to appear (usually at the end of the document).
2. Go to the **References** tab and click **Bibliography** in the **Citations & Bibliography** group.
3. Choose a built-in bibliography or works cited style from the dropdown.

4. FORMATTING CITATIONS AND BIBLIOG-RAPHIES

Word supports various citation styles, including APA, MLA, and Chicago.

Changing the Citation Style

1. Go to the **References** tab and select a style from the **Style** dropdown in the **Citations & Bibliography** group.
2. Word will automatically update all citations and the bibliography to match the selected style.

Customizing the Appearance

1. Highlight the citation or bibliography text.
2. Use the formatting tools in the **Home** tab to adjust font, size, or spacing.

5. USING CROSS-REFERENCES

Cross-references link to specific elements within the document, such as tables, figures, or headings.

Steps to Add a Cross-Reference

1. Place your cursor where you want the reference to appear.
2. Go to the **References** tab and click **Cross-reference**.
3. Select the type of reference (e.g., heading, figure, table).
4. Choose the specific item from the list and click **Insert**.

6. TIPS FOR WORKING WITH CITATIONS AND REFERENCES

- **Keep Your Sources Organized**: Use the Source Manager to maintain a master list of frequently used references.
- **Double-Check Accuracy**: Ensure that the citation style and source details meet the required guidelines.

CHAPTER 4: BORDERS AND TABLES

I.   BORDERS

Borders are an excellent way to add structure, emphasis, or a decorative touch to your document. You can apply borders to text, paragraphs, or entire pages in Microsoft Word.

1.   ADDING BORDERS TO TEXT

Text borders highlight specific content, such as headings or important notes.

Steps to Add a Text Border

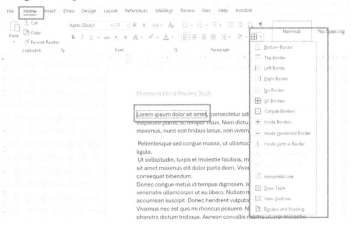

1.   Select the text you want to surround with a border.
2.   Go to the **Home** tab and click the **Borders** dropdown in the **Paragraph** group.
3.   Choose a border style (e.g., Bottom Border, All Borders).
4.   To customize the border:
     »   Select **Borders and Shading** from the dropdown.
     »   In the dialog box, choose the border style, color, and width.
     »   Click **OK** to apply the changes.

2.   ADDING BORDERS TO PARAGRAPHS

Borders around paragraphs can visually separate blocks of text or emphasize key sections.

Steps to Add a Paragraph Border

1.   Place your cursor inside the paragraph or select multiple paragraphs.
2.   Go to the **Home** tab and open the **Borders** dropdown.
3.   Choose **Borders and Shading** for more options.

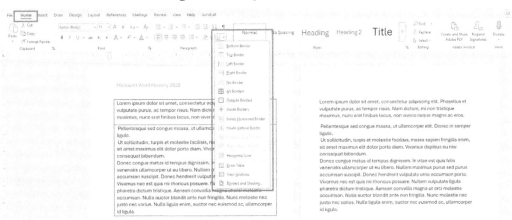

4. In the dialog box: Under **Settings**, select the desired border type (e.g., Box, Shadow, or Custom).

   » Adjust border style, color, and width.

5. Click **OK** to apply.

3. ADDING PAGE BORDERS

Page borders are ideal for adding a decorative or professional frame around the entire page.

Steps to Add a Page Border

1. Go to the **Design** tab and click **Page Borders** in the **Page Background** group.
2. In the **Borders and Shading** dialog box:

   » Under **Settings**, choose **Box**, **Shadow**, or **3D**.

   » Select the desired border style, color, and width. To use a decorative design, choose an option from the **Art** dropdown.

3. Under **Apply To**, select where the border should appear on.
4. Click **OK** to apply the border.

4. REMOVING BORDERS

1. Select the text, paragraph, or page with the border.
2. Open the **Borders** dropdown in the **Home** tab.
3. Select **No Border** to remove the applied border.

5. TIPS FOR USING BORDERS EFFECTIVELY

- **Keep It Simple**: Use subtle borders for professional documents and bold ones for creative or informal projects.
- **Combine with Shading**: Pair borders with background shading for added emphasis (found in the **Borders and Shading** dialog box).
- **Preview Before Finalizing**: Use the **Print Preview** feature to ensure borders align well with your document's layout.

II. CREATING AND FORMATTING TABLES FOR STRUCTURED DATA

Tables are an effective way to organize and present structured data in your document. Microsoft Word provides robust tools to create and customize tables for various purposes, from simple layouts to complex data presentations.

1. CREATING A TABLE

Using the Table Grid

1. Go to the **Insert** tab and click **Table** in the **Tables** group.
2. Hover over the grid to select the desired number of rows and columns.
3. Click to insert the table into your document.

Using the Insert Table Option

1. Go to the **Insert** tab and click **Table**.
2. Select **Insert Table** from the dropdown menu.
3. Specify the number of rows and columns in the dialog box. Click **OK** to insert the table.

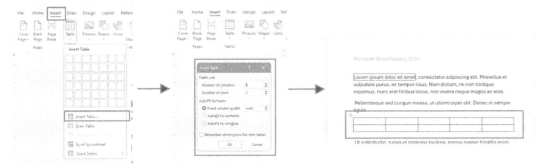

Drawing a Custom Table

1. Go to the **Insert** tab and click **Table**.
2. Select **Draw Table** from the dropdown menu.
3. Use the pencil tool to draw the table's borders manually. Click and drag to create cells, rows, or columns.

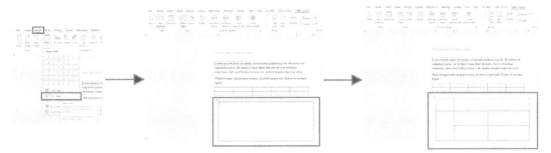

2. FORMATTING TABLES

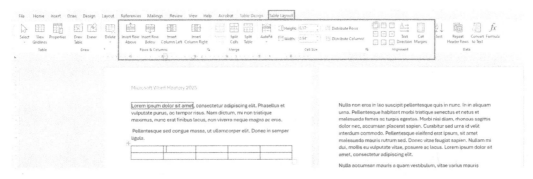

Adjusting Table Dimensions

1. Hover over a table border until you see the resize cursor (a double arrow). Drag the border to adjust row height or column width.
2. Alternatively, go to the **Layout** tab (under **Table Tools**) and use the **Height** and **Width** options to set precise dimensions.

Applying Table Styles

1. Click anywhere in the table.
2. Go to the **Table Design** tab (under **Table Tools**).
3. Choose a style from the **Table Styles** gallery for quick formatting.
4. Customize the style by selecting options like **Header Row**, **Banded Rows**, or **First Column** in the **Table Style Options** group.

Shading and Borders

1. Select the cells, rows, or columns you want to format.
2. Go to the **Table Design** tab:
   » Use **Shading** to add background color.
   » Use **Borders** to adjust the style, color, and width of cell borders.

Aligning Text in Cells

1. Select the cells you want to align.
2. Go to the **Layout** tab (under **Table Tools**) and use the **Alignment** group to choose text alignment (e.g., Top Left, Center, or Bottom Right).

Adding Rows or Columns

1. Click inside the table near where you want to add rows or columns.
2. Go to the **Layout** tab (under **Table Tools**) and use the options in the **Rows & Columns** group:
   » **Insert Above** or **Insert Below** for rows.
   » **Insert Left** or **Insert Right** for columns.

Deleting Rows or Columns

1. Select the rows or columns you want to remove.
2. Go to the **Layout** tab and click **Delete** in the **Rows & Columns** group.
3. Choose **Delete Rows**, **Delete Columns**, or **Delete Table** as needed.

Merging Cells

1. Select the cells you want to merge.
2. Go to the **Layout** tab and click **Merge Cells** in the **Merge** group.

Splitting Cells

1. Select the cell you want to split.
2. Go to the **Layout** tab and click **Split Cells** in the **Merge** group.
3. Specify the number of rows and columns for the split.

III. PLACING A COLUMN BREAK: MANAGING MULTI-COLUMN LAYOUTS

Multi-column layouts are a powerful way to format documents such as newsletters, brochures, and reports. Column breaks allow you to control the flow of content between columns, ensuring a polished layout.

1. CREATING A MULTI-COLUMN LAYOUT

Steps to Add Columns

1. Go to the **Layout** tab.
2. Click **Columns** in the **Page Setup** group.
3. Choose a preset option:
   » **One**: Standard single-column layout.
   » **Two** or **Three**: Splits content into the selected number of columns.
   » **Left** or **Right**: Creates one narrow and one wide column.
4. If none of the presets fit your needs, select **More Columns** to customize the width and spacing of each column.

Balancing Column Lengths

To balance the content across columns, insert a column break where necessary (explained below).

2. PLACING A COLUMN BREAK

Column breaks move content from one column to the next, giving you precise control over text placement.

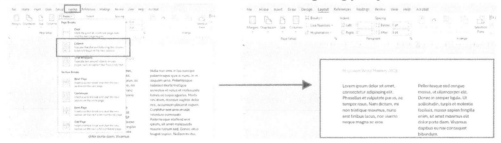

Steps to Insert a Column Break

1. Place your cursor where you want the content to move to the next column.
2. Go to the **Layout** tab.
3. Click **Breaks** in the **Page Setup** group.

4.   Select **Column** from the dropdown menu. The text after the break will move to the next column.

3.   CUSTOMIZING COLUMNS

Adjusting Column Width and Spacing

1.   Go to the **Layout** tab and click **Columns** > **More Columns**.
2.   In the dialog box:
   »   Adjust the width of each column.
   »   Modify the spacing between columns.
   »   Check **Line Between** to add a vertical line between the columns.
3.   Click **OK** to apply the changes.

Applying Columns to Specific Sections

1.   Highlight the text you want to format into columns.
2.   Go to the **Layout** tab and click **Columns**.
3.   Choose the desired column layout. Only the selected text will be formatted, leaving the rest of the document unchanged.

Removing Columns

1.   Highlight the content formatted into columns.
2.   Go to the **Layout** tab and click **Columns**.
3.   Select **One** to revert to a single-column layout.

IV.   GRAPHICAL WORKS IN MICROSOFT WORD

Visual elements like shapes, images, icons, and SmartArt enhance the impact and clarity of your documents. Microsoft Word provides tools to insert and customize these elements, making your documents more engaging and visually appealing.

1.   INSERTING AND CUSTOMIZING SHAPES, IMAGES, AND ICONS

Adding Shapes: Shapes can highlight important information or create visual interest.

1.   Go to the **Insert** tab and click **Shapes** in the **Illustrations** group.
2.   Select a shape (e.g., rectangle, arrow, circle) from the dropdown menu.
3.   Click and drag on the document to draw the shape.

Customizing Shapes

1.   Select the shape to open the **Shape Format** tab.
2.   Use the following tools:
   »   **Fill**: Change the shape's color with **Shape Fill**.
   »   **Outline**: Adjust the color, thickness, or style of the border with **Shape Outline**.
   »   **Effects**: Add shadows, reflections, or 3D effects using **Shape Effects**.

3. Resize the shape by dragging its edges or corners.

Inserting Images: Images help convey information more effectively and add visual appeal.

1. Go to the **Insert** tab and click **Pictures** in the **Illustrations** group.
2. Choose **This Device** to upload an image from your computer or **Online Pictures** to search for web-based images. Select the image and click **Insert** to add it to your document.

Customizing Images

1. Select the image to open the **Picture Format** tab.
2. Use tools like:
   » **Crop**: Trim unnecessary parts of the image.
   » **Corrections**: Adjust brightness, contrast, or sharpness.
   » **Picture Styles**: Add frames, borders, or effects to your image.

Inserting Icons: Icons are modern, scalable graphics that work well for visual communication.

1. Go to the **Insert** tab, click **Icons** in the **Illustrations** group.
2. Browse or search for an icon from Word's library.
3. Select an icon and click **Insert**.
4. Customize the icon's size, color, or position using the **Graphics Format** tab.

2. USING SMARTART FOR VISUAL HIERARCHY

SmartArt provides pre-designed diagrams to visually represent relationships, processes, or hierarchies.

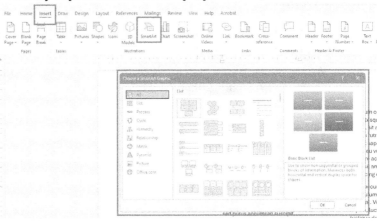

Inserting SmartArt

1. Go to the **Insert** tab and click **SmartArt**.
2. Choose a category (e.g., List, Process, Cycle, Hierarchy).
3. Select a layout and click **OK**.

Customizing SmartArt

1. Click inside the SmartArt graphic to add text.
2. Use the **SmartArt Design** tab to customize:
   » **Styles**: Apply pre-set styles for 3D effects, shadows, or outlines.
   » **Colors**: Change the color scheme to match your document's theme.
3. Resize or rearrange elements within the diagram by dragging or using the **Promote/Demote** options.

CHAPTER 5: ADVANCED LAYOUT & DESIGN

I.   PAGE SETUPS FOR PRINTING

Proper page setup is critical for creating print-ready documents that meet professional standards. Microsoft Word offers tools to adjust margins, paper size, and layout while providing a preview to ensure everything looks perfect before printing.

1.   ADJUSTING MARGINS

Margins define the blank space between your content and the edges of the page. Correct margins improve readability and give your document a polished look.

Setting Margins

1. Go to the **Layout** tab and click **Margins** in the **Page Setup** group.
2. Select a preset option (e.g., Normal, Narrow, Wide) from the dropdown menu.
3. For custom margins:
    » Click **Custom Margins** at the bottom of the dropdown.
    » In the dialog box, specify the values for top, bottom, left, and right margins.
    » Click **OK** to apply.

Tips for Margins

- Use **Normal (1-inch margins)** for standard documents like essays or reports.
- Adjust margins for special documents (e.g., Narrow margins for flyers or Wide margins for formal letters).

2.   SELECTING PAPER SIZE

Choosing the correct paper size ensures your document prints correctly on the intended medium.

Steps to Change Paper Size

1. Go to the **Layout** tab and click **Size** in the **Page Setup** group.
2. Select a preset size (e.g., Letter, Legal, A4) from the dropdown menu.
3. For custom sizes:
    » Click **More Paper Sizes** at the bottom of the dropdown.
    » Specify the width and height in the dialog box.
    » Click **OK** to apply.

Tips for Paper Size

- Use **Letter (8.5 x 11 inches)** for most standard documents.

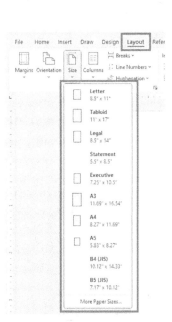

- Choose **A4 (8.27 x 11.69 inches)** for international printing.

3. PAGE ORIENTATION

Orientation determines whether your document is displayed vertically (Portrait) or horizontally (Landscape).

Changing Orientation

1. Go to the **Layout** tab and click **Orientation** in the **Page Setup** group.
2. Choose **Portrait** (default) or **Landscape** to adjust the layout.

4. PREVIEWING YOUR DOCUMENT BEFORE PRINTING

Previewing ensures your document looks as intended before sending it to the printer.

Steps to Preview

1. Go to **File > Print** to open the Print Preview screen.
2. Review the layout, margins, and overall formatting.
3. Use the zoom slider to examine details like alignment and spacing.

Making Adjustments from Print Preview

- If something doesn't look right, click **Back** to return to your document and make changes.
- Revisit the **Layout** tab to adjust margins, paper size, or orientation.

II. ALIGNING AND POSITIONING OBJECTS WITH PRECISION

Precise alignment and positioning of objects like text boxes, images, and shapes are essential for creating professional and visually appealing documents. Microsoft Word provides tools to ensure your layouts are polished and well-organized.

1. ALIGNING OBJECTS

Using the Align Tool

1. Select the object(s) you want to align.
2. Go to the **Shape Format** or **Picture Format** tab (depending on the type of object).
3. Click **Align** in the **Arrange** group.
4. Choose an alignment option:
   » **Align Left**: Aligns objects to the left margin.
   » **Align Center**: Centers objects horizontally.
   » **Align Right**: Aligns objects to the right margin.

- » **Align Top, Middle, Bottom**: Aligns objects vertically relative to the page or other objects.
- » **Distribute Horizontally** or **Distribute Vertically:** Aligns objects evenly. These options only appear if you select at least 3 objects.

Using Grids and Guides

Grids and guides help position objects accurately on the page.

- • **Turning On Grids and Guides**
  - » Go to the **View** tab.
  - » Check **Gridlines** or **Guides** in the **Show** group.
- • **Customizing Grid Settings**
  - » Go to **File > Options > Advanced** and scroll to the **Display** section.
  - » Adjust grid spacing or enable **Snap objects to grid when the gridlines are not displayed** for precise placement.

2. POSITIONING OBJECTS

Wrapping Text Around Objects

1. Select the object.
2. Go to the **Picture Format** or **Shape Format** tab and click **Wrap Text** in the **Arrange** group.
3. Choose a text-wrapping option:
   - » **Square**: Text flows around the object in a square pattern.
   - » **Tight**: Text closely follows the shape of the object.
   - » **Behind Text** or **In Front of Text**: Places the object behind or in front of the text.

Anchoring Objects

1. Select the object and go to the **Layout Options** icon that appears next to it.

2. Choose a specific position on the page or relative to text.

3. Enable **Fix position on page** to keep the object in place, regardless of text changes.

3. GROUPING AND LAYERING OBJECTS

Grouping Objects

1. Select multiple objects by holding **Ctrl** (Windows) or **Command** (Mac) while clicking each object.

2. Right-click and choose **Group** > **Group** to combine them into one element.

Layering Objects

1. Select an object and go to the **Shape Format** or **Picture Format** tab.

2. Use **Bring Forward** or **Send Backward** in the **Arrange** group to adjust the stacking order.

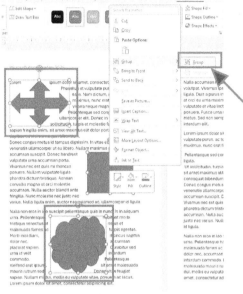

III. USING CHARTS

Charts visually represent data, making it easier to understand trends and comparisons.

Inserting a Chart

1. Go to the **Insert** tab and click **Chart** in the **Illustrations** group.

2. Choose a chart type, such as:

   » **Column**: Compare values across categories.

   » **Line**: Show trends over time.

   » **Pie**: Display proportions within a dataset.

3. Click **OK** to insert the chart and open an embedded Excel worksheet.

Editing Chart Data

1. Modify the data in the Excel worksheet.

2. Close the Excel window to update the chart in Word.

Customizing Chart Appearance

1. Select the chart to open the **Chart Tools** tab.

2. Use the **Design** and **Format** tabs to:

   » Change chart styles and colors.

   » Add or remove chart elements (e.g., axis titles, legends, data labels).

   » Adjust the layout and positioning.

IV. PREPARING DOCUMENTS FOR PUBLISHING

Creating publish-ready documents requires attention to detail and careful preparation. Microsoft Word provides tools to ensure your document is polished, properly formatted, and optimized for its purpose.

1. FINALIZING LAYOUT AND CONTENT

Before printing or publishing, ensure your document is free of errors and visually consistent.

Steps to Review Layout and Content

1. **Proofread Thoroughly**:
   » Use the **Review > Spelling & Grammar** tool to catch typos and grammatical errors.
   » Read through the document manually to ensure clarity and accuracy.

2. **Check Consistency**:
   » Verify uniform use of fonts, colors, and styles throughout the document.
   » Ensure headers, footers, and page numbers are properly formatted and consistent.

3. **Preview the Document**:
   » Go to **File > Print** to open the Print Preview screen.
   » Examine margins, alignment, and overall layout.

2. PREPARING FOR DIGITAL PUBLISHING

When publishing your document online or sharing it digitally, consider converting it to a PDF or another compatible format.

Saving as PDF

1. Go to **File > Save As**.
2. Choose the location and select **PDF** from the **Save as Type** dropdown.
3. Click **Options** to customize settings:
   » Optimize for **Standard (publishing online and printing)** or **Minimum size (publishing online only)**.
   » Include non-printing elements like comments or markup if needed.
4. Click **Save** to generate the PDF.

Embedding Fonts for Portability

1. Go to **File > Options > Save**.
2. Check Embed fonts in the file under the Preserve fidelity when sharing this document section. This ensures your document appears the same on all devices, even if the fonts are not installed.

3. TIPS FOR PROFESSIONAL DOCUMENTS

- **Use High-Resolution Images**: Low-quality images may appear pixelated in print or online.
- **Keep File Sizes Manageable**: Optimize images and content to prevent excessively large file sizes.
- **Check Copyrights**: Ensure all content, especially images, complies with copyright laws.

CHAPTER 6: AUTOMATING & ADVANCED FEATURES

I. USING MAIL MERGE FOR LETTERS, LABELS, AND ENVELOPES

Mail Merge is a powerful feature in Microsoft Word that allows you to personalize letters, labels, and envelopes for multiple recipients efficiently. By combining a main document with a data source, you can automate the creation of customized documents.

1. WHAT IS MAIL MERGE?

Mail Merge connects your Word document to a data source (e.g., Excel spreadsheet, Access database) to populate fields like names, addresses, and other details.

Examples of Use Cases

- Personalizing invitation letters for a large group.
- Printing address labels for mailing campaigns.
- Creating envelopes with recipient information.

2. STEPS TO PERFORM MAIL MERGE

1. Choose the Document Type

- Go to the **Mailings** tab.
- Click **Start Mail Merge** and select the type of document:
  - » **Letters**: For personalized letters.
  - » **Email Messages**: For sending emails (requires Outlook).
  - » **Envelopes** or **Labels**: For postal mailings.
  - » **Directory**: For creating lists or catalogs.

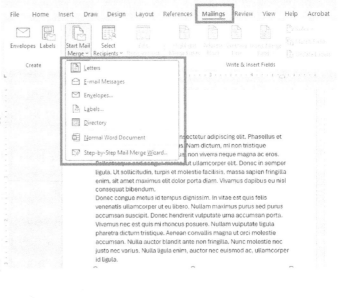

2. Select a Data Source

- Click **Select Recipients** in the **Mailings** tab.
- Choose an option:
  - » **Type a New List**: Enter recipient details directly into Word. After entering, you have to save the recipient details as a data source in order to continue.
  - » **Use an Existing List**: Browse and select an external data source (e.g., Excel file).
  - » **Choose from Outlook Contacts**: Use your Outlook contact list.

- Verify the data by clicking **Edit Recipient List** to ensure accuracy.

3. Insert Merge Fields

- Place your cursor where you want personalized information to appear.
- Click **Insert Merge Field** in the **Mailings** tab.
- Select fields like **First Name**, **Last Name**, or **Address** to insert placeholders in the document.

4. Preview and Finalize

- Click **Preview Results** in the **Mailings** tab to view how the data populates the document.
- Use the navigation arrows to preview each recipient's document.

- Click **Finish & Merge** and choose:
  - » **Edit Individual Documents**: Create a separate document for each recipient.
  - » **Print Documents**: Send the merged documents directly to the printer.
  - » **Send Email Messages**: Email the documents (if using the email option).

3. MAIL MERGE FOR LABELS AND ENVELOPES

Creating Labels

1. Go to **Mailings > Start Mail Merge > Labels**.
2. Select the label type and size from the dialog box.
3. Follow the same steps to select recipients and insert merge fields.
4. Preview the labels and print them using **Finish & Merge**.

Creating Envelopes

1. Go to **Mailings > Envelopes**.
2. Enter the return and recipient addresses or use merge fields for recipient details.
3. Click **Add to Document** to include the envelope in your main document.

4. TIPS FOR SUCCESSFUL MAIL MERGE

- **Organize Your Data Source**: Ensure the data source is clean and well-structured, with clear headers and no blank rows.
- **Test with a Few Records**: Preview a small batch of records to confirm the merge works.
- **Save Time with Templates**: Create reusable templates for letters, labels, and envelopes.

II. CREATING AND MANAGING MACROS TO AUTOMATE TASKS

Macros are powerful tools in Microsoft Word that automate repetitive tasks by recording a series of actions. By creating and managing macros, you can save time and increase efficiency in your workflow.

1. WHAT IS A MACRO?

A macro is a recorded sequence of commands and actions that can be played back to perform tasks automatically. Macros are especially useful for:

- Formatting documents consistently.
- Applying complex styles to text.
- Automating repetitive actions like inserting boilerplate text.

2. CREATING A MACRO

1. Go to the **View** tab and click **Macros > Record Macro**.
2. In the **Record Macro** dialog box:

- Enter a name for the macro (e.g., "ApplyHeaderStyle").
- Choose where to store the macro:
  - » **All Documents** (Normal.dotm): Makes the macro available in all Word documents.
  - » **This Document**: Limits the macro to the current document.
- Assign a shortcut key or a button if desired.

3. Click **OK** to start recording.
4. Perform the actions you want the macro to automate. For example:

- Format a heading.

- Insert a specific table or logo.
- Apply a particular style.

5. Once finished, go back to the **View** tab and click **Macros > Stop Recording**.

3. RUNNING A MACRO

Using the Ribbon or Shortcut Key

1. Select the text where you want to apply the Macro.
2. Go to the **View** tab and click **Macros > View Macros**.
3. Select the macro you want to run and click **Run**.
4. If you assigned a shortcut key or button, use it to execute the macro directly.

4. MANAGING MACROS

Editing a Macro

Macros are written in VBA (Visual Basic for Applications). To edit a macro:

1. Go to the **View** tab and click **Macros > View Macros**.
2. Select the macro and click **Edit**.
3. Modify the VBA code in the editor. (Basic programming knowledge is helpful here.)

Deleting a Macro

1. Go to **View > Macros > View Macros**.
2. Select the macro you want to delete and click **Delete**.

5. SECURITY AND PERMISSIONS

Macros can contain harmful code, so it's important to manage security settings:

1. Go to **File > Options > Trust Center > Trust Center Settings**.
2. Select **Macro Settings** and choose the appropriate level:
   » **Disable all macros without notification**: Safest option but prevents macros from running.
   » **Disable all macros with notification**: Allows you to enable trusted macros.
   » **Enable all macros**: Not recommended due to security risks.

III. EMBEDDING AND LINKING OBJECTS

Embedding and linking objects in Microsoft Word allows you to integrate external content such as Excel charts or PowerPoint slides directly into your documents. These features are essential for creating dynamic and informative documents.

1. EMBEDDING OBJECTS

When you embed an object, it becomes part of the Word document, and you can edit it using its native application without needing the original file.

Steps to Embed an Object

1. Go to the **Insert** tab and click **Object** in the **Text** group.
2. In the **Object** dialog box, select the **Create from File** tab.
3. Click **Browse** to locate the file you want to embed (e.g., an Excel or PowerPoint file).
4. Check **Display as Icon** if you want to show an icon instead of the content.
5. Click **OK** to embed the object into your document.

Editing an Embedded Object

1. Double-click the embedded object to open it in its native application (e.g., Excel or PowerPoint).
2. Make changes and save them; the updates will appear in the Word document.

2. LINKING OBJECTS

Linking objects keeps the Word document connected to the original file. Updates to the source file are automatically reflected in the Word document.

Steps to Link an Object

1. Go to the **Insert** tab and click **Object** in the **Text** group.
2. In the **Object** dialog box, select the **Create from File** tab.
3. Click **Browse** to locate the file you want to link.
4. Check **Link to File** and click **OK**.
5. The linked content will appear in your document.

Editing a Linked Object

1. Right-click the linked object and choose **Linked Worksheet Object > Edit Link** (or a similar option depending on the object type).
2. Open the source file, make edits, and save it.

3. DIFFERENCES BETWEEN EMBEDDING AND LINKING

Feature	Embedding	Linking
Connection	Independent of the source file.	Dependent on the source file.
File Size	Larger, as the object is stored.	Smaller, as only a link is stored.
Updates	Static; doesn't reflect source changes.	Dynamic; reflects source changes.

IV. USING COPILOT IN WORD

Copilot is one of the major new additions to Microsoft Word. It serves as an intelligent writing assistant built directly into the app, helping you draft, summarize, rewrite, and transform content with simple prompts. Whether you are creating a document from scratch or refining an existing one, Copilot can significantly speed up your writing process.

Copilot works through the sidebar, the Home tab, or the sparkle icon that appears when you select text.

1. WHAT COPILOT CAN DO

Copilot supports a wide range of tasks, including:

- Summarizing long documents
- Rewriting existing text
- Transforming content into different formats
- Generating new text from a prompt
- Creating structured documents such as letters, proposals, and reports
- Drafting content based on uploaded files

These features help you produce high-quality writing with less effort and greater consistency.

2. SUMMARIZING CONTENT

Copilot can summarize either the entire document or only the text you select.
1. Go to the Home tab and click Copilot, or click the sparkle icon next to selected text.
2. Choose Summarize.
3. Select whether you want a brief, detailed, or bullet-point summary.

3. REWRITING TEXT

Rewrite suggestions improve clarity, tone, or structure without changing the meaning of your content.
4. Highlight the text.
5. Click the sparkle icon or open Copilot.
6. Choose Rewrite and select one of the suggested versions.

You can insert the improved version directly or compare multiple alternatives before choosing.

4. TRANSFORMING CONTENT

Copilot can convert your content from one format to another.

- Convert bullet points into a paragraph
- Convert a paragraph into bullet points
- Turn rough notes into an email
- Turn a section into an executive summary
- Convert a block of text into a structured outline

Steps:

1. Select the text you want to transform.
2. Open Copilot → Transform.
3. Choose the format you want.

This is especially useful for repurposing content for different audiences.

5. GENERATING NEW TEXT

Copilot can draft new content using your instructions.

1. Open the Copilot sidebar.
2. Type a prompt such as: "Create a short introduction explaining the purpose of this report."

Copilot will generate a draft, which you can insert into your document and edit as needed.

6. CREATING STRUCTURED DOCUMENTS

Copilot can help you generate complete document structures. This is helpful when you know what you want to create but don't want to build the layout manually.

Example Prompt: "Create a one-page project proposal layout with sections for overview, objectives, timeline, and next steps."

Copilot will insert the structure and allow you to fill it in or ask for additional content.

7. DRAFTING FROM A FILE

You can instruct Copilot to create content from an existing document such as a Word file, or PowerPoint.

What Copilot Can Do with a File:

- Summarize the document
- Extract key points
- Rewrite the content in a different format
- Generate a new draft based on multiple files
- Create an outline of the document

Steps:

1. Open Copilot.
2. Write a prompt such as: "Summarize this PDF and rewrite it in a formal tone."
3. Attach or reference the file stored in OneDrive.

This feature is helpful when working with long documents or combining information from several sources.

8. DRAFTING FROM A PROMPT

If you don't have an existing document, Copilot can create content entirely from your instructions. Examples:

- "Draft an introduction for a classroom handbook."
- "Write a summary explaining the main updates in this policy."
- "Create a short paragraph describing our team's objectives."
- Copilot will generate text directly in the Word document.

9. LIMITATIONS, PRIVACY, AND DATA BEHAVIOR

While Copilot is powerful, it operates within Microsoft 365's security framework and has several built-in restrictions.

Limitations:

- Copilot cannot access files you do not have permission to open.
- It cannot bypass password-protected or restricted content.
- Offline mode disables Copilot completely.
- Complex formatting (tables, multi-column layouts, forms) may reduce accuracy.
- Very large files may result in partial or incomplete responses.

Privacy and Security:

- Copilot follows your organization's security and compliance policies.
- Content used with Copilot is not used to train public Microsoft models.
- Copilot respects existing permissions and cannot see private information you cannot access.
- It cannot retrieve or expose hidden metadata unless visible in the document.

Good Practices:

- Always review Copilot output for accuracy.
- Confirm factual information, especially in legal, financial, and technical documents.
- Use Copilot to assist your writing, not replace your critical judgment.

POWERPOINT MASTERY 2026

FROM BEGINNER TO EXPERT

THE ULTIMATE GUIDE TO CREATING STUNNING PRESENTATIONS

CHAPTER 1: GETTING STARTED

I.   INSTALLING AND LAUNCHING POWERPOINT

Before you can dive into creating presentations, it's essential to ensure PowerPoint is properly installed on your device and ready to use. This section walks you through the steps to install and launch PowerPoint smoothly.

1.   INSTALLING POWERPOINT:

Via Microsoft 365 Subscription:

- After purchasing a subscription, sign in with your Microsoft account..
- Download and install the Office apps package, which includes PowerPoint.

Free Versions:

- A limited, web-based version of PowerPoint is available for free at office.com.
- You can also download the PowerPoint mobile app from the App Store or Google Play Store.

2.   LAUNCHING POWERPOINT:

On Windows:

- Click the **Start Menu**, then type "PowerPoint" in the search bar and select the app.
- Alternatively, find it in the **All Apps** section of the Start Menu.

On Mac:

- Open the **Applications** folder, locate PowerPoint, and double-click to open it.
- You can also use **Spotlight Search** by pressing Command + Space, typing "PowerPoint," and hitting Enter.

II.   OVERVIEW OF MICROSOFT POWERPOINT AND ITS INTERFACE

The Ribbon:

- The Ribbon is a central part of the interface, located at the top of the screen.
- It is divided into tabs such as **Home**, **Insert**, **Design**, and more.
- Each tab contains groups of commands for specific tasks, like formatting text or inserting media.

Slide Pane:

- The main working area where you create and edit slides.
- Includes placeholders for adding content like text, images, charts, and videos.
- You can switch between **Normal View** and other views like **Slide Sorter** for arranging slides.

Thumbnail Panel:

- Found on the left side of the screen, this vertical panel shows miniature previews of your slides.
- It allows you to quickly navigate, reorder, or delete slides.

Notes Section:

- Located below the Slide Pane, this area is for adding speaker notes.
- Notes are visible in **Presenter View** during your presentation but hidden from your audience.

Quick Access Toolbar:

- Positioned at the very top of the interface.
- Includes shortcuts to frequently used actions like **Save**, **Undo**, and **Redo**.
- Fully customizable to suit your workflow.

Status Bar:

- Displays slide count, language settings, and options to adjust views (e.g., Normal, Slide Sorter, Reading View).
- A zoom slider on the right lets you resize the slide display.

Start Screen (upon opening PowerPoint):

- Offers quick access to recently opened files.
- Provides a range of templates to jumpstart your design.
- Features a search bar for locating templates, tools, or help resources.

III. NAVIGATING THE START SCREEN

The **Start Screen** is the first thing you'll see when you open PowerPoint. It's designed to help you quickly access your recent work, explore templates, or start a new presentation. Familiarizing yourself with this screen will streamline your workflow and get you into the action faster.

1. KEY COMPONENTS OF THE START SCREEN:

Home Tab:

- Displays a mix of your **recent presentations** and commonly used templates.
- Offers quick access to create a **Blank Presentation** or choose from pre-designed templates.

Search Bar: Found at the top of the screen, it allows you to search for:

- Built-in and online templates.
- PowerPoint features and help topics.

Templates Section:

- You'll find a selection of PowerPoint's professionally designed templates categorized by themes, such as **Business**, **Education**, and **Personal**.
- You can click **More Themes** to explore additional template options.

Pinned Presentations:

- Displays presentations you've marked as important for quick access.
- To pin a file, click the **pushpin icon** next to the file name in your recent list.

Recent Presentations:

- Shows a chronological list of presentations you've recently opened.
- Helps you quickly resume your work without searching for the file.

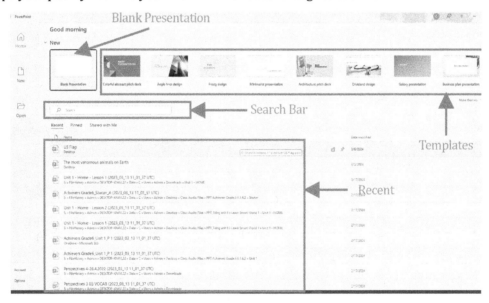

Open Other Presentations:

- Located at the bottom-left corner of the Start Screen.
- Use this option to browse your computer, OneDrive, or other locations for presentations.

2. NAVIGATING THE START SCREEN:

Starting a New Presentation:

- Select **Blank Presentation** to start from scratch.

- Click on a template to begin with a pre-designed layout.

Opening an Existing Presentation:

- Click a file from the **Recent Presentations** list or **Pinned Presentations**.
- Use the **Open Other Presentations** option if your file isn't listed.

Exploring Template Options:

- Click on New tab to display Templates.
- Click on a category in the **Templates Section** or use the search bar to find a specific type of template. Templates are a great way to jumpstart your design with minimal effort.

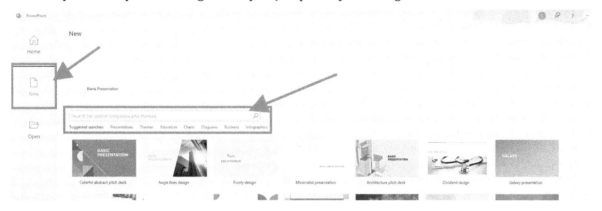

IV.   BASIC TERMINOLOGIES IN MICROSOFT POWERPOINT

Understanding key terms in PowerPoint will help you navigate its features with ease and communicate effectively when discussing presentations with others. Here are the most essential terminologies you'll encounter:

Slide:

- A single page in your presentation where you add content like text, images, charts, or videos.
- Slides are the building blocks of a PowerPoint presentation.

Presentation (PPTX File):

- A collection of slides saved as a PowerPoint file with the extension .pptx.
- It's the main file format used to create and share presentations.

Placeholder:

- Predefined areas on a slide where you can insert specific content, such as text, images, or charts.
- Placeholders guide the layout and keep your slides organized.

Themes:

- Pre-designed slide layouts with coordinated colors, fonts, and effects. Themes provide consistency and save time during the design process.

Slide Layout:

- The arrangement of placeholders on a slide, such as title, content, or image placeholders.

- Common layouts include **Title Slide**, **Two-Content**, and **Blank**.

Slide Master:

- A template that controls the design and layout of all slides in your presentation.
- Changes made to the Slide Master affect all slides, ensuring consistent formatting.

Transitions:

- Visual effects applied when moving from one slide to the next during a presentation.
- Examples include fades, wipes, and morph effects.

Animations:

- Effects applied to objects on a slide, such as text, images, or shapes. Animations can control how objects appear, move, or disappear.

Notes:

- A section where you can write additional information or speaker prompts for each slide. Notes are visible only to the presenter during a slideshow..

Presenter View:

- A special mode that allows you to see your notes and upcoming slides while presenting to an audience. This view is only visible on your device and not to your audience.

V.   CREATING AND SAVING PRESENTATIONS

Creating a Blank Presentation or Using Templates:

- From the Start Screen, select **Blank Presentation** to start with a clean slate or select a template for pre-designed layouts and themes.
- With Blank Presentation, PowerPoint opens a single slide using the default layout, typically a **Title Slide**.

Importing Content: Use the **Insert Tab** to add content such as text, images, or charts to your new presentation.

Saving a Presentation

- Save for the First Time:
  » Click **File > Save As**.
  » Choose a location: your computer, OneDrive, or other cloud storage.
  » Enter a file name and click **Save**.
- Quick Save: Use Ctrl + S (Windows) or Command + S (Mac) to save changes instantly.
- AutoSave: Ensure AutoSave is enabled (available for files stored in OneDrive or SharePoint) to save changes in real time.
- Save As Different Formats: Save your presentation in other formats via File > Save As and choose the format you want.

CHAPTER 2:
ADDING AND FORMATTING SLIDES

I.   CREATING, DUPLICATING, AND DELETING SLIDES

Slides are the foundation of any PowerPoint presentation. Learning how to create, duplicate, and delete slides is essential for building and managing your presentation effectively.

Creating Slides

- Adding a New Slide:
  » Navigate to the **Home** tab and click on **New Slide**.
  » Select a layout from the dropdown menu, such as **Title Slide**, **Two Content**, or **Blank**.
- Keyboard Shortcut: Use Ctrl + M (Windows) or Command + M (Mac) to quickly add a new slide with the default layout.
- Adding Slides with Templates: Open a template or theme and add slides that follow the pre-designed styles and placeholders.

Duplicating Slides

- Using Right-Click:
  » Right-click on the slide thumbnail in the **Thumbnail Panel** (left side of the screen).
  » Select **Duplicate Slide** to create an exact copy.
- Ribbon Option: In the Home tab, click on the New Slide dropdown and choose Duplicate Selected Slides.
- Keyboard Shortcut: Select the slide, then press Ctrl + D (Windows) or Command + D (Mac) to duplicate it.

Deleting Slides

- From the Thumbnail Panel: Right-click the slide thumbnail and select Delete Slide.
- Ribbon Option: Go to the Home tab and click Delete in the Slides group.
- Keyboard Shortcut: Select the slide and press the Delete key on your keyboard.

Rearranging Slides

- Drag and Drop:
  » Click and hold a slide thumbnail, then drag it to the desired position in the **Thumbnail Panel**.
  » Release to drop the slide into its new position.
- Using Slide Sorter View:
  » Go to the **View** tab and select **Slide Sorter**.
  » Rearrange slides visually by dragging and dropping them into order.

II.   ORGANIZING SLIDES WITH SECTIONS

Sections are groupings of slides that help divide your presentation into manageable parts. Think of sections as chapters in a book—they give structure and make it easier to rearrange, review, and focus.

Adding Sections

- From the Thumbnail Panel:
  » Right-click on the slide where you want to start a new section.
  » Select **Add Section** from the context menu. A section header will appear above the selected slide.

- Using the Ribbon:
  » Go to the **Home** tab. In the **Slides** group, click **Section** and then select **Add Section**.

Collapsing and Expanding Sections

- Collapsing: Click the small arrow next to a section header to collapse all slides within that section, reducing clutter in the Thumbnail Panel.
- Expanding: Click the same arrow to expand the section and view all slides.

Rearranging Sections

- Drag and Drop: Click and drag a section header in the Thumbnail Panel to move the entire section to a new position.
- Using Slide Sorter View:
  » Switch to **Slide Sorter View** from the **View** tab for a bird's-eye view of all slides and sections.
  » Drag and rearrange sections as needed.

Deleting Sections

- From the Thumbnail Panel: Right-click on the section header and select **Remove Section**. Choose whether to keep or delete the slides within the section.
- Using the Ribbon: Go to the Home tab, click Section, and select Remove Section.

III.   SLIDE LAYOUTS AND THEMES

Slide layouts define the arrangement of placeholders on a slide, such as text boxes, images, or charts. PowerPoint includes several default layouts, but you can customize them to fit your needs.

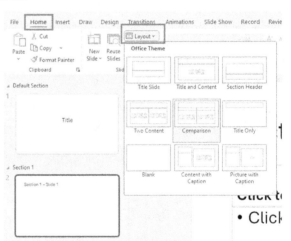

Slide Layouts

- Applying a Layout:
  » Select a slide in the Thumbnail Panel.
  » Go to the Home tab and click on the Layout button in the Slides group.
  » Choose a layout from the dropdown menu, such as Title Slide, Two Content, or Blank.

- Customizing Placeholders:
  » Click on a placeholder to adjust its size, position, or content type.
  » Add new placeholders by switching to Slide Master View (explained below).

- Incorporating Media: Use layouts with placeholders for images, videos, or charts to streamline the addition of multimedia content.

Themes and Design Options

Themes control the overall look of your presentation by defining color schemes, fonts, and background styles. PowerPoint's built-in themes offer a quick way to create professional presentations.

- Applying a Theme:
  » Go to the **Design** tab.
  » Select a theme from the gallery. Hover over a theme to preview it on your slides.
- Customizing a Theme:
  » Click on Variants in the Design tab to adjust the color scheme, font, or background style.
  » Use Customize Fonts and Customize Colors to create a personalized theme.
- Saving a Custom Theme:
  » Click More in the Themes gallery, then select Save Current Theme.
  » Assign a name and save it to the default location for quick access later.

IV.   WORKING WITH THE SLIDE MASTER

Accessing Slide Master View

- Opening Slide Master:
  » Go to the **View** tab on the Ribbon.
  » Click **Slide Master** in the Master Views group.
- Understanding the Layout:
  » The Slide Master is the top slide in the hierarchy and controls the overall design.
  » Below the Slide Master are individual slide layouts that inherit its design elements.

Customizing the Slide Master

- Editing the Master Slide:
  » Make global changes (e.g., fonts, background styles, logos) on the Slide Master.
  » These changes will apply to all layouts linked to the master.
- Modifying Layouts:
  » Select an individual layout below the Slide Master to customize specific slide types.
  » Add or remove placeholders (text, image, chart, etc.) based on the layout's purpose.
- Changing the Theme:
  » In the Slide Master tab, use the **Themes** dropdown to apply or modify the presentation's theme.
  » Customize colors, fonts, and effects via the **Variants** menu.
- Adding Branding:
  » Insert your organization's logo or other branding elements on the Slide Master.
  » These will appear on every slide, ensuring a professional and consistent look.

Using Placeholders

- Adding Placeholders:
  - » In the Slide Master tab, click **Insert Placeholder** and select a content type (e.g., Text, Picture, Chart).
  - » Position and size the placeholder on the layout.

- Editing Placeholder Properties:
  - » Customize the font, alignment, and formatting of placeholders to maintain a consistent style.
  - » Placeholder properties set in the Slide Master cannot be altered in Normal View.

Applying Custom Slide Layouts

- Using Customized Layouts:
  - » Return to Normal View by closing the Slide Master tab.
  - » Select a slide, go to the **Home** tab, and click **Layout** to apply your customized layouts.

- Consistency Across Slides: Slides that use customized layouts from the Slide Master automatically reflect changes made to the master.

Saving a Slide Master as a Template

- Save Your Master Design:
  - » After making all customizations, save the presentation as a template.
  - » Go to File > Save As > Choose PowerPoint Template (.potx) as the file type.

- Using Templates: Access your saved templates from the Start Screen under Custom templates or browse to locate them.

CHAPTER 3:
ADDING TEXT & VISUAL CONTENT

I. ADDING AND FORMATTING TEXT BOXES

Text boxes are essential for presenting information in PowerPoint. They allow you to place text anywhere on a slide, making it easy to create flexible and customized layouts.

Adding Text Boxes

- Using the Ribbon:
  - » Go to the **Insert** tab on the Ribbon.
  - » Click **Text Box** in the Text group.
  - » Click anywhere on the slide, then drag to draw the size of the text box.
- Direct Placement: Click on a placeholder on the slide (e.g., Title or Content placeholder) and start typing.

Editing and Formatting Text

- » Click inside the text box and type your content.
- » Use **Ctrl + Enter** (Windows) or **Command + Enter** (Mac) to quickly exit the text box.

Resizing and Positioning Text Boxes

- Resizing:
  - » Click and drag the corner handles of a text box to adjust its size.
  - » Hold **Shift** while resizing to maintain proportions.
- Positioning:
  - » Drag the text box to move it to the desired location.
  - » Use the **Arrange** group in the **Format** tab to align it with other elements.

II. TEXT FORMATTING: FONTS, ALIGNMENT, SPACING, AND EFFECTS

Formatting Fonts

- Changing Font Style:
  - » Highlight the text and select a font from the Font dropdown in the Home tab.
  - » Use fonts that are clear and appropriate for your presentation's tone (e.g., formal fonts like Arial for business, playful fonts like Comic Sans for casual use).
- Adjusting Font Size: Increase or decrease font size using the Font Size dropdown or the Increase/Decrease Font Size buttons in the Home tab.
- Adding Font Attributes: Apply bold, italic, or underline using the buttons in the Font group or shortcuts: Bold: Ctrl + B, Italic: Ctrl + I, Underline: Ctrl + U.
- Changing Font Color:
  - » Use the **Font Color** dropdown to apply a color.

» Click **More Colors** to define custom colors for branding or thematic consistency.

Text Alignment and Spacing

- Aligning Text:
  » Align text left, center, right, or justify using the Paragraph group in the Home tab.
  » Use the Align Text options in the Format Shape pane to adjust alignment within a text box.

- Adjusting Line Spacing:
  » Highlight the text, click the Line Spacing button in the Paragraph group, and choose a spacing option. For more precise adjustments, select Line Spacing Options.

- Paragraph Spacing: Modify spacing before or after paragraphs in the Paragraph group or in the Format Shape pane.

Applying Text Effects

- Adding Text Effects:
  » Select the text and go to the Format tab (or Shape Format for text in a shape).
  » Choose Text Effects to apply shadows, reflections, glows, bevels, or 3D rotation.

- Transforming Text: Use Text Effects > Transform to apply curved, arched, or wavy effects.
- Combining Effects: Layer multiple effects (e.g., shadow + reflection) for a dynamic look.

III.   USING SMARTART FOR VISUAL HIERARCHIES

SmartArt is a feature that converts text into visually appealing graphics. It's especially useful for representing hierarchical structures (e.g., organizational charts), illustrating processes and highlighting relationships between elements.

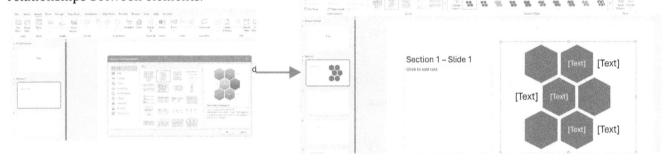

Inserting SmartArt

- From the Ribbon:
  » Go to the **Insert** tab and click **SmartArt** in the Illustrations group.
  » Select a SmartArt graphic type from the dialog box (e.g., List, Process, Cycle, Hierarchy).

- From a Placeholder: If your slide layout includes a content placeholder, click the SmartArt icon.

Customizing SmartArt

- Adding Text:
  » Click on a shape within the SmartArt graphic and type directly.
  » Use the Text Pane (on the left side) to enter or edit text.

- Changing Layouts: Select the SmartArt graphic, go to the SmartArt Design tab, and choose a different layout from the Layouts group.
- Styling SmartArt:
  » Use the SmartArt Styles group in the SmartArt Design tab to apply effects like shadows, 3D styles, or color schemes.
  » Click Change Colors to select a color palette that complements your slide's theme.

Converting Existing Text to SmartArt

- Select Text: Highlight a bulleted or numbered list on your slide.
- Convert to SmartArt:
  » Right-click the text and choose **Convert to SmartArt** from the context menu. Select a SmartArt layout that suits your content.

IV. ADDING IMAGES AND SCREENSHOTS

Visual elements like images and screenshots enhance the appeal of your presentation and help communicate ideas effectively. PowerPoint makes it easy to integrate and customize these visuals.

Adding Images

- Inserting an Image from Your Device:
  » Go to the **Insert** tab and click **Pictures** > **This Device**.
  » Browse your computer, select the image, and click **Insert**.

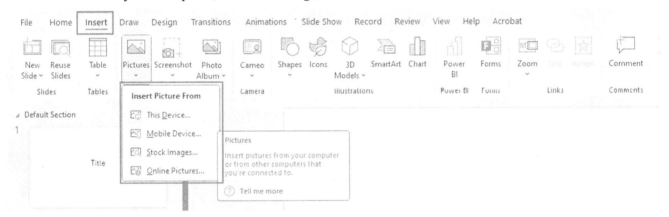

- Using Online Pictures:
  » In the **Insert** tab, select **Pictures** > **Online Pictures**.
  » Use the search bar to find royalty-free images or photos licensed through Creative Commons.
- Adjusting Image Properties:
  » Resize images using corner handles to maintain aspect ratio.
  » Use the **Picture Format** tab to apply styles like borders, shadows, or reflections, crop images or adjust brightness, contrast, and color.

Adding Screenshots

- Using the Screenshot Tool:
  » Go to the **Insert** tab and click **Screenshot** in the Images group.

» Choose a thumbnail from the list of available windows to capture the entire window.

- Using the Screen Clipping Tool:
  » Click **Screenshot** > **Screen Clipping**.
  » Select a portion of your screen to capture and insert directly into the slide.

- Editing Screenshots: Use the Picture Format tab to crop or apply effects to the screenshot.

V.   PHOTO ALBUMS FOR QUICK SLIDESHOW CREATION

A Photo Album is a PowerPoint presentation automatically generated from a set of images. It saves time by organizing and formatting pictures into slides, which you can customize further if needed.

Creating a Photo Album

- Access the Photo Album Tool: Go to the Insert tab and click Photo Album in the Images group.
- Add Pictures:
  » In the **Photo Album** dialog box, click **File/Disk** to select images from your computer.
  » Hold **Ctrl** (Windows) or **Command** (Mac) to select multiple images, then click **Insert**.

- Organize Pictures:
  » Use the **Up** and **Down** arrows in the dialog box to reorder the images.
  » Check the **Captions Below ALL Pictures** box to add captions based on file names.

- Select Album Options:
  » Choose a layout for your album under the **Picture Layout** dropdown.
  » Customize frame shapes using the **Frame Shape** dropdown.
  » Add a title slide by checking the **Include Text** box and typing a title.

- Create the Album: Click Create to generate the photo album as a new PowerPoint presentation.

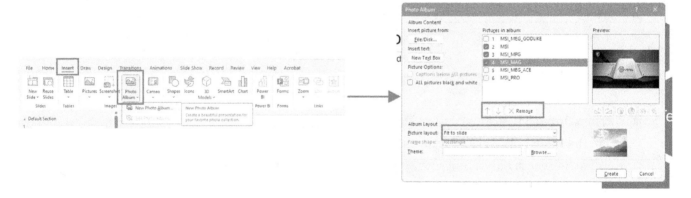

152

CHAPTER 4: CREATING SHAPES, CHARTS, AND 3D MODELS

I.   DRAWING AND CUSTOMIZING SHAPES

Shapes in PowerPoint are versatile tools that help you create diagrams, illustrations, and visual elements to enhance your presentations.

Adding Shapes

- Using the Ribbon:
  - » Go to the **Insert** tab and click **Shapes** in the Illustrations group.
  - » Select a shape from categories like Lines, Rectangles, Basic Shapes, or Flowchart.
- Drawing a Shape:
  - » Click on the slide and drag to draw the shape.
  - » Hold **Shift** while dragging to maintain proportions (e.g., create a perfect square or circle).

Customizing Shapes

- Resizing and Rotating:
  - » Resize shapes by dragging the corner handles. Hold **Shift** to maintain proportions.
  - » Rotate shapes using the circular rotation handle above the shape or by specifying an angle in the **Format Shape** pane.
- Changing Fill and Outline:
  - » Select the shape and go to the **Shape Format** tab.
  - » Use **Shape Fill** to apply solid colors, gradients, textures, or images.
  - » Use **Shape Outline** to customize the border's color, thickness, and style (e.g., dashed or solid).
- Merging Shapes:
  - » Select two or more shapes, go to the **Shape Format** tab, and click **Merge Shapes** in the Insert Shapes group.
  - » Choose options like Union, Combine, Intersect, Subtract, or Fragment to create new designs.
- Grouping Shapes:
  - » Select multiple shapes, right-click, and choose **Group** to combine them into one object.
- Aligning Shapes: Use the **Align** tool in the **Shape Format** tab to align shapes horizontally, vertically, or distribute them evenly across the slide.

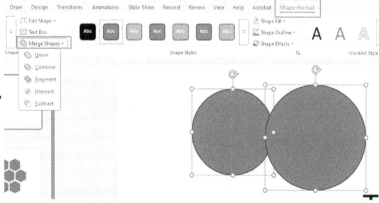

II. CREATING AND CUSTOMIZING ICONS

Icons are a fantastic way to represent ideas visually and add style to your presentation. PowerPoint's built-in icon library provides a wide range of scalable vector graphics that you can customize to fit your slide design.

Adding Icons

- Using the Insert Tab:
  » Go to the **Insert** tab and click **Icons** in the Illustrations group.
  » Browse the icon library, which includes categories like People, Business or Education.
- Searching for Icons: Use the search bar in the icon library to quickly find specific icons.
- Inserting Icons:
  » Select one or more icons and click **Insert**.
  » The icons will appear on your slide and can be moved or resized.

Customizing Icons

- Resizing Icons: Click and drag the corner handles to resize the icon while maintaining its proportions.
- Changing Colors:
  » Select the icon, then go to the **Graphics Format** tab.
  » Use the **Graphics Fill** and **Graphics Outline** options to change the color or border.
- Applying Effects: Use Graphics Effects to add shadows, glows, or 3D rotation for a polished look.
- Ungrouping Icons:
  » Right-click on an icon and choose **Convert to Shape** to break it into editable parts.
  » Customize individual elements of the icon (e.g., changing the color of specific components).

3. Organizing Icons

- Aligning Icons: Select multiple icons, go to the Graphics Format tab, and use the Align tool to align them horizontally, vertically, or to distribute them evenly.
- Layering Icons: Use Bring to Front or Send to Back in the right-click menu to position icons relative to other objects.
- Grouping Icons: Combine multiple icons into a single object by selecting them, right-clicking, and choosing Group.

III. DESIGNING IMAGES WITH 3D MODELS AND ICONS

PowerPoint allows you to incorporate 3D models and icons into your presentations, enabling you to create dynamic, interactive, and visually striking content.

Adding 3D Models

- Using the Ribbon:
  » Go to the **Insert** tab and click **3D Models** in the Illustrations group.
  » Choose from **This Device** or **Stock 3D Models**.
- Inserting a 3D Model:

- » Select the desired model and click **Insert**.
- » The 3D model will appear on your slide, ready for customization.

Customizing 3D Models

- Rotating Models:
  - » Select the 3D model, then use the 3D rotation handle to adjust its angle.
  - » Alternatively, use the 3D Model Views menu in the 3D Model tab to apply preset angles.

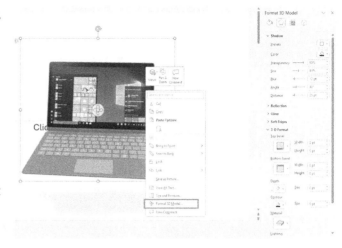

- Resizing Models:
  - » Drag the corner handles to resize the model proportionally. Hold Shift to maintain proportions while resizing.

- Applying Effects:
  - » Right-click the 3D model and select Format 3D Model, from there, you can use tools to add shadows, reflections, or soft edges for enhanced visuals.

- Animating 3D Models:
  - » Select the 3D model, go to the Animations tab, and apply animations.
  - » Customize the animation settings in the Animation Pane.

Combining 3D Models and Icons

- Layering for Depth:
  - » Combine icons and 3D models to create layered visuals.
  - » Use Bring to Front and Send to Back to adjust layering.

- Interactive Visuals:
  - » Add 3D models to interactive slides where users can click or hover to explore.
  - » Pair icons with 3D models to create visual guides or process diagrams.

IV.   CREATING AND FORMATTING CHARTS

Inserting a Chart

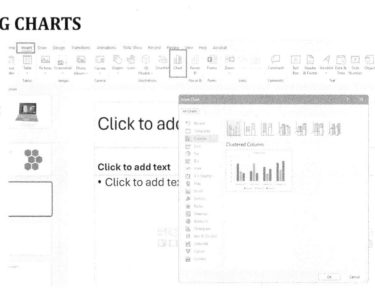

- Using the Insert Tab:
  - » Go to the Insert tab and click Chart in the Illustrations group.
  - » Select a chart type from categories like Column, Line or Pie.
  - » Click OK to insert the chart.
- Using a Placeholder: If your slide layout includes a content placeholder, click the Insert Chart icon and follow the same steps.

Types of Charts and Their Uses

Type of Charts	When to use
Column and Bar Charts	Best for comparing values across categories (e.g., sales by region).
Line Charts	Ideal for showing trends over time (e.g., monthly revenue).
Pie Charts	Effective for illustrating proportions or percentages (e.g., market share).
Scatter Charts	Useful for visualizing relationships between variables (e.g., height vs. weight).
Combination Charts	Combine different chart types for multi-dimensional insights.

Entering and Editing Chart Data

- Opening the Chart Data Sheet:
  » After inserting a chart, PowerPoint opens an Excel-like data sheet.
  » Enter your data directly into the sheet.

- Editing Data:
  » Select the chart, go to the Chart Design tab, and click Edit Data.
  » Update the values in the datasheet to reflect changes in your chart.

Formatting Charts

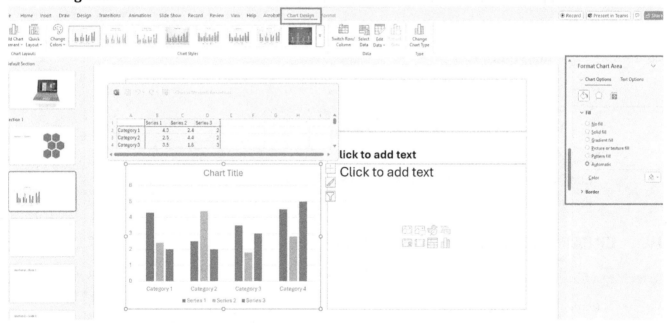

- Customizing Chart Elements:
  » Use the Chart Elements button to toggle elements like titles, legends, gridlines, and data labels.

- Applying Chart Styles: Go to the Chart Design tab and select a style from the Chart Styles gallery for a professional look.

- Adjusting Colors: Click Change Colors in the Chart Design tab to apply a color scheme that matches your presentation theme.

- Formatting Axes: Right-click an axis and select Format Axis to adjust scale, labels, and appearance.

- Adding Data Labels: Enable data labels to display values directly on the chart for better readability.

V. LINKING AND EMBEDDING EXCEL DATA INTO CHARTS

PowerPoint enables you to link or embed Excel data directly into your charts, ensuring accuracy and seamless updates. This feature is particularly useful for presentations that rely on dynamic data.

Linking vs. Embedding Excel Data

- Linking Data:
  » Establishes a connection between your PowerPoint chart and the Excel source file.
  » Updates in the Excel file are automatically reflected in the PowerPoint chart.

- Embedding Data:
  » Inserts the data directly into the PowerPoint file.
  » The data becomes static and doesn't update when changes are made in Excel.

Linking Excel Data to a Chart

1. Insert a Chart:
   » Go to the **Insert** tab, click **Chart**, and select a chart type.
   » A placeholder chart and an Excel-like data table will appear.

2. Replace Placeholder Data:
   » Click **Edit Data** in the **Chart Design** tab to open the linked Excel workbook.
   » Replace the placeholder data with your actual Excel data.

3. Maintain Link: Save both the PowerPoint and Excel files in the same folder to preserve the link.

Embedding Excel Data in a Chart

1. Copy Data from Excel: Open your Excel file, select the data you want, and press **Ctrl + C** to copy it.
2. Paste Data into PowerPoint:
   » Insert a chart in PowerPoint, then go to **Edit Data** in the **Chart Design** tab.
   » Replace the placeholder data by pasting your Excel data directly.
3. Save the Embedded Data: The data is now stored within the PowerPoint file, independent of the Excel file.

Updating Linked Data

1. **Open Linked Chart**:
   » Right-click the chart in PowerPoint and select **Edit Data** to view the linked Excel file.

2. **Refresh Data**:
   » Go to the **Chart Design** tab and click **Refresh Data** to sync changes from Excel.

CHAPTER 5: ANIMATIONS & TRANSITIONS

I.   ADDING AND CUSTOMIZING TRANSITIONS TO SLIDES

Transitions are effects that occur when moving from one slide to the next during a presentation. Using transitions effectively can enhance the flow and impact of your presentation.

Adding Transitions

1. **Select a Slide**: In the **Thumbnail Panel**, click on the slide to which you want to apply a transition.
2. **Open the Transitions Tab**: Go to the **Transitions** tab on the Ribbon.
3. **Choose a Transition**: Click on a transition effect in the **Transition to This Slide** group.
4. **Apply to All Slides**: After selecting a transition, click **Apply to All** to use the same effect across your entire presentation.

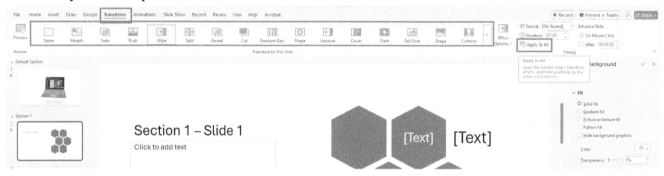

Customizing Transitions

- Effect Options: Many transitions have customization options. Click Effect Options in the Transitions tab to adjust settings (e.g., direction of the transition, such as left, right, up, or down).
- Duration: Use the Duration box to specify how long the transition lasts.
- Sound: Add a sound effect to the transition by selecting an option from the Sound dropdown.
- Trigger Timing: In the Timing group, choose whether the transition happens On Mouse Click or After a set amount of time.

Removing Transitions

1. **Select the Slide**: Click the slide in the **Thumbnail Panel**.
2. **Remove Transition**: Go to the **Transitions** tab and select **None** to remove the applied transition.

II.   ANIMATING TEXT AND OBJECTS

Animations in PowerPoint bring your slides to life by adding movement to text, images, shapes, and other objects. When used thoughtfully, animations can emphasize key points and maintain audience engagement.

Types of Animations

- Entrance Animations: Control how objects appear on the slide (e.g., Fade In, Fly In, Wipe).
- Emphasis Animations: Draw attention to objects already on the slide (e.g., Pulse, Spin, Grow/ Shrink).

158

- Exit Animations: Define how objects leave the slide (e.g., Fade Out, Fly Out, Disappear).
- Motion Path Animations: Move objects along a predefined or custom path (e.g., lines, curves, or freehand paths).

Adding Animations

1. **Select an Object**: Click on the text, image, or s hape you want to animate.
2. **Go to the Animations Tab**:
   » Select an animation from the gallery in the **Animation** group.
   » Hover over animations to preview them on the selected object.
3. **Add Multiple Animations**: Use the **Add Animation** button in the Animations tab to apply additional effects to the same object.

III.   MANAGING ANIMATIONS WITH THE ANIMATION PANE

The Animation Pane is a tool that lists all animations applied to objects on a slide in chronological order. It provides options to adjust timing, sequence, and other animation properties.

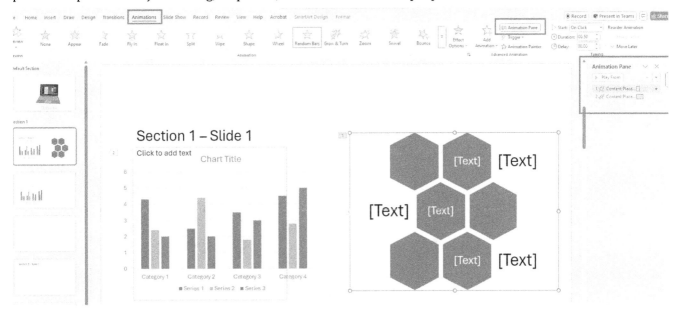

Opening the Animation Pane

1. **Accessing the Animation Pane**: Go to the **Animations** tab on the Ribbon. Click **Animation Pane** in the Advanced Animation group. A panel will appear on the right side of the screen.
2. **Viewing Animations**: The pane displays a list of all animations on the current slide. Each animation is labeled by the object it affects and the type of animation applied.

Managing Animations

- Reordering Animations:
  » Drag and drop animations in the Animation Pane to change their order.
  » Alternatively, select an animation and use the Move Up or Move Down buttons.

- Editing Timing: Select an animation in the Animation Pane. Use the Timing options in the pane or the Animations tab to adjust.

- Grouping Animations: Group multiple animations by selecting them and adjusting their Start settings to With Previous or After Previous.

Advanced Features

- Using Triggers:
  » Assign animations to be triggered by specific actions, like clicking a button or another object.
  » Select the animation, click Triggers in the Advanced Animation group, and choose an event.
- Copying Animations: Use the Animation Painter (covered in the next section) to duplicate animations across objects.

IV.   USING ANIMATION PAINTER FOR CONSISTENT EFFECTS

The Animation Painter is a feature that duplicates the animation effects applied to one object and transfers them to another. It's similar to the Format Painter but works specifically for animations. The Animation Painter duplicates: animation type (e.g., Entrance, Emphasis, Exit), timing settings (e.g., Start, Duration, Delay), effect options (e.g., direction, transparency).

Where to Find the Animation Painter

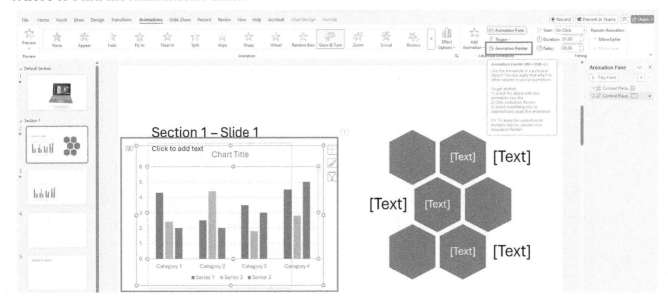

1. **Access the Animation Painter**:
    » Select an object with an existing animation.
    » Go to the **Animations** tab on the Ribbon.
    » Click the **Animation Painter** in the Advanced Animation group.

2. **Shortcut to Animation Painter**: Right-click the object with the animation, then choose **Animation Painter** from the context menu.

How to Use the Animation Painter

1. **Single Application**:
    » Select the object with the animation.

» Click **Animation Painter** and then click the target object to apply the animation.

2. **Multiple Applications**:
   » Double-click the **Animation Painter** to keep it active.
   » Click on multiple objects to apply the animation settings to each.
   » Press **Esc** to deactivate the tool.

V.   ADVANCED ANIMATIONS: MORPH TRANSITION

Advanced animations in PowerPoint allow you to create complex and interactive effects that elevate the professionalism and engagement of your presentation. By using features like **Morph Transition** you can achieve a highly dynamic result.

What is the Morph Transition?

- The Morph Transition creates smooth, seamless animations between slides by moving objects, changing shapes, or modifying properties like size and color.

Setting Up a Morph Transition:

- Create two slides with similar objects (e.g., text boxes, shapes, or images).
- Make changes to the objects on the second slide (e.g., resize, move, rotate, or recolor them).
- Apply the **Morph** transition to the second slide by selecting it, going to the **Transitions** tab, and clicking **Morph**.

Customizing Morph:

- Use the **Effect Options** menu in the Transitions tab to specify how the morph transition should behave (e.g., objects, words, or characters).

Applications of Morph:

- Showcase before-and-after scenarios.
- Create smooth zoom-ins or pans on images.
- Demonstrate flowcharts or processes dynamically.

CHAPTER 6: USING COPILOT

I.   COPILOT IN POWERPOINT

Copilot is a new AI-powered assistant built into Microsoft 365, including PowerPoint. It helps you draft presentations, reorganize content, generate speaker notes, and even create visuals with simple prompts. Copilot works directly within PowerPoint, making it easier to build professional presentations quickly.

You can access Copilot from:

- The Home tab
- The Copilot button on the Ribbon
- The Copilot sidebar on the right side of the screen

II.   CREATING A PRESENTATION WITH COPILOT

Copilot can create a complete presentation based on a prompt, outline, or file you provide.

Creating a Presentation from a Prompt

1. Go to the Home tab and click Create with Copilot.
2. Enter a prompt such as: "Create a 6-slide presentation explaining solar energy for beginners."
3. Copilot generates slides with titles, text, and suggested layouts.
4. Review the draft and make edits as needed.

Creating a Presentation from a File

1. Open Copilot.
2. Select Create from File.
3. Choose a Word document, PDF, or outline stored in OneDrive.
4. Copilot analyzes the file and generates a presentation based on the content.

This is useful when you already have written material and want a quick presentation version.

III.   REWRITING SLIDE CONTENT

Copilot can help refine and improve the text on your slides.

1. Select the text on your slide.
2. Click the sparkle icon that appears or open the Copilot sidebar. Choose Rewrite.
3. Select from options such as: Make clearer, Shorter, More detailed, More professional, Friendlier tone.

IV.   TRANSFORMING SLIDE CONTENT

Copilot can convert your content into a different format based on the needs of your presentation.

- Turn bullet points into a paragraph or turn a paragraph into bullet points.

- Summarize long text into key highlights,
- Convert slide text into an email or outline and convert notes into presentation content

How to Use Transform

1. Highlight the content.
2. Open Copilot → select Transform.
3. Choose the format you want.

V.   GENERATING SPEAKER NOTES

Copilot can automatically create speaker notes to accompany your slides.

1. Select a slide.
2. Open Copilot in the sidebar.
3. Choose Generate Speaker Notes.

Copilot creates notes that explain the slide's key points, helping you present confidently without writing notes manually.

VI.   ENHANCING VISUAL DESIGN WITH COPILOT

Copilot can suggest visual improvements to your slides.

- Recommend layouts
- Suggest images based on your slide content
- Improve visual balance and spacing
- Generate AI images directly inside PowerPoint using DALL·E models

Adding AI Images

1. Open Copilot.
2. Type a prompt such as: "Create a simple illustration of a wind turbine on a blue background."
3. Select the generated image and insert it into your slide.

VII.   SUMMARIZING YOUR PRESENTATION

Copilot can produce a summary of the entire presentation or selected slides.

1. Open Copilot. Select Summarize Presentation.
2. Choose whether you want:
   » A brief overview
   » A detailed summary
   » Bullet-point highlights

This is useful for creating executive summaries or preparing handouts.

CHAPTER 7: MANAGING PRESENTATIONS

I.   PRESENTER AND NAVIGATING

Presenter View in PowerPoint is a powerful tool that helps you deliver your presentation smoothly by giving you access to tools like notes, slide previews, and timers—visible only to you while the audience sees the slides.

How to Enable Presenter View

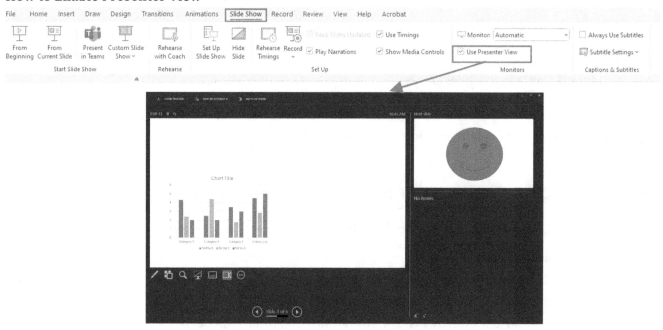

1. Start the Slide Show: Click Slide Show on the Ribbon, then select From Beginning or From Current Slide.

2. Enable Presenter View:

    »   Go to Slide Show > Use Presenter View.

    »   PowerPoint will automatically detect if you are using a dual-monitor setup (e.g., a projector or external screen) and enable Presenter View.

3. Manually Configure Displays: If Presenter View doesn't start automatically: go to Slide Show > Monitor > Primary Monitor to set the correct display for your audience.

Features of Presenter View

*   Current Slide Display: Shows the slide currently visible to the audience.

*   Next Slide Preview: Displays a thumbnail of the upcoming slide for smooth transitions.

*   Speaker Notes: Your notes appear below the current slide, providing prompts and additional information.

*   Timer and Clock: Tracks the duration of your presentation and displays the current time.

*   Slide Navigation: Use the navigation tools to jump between slides without disrupting the flow. The thumbnail strip allows you to select specific slides easily.

*   Annotation Tools: Use tools like laser pointers, highlighters, or pens to emphasize points during your presentation.

Customizing Presenter View

- Adjusting Note Size: Use the zoom controls in the notes section to enlarge or reduce the text size for better readability.
- Reordering Displays: Click Swap Displays if the audience view and Presenter View are reversed.
- Pointer and Laser Options: Activate these tools directly from Presenter View for more interactive presentations.

Navigating during the slide shows

- Using Slide Show Controls:
  » Start the presentation by clicking **Slide Show** > **From Beginning** or pressing **F5**.
  » Use the arrow keys or spacebar to move forward and backward between slides.
- Jumping to a Specific Slide:
  » Right-click during the presentation and select **See All Slides** to view a thumbnail overview.
  » Click the desired slide to navigate directly to it.
- Using the Keyboard: Press the slide number followed by Enter to jump directly to a specific slide.
- Pause or End the Slide Show: Right-click and select Pause Show to freeze the presentation temporarily. Press Esc to exit Slide Show mode.

II.   COLLABORATING IN REAL-TIME WITH OTHERS

PowerPoint's real-time collaboration features allow multiple users to work on the same presentation simultaneously, making teamwork more efficient and seamless.

Working Together in Real-Time

- Live Editing:
  » Collaborators can edit slides simultaneously, with changes appearing in real time.
  » A colored cursor or tag shows who is editing a specific part of the slide.
- Tracking Changes: View recent changes by clicking See What's Changed in the Review tab.
- AutoSave: Changes are automatically saved for all collaborators when AutoSave is enabled.

Communicating Through Comments

- Adding Comments:
  » Click **Review** > **New Comment** or right-click on an object and select **New Comment**.
  » Enter your feedback in the comment box.
- Replying to Comments:
  » Click on a comment and type your response in the thread.
  » Use @mentions (e.g., @JohnDoe) to notify specific collaborators.
- Resolving Comments: Once addressed, mark comments as resolved to keep the collaboration organized.

III.   CREATING BRANCHING SLIDES FOR INTERACTIVE PRESENTATIONS

Branching slides let the presenter or audience choose different paths or topics within the presentation. For example:

- Clicking a button or hyperlink takes the user to a specific slide.
- Users can explore content non-linearly, returning to the main menu or moving to related sections.

Setting Up Branching Slides

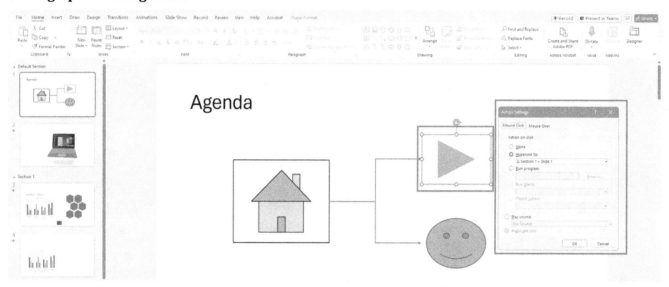

1. **Design a Main Menu**:

- Create a slide that serves as the central hub or menu.
- Use shapes, images, or text as buttons to represent different paths or topics.

2. **Add Destination Slides**:

- Create slides that correspond to each option on your main menu.
- Clearly label each destination slide for easy navigation.

3. **Adding Hyperlinks**

- **Link Buttons to Slides**:
  - » Select the object (shape, text, or image) you want to use as a button.
  - » Right-click and select **Link** (or **Hyperlink**).
  - » Choose **Place in This Document** and select the slide you want to link to.
  - » Click **OK** to create the link.

- **Create a Return Button**:
  - » Add a button on each destination slide that links back to the main menu.
  - » Use the same steps to hyperlink it to the main menu slide.

4. **Using Slide Master for Consistent Design**

- **Set Up a Template**:
  - » Go to the **View** tab and click **Slide Master**.
  - » Design your branching layout, including buttons and navigation elements.

- **Apply to All Slides**: Use the Slide Master to maintain consistent navigation buttons and design across all slides.

5. **Testing the Branching Presentation**

- **Run the Slide Show**:
  » Press **F5** or go to the **Slide Show** tab and click **From Beginning**.
  » Test all buttons and links to ensure they direct to the correct slides.

- **Fix Broken Links**: Return to the relevant slides and update any incorrect or broken links.

IV. RECORDING AND NARRATING SLIDESHOWS

PowerPoint's recording feature enables you to add narration, annotations, and timings to your slides, creating self-contained presentations or video exports. This is ideal for webinars, online courses, and self-paced training materials.

Starting the Recording

1. Access the Recording Tab: Go to the Recording tab on the Ribbon. If not visible, enable it via File > Options > Customize Ribbon and check the Recording option.
2. Record from Beginning or Current Slide: Click Record Slide Show > Record from Beginning or Record from Current Slide.
3. Recording Options:
   » Narration: Record audio for each slide.
   » Video: Include webcam footage for a more personal touch.
   » Ink and Laser Pointer: Annotate slides using the pen, highlighter, or laser pointer tools.

Recording Tools

- Slide Timer: Tracks the time spent on each slide. Use this to maintain consistent pacing.
- Annotation Tools: Access tools like pens, highlighters, and erasers to draw or emphasize points during the recording.
- Pause and Resume: Use the Pause button to stop recording temporarily and Resume Recording when ready.

Reviewing and Editing Recordings

1. Preview the Recording: Go to Slide Show > Rehearse Timings to review your recorded slides.
2. Edit Audio/Video: Select the slide with the recorded media. Use the playback controls to review and trim recordings as needed.
3. Re-Record Individual Slides: Go to the specific slide and click Record Slide Show > Record from Current Slide to overwrite the recording for that slide.

Exporting the Recorded Presentation

- Save as Video: Go to File > Export > Create a Video. Choose a resolution and ensure recorded timings and narrations are included.
- Share as PowerPoint Show: Save the presentation as a PowerPoint Show (.ppsx) for a seamless playback experience.

MASTERING MICROSOFT OUTLOOK

FROM EMAIL MANAGEMENT TO ADVANCED PRODUCTIVITY

CHAPTER 1: GETTING STARTED WITH OUTLOOK

I.   SETTING UP OUTLOOK

The new Outlook offers an experience designed for modern communication and productivity. It supports most email accounts, including Microsoft accounts (Outlook.com, Hotmail.com), work or school accounts, and third-party accounts like Gmail and Yahoo! You can also add IMAP accounts for broader compatibility.

Switching to the New Outlook

- From Classic Outlook:
  - » Look for the **Try the new Outlook** toggle in the upper-right corner of your classic Outlook app.
  - » Enable the toggle to download and switch to the new Outlook. If prompted, sign in with your account credentials. The app will launch with your default account settings.

- From Windows Mail and Calendar:
  - » If supported, you'll see a **Try the new Outlook** toggle in the upper-right corner of the Mail app in Windows 10 or 11.
  - » Enabling the toggle will download and activate the new Outlook as your default email client.

- Adding an Email Account
  - » Navigate to **Add Account** at the bottom of the folder list or go to **Settings** > **Accounts** > **Add Account**.
  - » Enter your email address and follow the prompts to complete the setup. For Gmail or similar accounts, ensure that IMAP is enabled and use an app-specific password if two-factor authentication is active.

- Managing Multiple Accounts
  - » Add and manage multiple email accounts within the same interface. Use the **Favorites** feature to mark important folders, categories, or contacts for quick access.
  - » Switch between accounts using the Navigation Pane on the left.

II.   EXPLORING THE OUTLOOK INTERFACE

The Ribbon

The Ribbon serves as the primary command center in Outlook, designed for quick access to essential tools and features. You can toggle between the detailed and minimal layout using the dropdown arrow on the right.

Navigation Pane

Located on the left side, the Navigation Pane lets you quickly switch between primary modules:

1. Mail: Access and organize your emails.
2. Calendar: View and manage your schedule.
3. People: Store and search for contacts.

My Day

The My Day feature allows you to view your calendar or tasks alongside your inbox without switching modules. To use My Day:

1. Click the My Day icon in the upper-right corner.
2. Toggle between your upcoming events and task lists.

This feature helps keep your schedule and to-do list visible while you work through emails.

The Reading Pane

The Reading Pane lets you preview emails without opening them fully, saving time and providing context at a glance. To customize:

1. Navigate to View > Layout > Reading Pane.
2. Choose the placement (Right, Bottom, or Off) based on your preference.

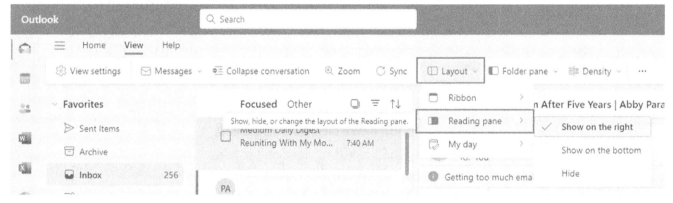

Search Bar

The Search Bar, located at the top of the Outlook window, is a powerful tool for finding emails, events, contacts, or settings.

III.   CUSTOMIZING YOUR OUTLOOK EXPERIENCE

Outlook offers extensive customization options to create a workspace tailored to your needs.

Customizing the Ribbon

The Ribbon is the primary command center in Outlook, and you can adjust it to include your most-used tools.

1. Add or Remove Commands:
   » Click on three dot ... > Customize.
   » Add or remove groups and buttons.

2. Reorder Tabs:
   » Drag and drop tabs within the customization menu to reorder them.

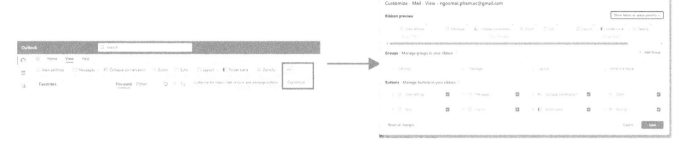

Changing Themes

Give Outlook a fresh look by selecting a theme that suits your preferences.

1. Select a Theme: Go to Settings > General > Appearance.
2. Choose Dark Mode: Choose between the Dark or Light theme.
3. Choose background and color.

Adjusting Layout

Modify how your mail, calendar, and tasks are displayed to match your workflow.

1. Mail View: Go to Settings > Mail > Layout.
2. Calendar View: Show work week, adjust time scale and meeting hour. Go to Settings > Calendar.

Customizing Categories

Categories help you organize emails, tasks, and calendar events with color-coded labels. To create or Edit Categories:

1. Go to Settings > Accounts > Categories.
2. Create new category and assign color to it.

CHAPTER 2:
EMAIL MANAGEMENT ESSENTIALS

I. MANAGING CONTACTS AND PEOPLE

Adding and Organizing Contacts

Contacts are central to efficient communication in Outlook. To add and organize your contacts:

1. Go to the People module from the Navigation Pane.
2. Click New Contact to add a contact manually.
3. Fill in the contact's details such as name, email, phone, and address.
4. Use the **Save** button to save the contact.

Importing and Exporting Contact Lists

1. Navigate to People > Home > Manage contacts.
2. Select the appropriate option to import contacts from a CSV file or export them for backup.
3. Follow the wizard to complete the process.

II. COMPOSING AND FORMATTING EMAILS

Outlook offers a variety of tools to enhance your emails, from formatting options to advanced features like templates and scheduling.

Composing Emails

1. Starting a New Email:
   » Click New mail in the Ribbon or use the shortcut Ctrl + N (Windows) to open a blank message.
   » Enter the recipient's email address in the To field. Use Cc for additional recipients or Bcc for hidden recipients.

2. Replying and Forwarding:
   » Reply: Use Reply or Reply All to respond to one or multiple recipients.
   » Forward: Select Forward to share the email with someone else.

3. Adding Attachments:
   » Click the Attach File button in the Ribbon and select a file from your computer or cloud storage.
   » Use Insert > Pictures to embed images directly into the email body.

Formatting Options

Outlook provides rich formatting tools to ensure your emails are clear and engaging:

1. Basic Formatting:
   - » Use the formatting toolbar to apply styles like bold (Ctrl + B), italics (Ctrl + I), and underline (Ctrl + U).
   - » Change fonts, sizes, and colors to match your tone or brand.
2. Paragraph Styles:
   - » Align text (left, center, or right).
   - » Create numbered or bulleted lists.
   - » Adjust line spacing and indentation for better readability.
3. Advanced Formatting:
   - » Use Styles to apply predefined text formatting (e.g., headings or quotes).
   - » Highlight key points with the Highlight tool.

Adding Signatures

1. Creating a Signature:
   - » Navigate to Settings > Accounts > Signatures.
   - » Create a new signature with your name, title, and contact information.
   - » Add images or hyperlinks (e.g., your company logo or website).
2. Assigning Signatures:
   - » Assign a default signature for new messages and replies.
   - » Select a signature manually by clicking Signature in the Ribbon.

Inserting Links and Tables

1. Hyperlinks:
   - » Highlight text, then click Insert > Link to add a clickable hyperlink.
   - » Use Ctrl + K (Windows) as a shortcut to insert links quickly.
2. Tables:
   - » Use Insert > Table to add structured information to your emails.
   - » Adjust the rows, columns, and formatting for clarity.

Spell Check and Proofing Tools

1. AutoCorrect: Outlook automatically fixes common typos while you type.
2. Spell and Grammar Check: Press F7 to review spelling and grammar before sending.

III. ORGANIZING YOUR INBOX

Managing your inbox effectively ensures you can stay on top of communication and prioritize what matters most. Outlook offers several tools to help organize your email seamlessly.

Creating and Managing Folders

Folders are a great way to sort emails by project, topic, or contact:

1. Right-click on the account you want to create a folder under and click Create new folder.

2. Name the folder and place it under the desired parent folder.

3. Drag and drop emails into the folder or use rules to automate sorting (see below).

Using Focused Inbox

Focused Inbox automatically separates important emails from less relevant ones:

1. Enable it under Settings > Mail > Layout.

2. Switch between the Focused and Other tabs in your inbox to review emails.

3. Move misclassified emails to the correct tab by right-clicking and selecting Move to Focused/Other.

Flagging and Categorizing Emails

- Flags: Mark emails for follow-up by clicking the flag icon in the email list.

- Categories: Assign color-coded categories to emails for easier identification.
  - » Right-click an email, choose Categorize, and select or create a category.
  - » View all categorized emails by filtering for a specific category.

Archiving Emails

Reduce inbox clutter by archiving old emails:

1. Right-click the emails and select Archive or click Archive in the Ribbon.

2. Archived emails are moved to the Archive Folder, where they remain searchable.

IV.   RULES AND AUTOMATION

Creating Rules for Automatic Actions

Rules enable you to automate email organization by setting conditions and actions.

1. Access Rules: Go to Settings > Mail > Rules and click Add new rule.

2. Set Conditions: Define criteria like sender, subject, or keywords.

3. Choose Actions: Options include moving emails to folders, marking them as read, or flagging them.

4. Apply the Rule: Run the rule or stop processing more rules if the new rule conflicts with previous rules.

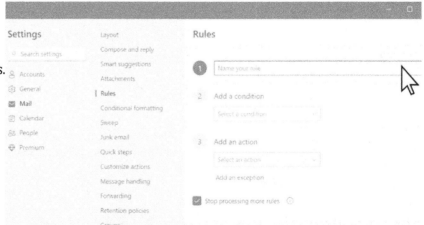

You can access and edit all the rules you've created by going to Settings > Mail > Rules.

Using Focused Inbox with Rules

Combine Focused Inbox and rules for smarter prioritization:

- Set rules to automatically mark important emails so that they appear in the Focused tab.

174

- Move less relevant emails to the Other tab or specific folders.

V.   SEARCH AND FILTERING TOOLS

Basic Search:

- Type keywords in the Search Bar (e.g., sender's name, subject, or a specific phrase).
- Results appear instantly, filtered by relevance.

Advanced Search Options with Filters:

- Click on Filters symbol in the Search Bar.
- Apply filters like From, Has Attachments, or Keywords to narrow results.

Example: Searching "project" and filtering by Last Month shows all emails containing "project" sent or received in the last 30 days.

VI.   PIN, SNOOZE, AND SCHEDULE SEND

Pin Emails keep essential emails at the top of your inbox for quick reference.

1. Pinning an Email:
   » Right-click the email in your inbox and select Pin.
   » The email will remain at the top of your inbox until manually unpinned.

2. Unpinning an Email:
   » Right-click the pinned email and select Unpin to return it to its original position.

3. Use Cases:
   » Key Conversations: Keep important threads easily accessible during a project.
   » Action Items: Highlight emails requiring follow-up or further action.

Snooze Emails: snooze delays the visibility of an email for some time, removing it from your inbox temporarily.

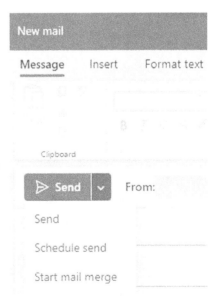

1. How to Snooze:
   » Right-click the email and select Snooze.
   » Choose a time for the email to reappear in your inbox, such as later today, tomorrow, or a custom date and time.

2. Managing Snoozed Emails: Snoozed emails are stored in the Snoozed folder until they reappear.

3. Use Cases:
   » Time Management: Delay emails that aren't urgent but require your attention later.
   » Meeting Preparation: Snooze emails with materials for an upcoming meeting.

Schedule Send: control when your emails are delivered by scheduling them to send at a specific time.

1. Scheduling an Email:
   - » Compose your email as usual.
   - » Click the dropdown arrow next to Send and select Schedule Send.
   - » Choose a date and time for the email to be sent.
2. Modifying Scheduled Emails:
   - » Scheduled emails remain in the Outbox until delivery.
   - » Open the email in the Outbox to make changes or delete it before it is sent.

VII.   UNDO AND RECOVERY OPTIONS

Undo Send

Outlook allows you to delay email delivery, giving you a brief window to undo the action.

1. Enable Undo Send:
   - » Go to Settings > Mail> Compose and reply.
   - » Under Undo send, use the slider to set the desired delay (e.g., 10 seconds).
2. Cancel an Email:
   - » After clicking Send, the message stays in your Outbox for the configured delay period.
   - » Open the email in the Outbox to make edits or delete it before it's sent.

Recover Deleted Emails

Retrieve emails that were accidentally deleted from your inbox.

1. Recover from Deleted Items Folder:
   - » Open the Deleted Items folder in the Navigation Pane.
   - » Right-click the email you want to recover and select Move > Inbox or another folder.
2. Recover Permanently Deleted Emails:
   - » Go to Deleted Items.
   - » Click Recover Items Recently Deleted From This Folder at the top of the folder window.
   - » Select the items to recover and click Restore.

Note: Permanently deleted items are recoverable only if your account is configured to retain them for a specific period, as defined by your email provider or administrator.

Recover Drafts

If you accidentally close a draft email or experience an interruption:

1. Go to the Drafts folder in the Navigation Pane.
2. Open the draft email to continue editing.
3. Save changes by clicking **Save** or pressing **Ctrl + S**.

CHAPTER 3:
CALENDAR AND TASK MANAGEMENT

Outlook's calendar and task features provide a comprehensive solution for scheduling, planning, and staying organized. Whether you're managing meetings, appointments, or task deadlines, these tools make it easy to streamline your workflow.

I. CALENDAR BASICS

The calendar in Outlook is designed to help you manage your time efficiently. From scheduling events to setting reminders, it provides all the tools needed to stay on track.

Creating and Managing Events

1. **Creating a New Event**:
   - » Go to the **Calendar** module in the Navigation Pane.
   - » Click **New Event** in the Ribbon or double-click a time slot in the calendar.
   - » Add details such as title, location, and start/end times.
   - » Use the **Save & Close** button to finalize.

2. **Recurring Events**:
   - » For regular meetings or reminders, select **Make recurring** in the event window.
   - » Define the recurrence pattern (daily, weekly, monthly, etc.).
   - » Customize end dates or specific occurrences.

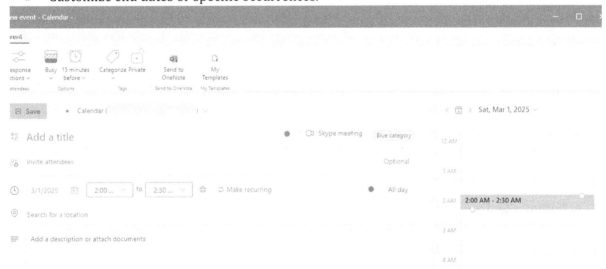

3. **Editing or Deleting Events**:
   - » Double-click an event to edit its details.
   - » Right-click and select **Delete** to remove an event from your calendar.

Setting Reminders and Notifications

- • Outlook allows you to set reminders for events:

» Open the event and select a reminder time (e.g., 15 minutes before).

» Notifications will appear as pop-ups or alerts based on your settings.

- Adjust global notification settings under **Settings** > **General** > **Notifications**.

II. SHARING AND COLLABORATION

Outlook's calendar-sharing and collaboration features make it easy to coordinate schedules, plan meetings, and stay aligned with your team. These tools are particularly helpful for work environments or shared family schedules.

Sharing Your Calendar

Sharing your calendar with others allows them to view your availability and, if permitted, make edits.

1. Share with Specific People:

» Go to your calendar and select **Share Calendar**.

» Enter the recipient's email address and define permissions: **Can view all details** (which allows the recipient to see all event details) or **Can edit** (which grants the ability to modify events).

» Click **Share** to share the invitation.

2. Manage Shared Permissions:

» Go to your calendar and select **Share Calendar**..

» Adjust or revoke permissions anytime.

Using Scheduling Assistant

The **Scheduling Assistant** simplifies meeting planning by finding time slots that work for everyone:

1. Open a new meeting request.
2. Add attendees and select the **Scheduling Assistant** tab.
3. View participants' availability and select a time that suits all.
4. Finalize the meeting details and send the invitation.

Collaborating with Shared Calendars

Shared calendars allow you to monitor and manage group schedules in real-time:

1. **Adding a Shared Calendar**: Click **Add Calendar** > **Add from directory** to add a team member's calendar.
2. **Viewing Shared Calendars**:

» Overlay calendars to see combined schedules, or view them side-by-side.

» Use the checkboxes in the Navigation Pane to toggle calendar visibility.

III. TASKS AND TO-DO LISTS

Tasks in Outlook integrate seamlessly with Microsoft To Do, providing you access to tasks from the To Do app directly within Outlook. By integrating tasks with your calendar and email, you can effectively manage both short-term and long-term responsibilities.

Creating and Completing Tasks

Tasks in Outlook allow you to track individual items with deadlines and additional details.

1. **Add a New Task**:
   » Navigate to **My Day** in the Ribbon, click To Do and click Open To Do symbol.
   » Click **Task** in the left pane. Name your task, due date, set reminder option and repeat option in the task window.
   » Click Add to add your task.

2. **Assign Categories**:
   » Categorize tasks with color codes for better organization.
   » Click the task and select **Pick a category** to assign a category.
   » Add file and note to the task if needed.

3. **Mark Tasks as Complete**: Check the box next to a task in the task list to mark it as completed.

Organizing Tasks

1. **Create Folders**: Organize tasks into folders by project, team, or personal categories.
2. **Sort and Filter**:
   » Sort tasks by due date, priority, or category to focus on what matters most.
   » Apply filters to view only active or overdue tasks.

CHAPTER 4:
USING COPILOT IN OUTLOOK

Copilot is now integrated directly into the new Outlook experience. It helps you write clearer emails, summarize long conversations, draft replies, schedule meetings, and manage your communication more efficiently. Copilot appears in the Outlook Ribbon and in the message window whenever you are composing or reading an email.

I.   DRAFTING EMAILS WITH COPILOT

Copilot can help you compose new emails by generating a first draft based on your instructions.

1. Click New mail.
2. Select Copilot in the toolbar.
3. Enter a prompt such as:
   » "Write a friendly reminder email about an overdue invoice."
   » "Draft an update to the team about tomorrow's meeting."
4. Review the draft and make changes as needed.

You can also ask Copilot to adjust tone, shorten, or expand your message.

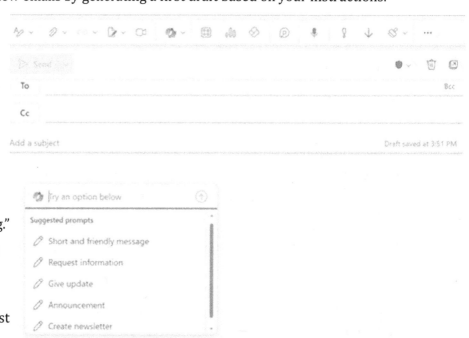

II.   SUMMARIZING LONG EMAIL THREADS

Copilot can summarize long conversations so you can quickly understand the key points without reading every message.

1. Open the email thread.
2. Click Copilot → Summarize.
3. Choose a summary format:
   » Key points
   » Action items
   » Short overview

This feature is especially helpful when returning to a long conversation after time away.

III.   REWRITING EMAILS

Copilot can rewrite the text of your email to improve clarity or adjust the tone to be more concise, more formal, more friendly, professional or explain in simpler language.

1.   Highlight the text you want to adjust.
2.   Select the sparkle icon or open Copilot. Choose Rewrite.
3.   Insert the version you prefer.

IV.   GENERATING REPLIES

When you're not sure how to respond, Copilot can draft a reply based on the content of the email you're reading.

1.   Open the email.
2.   Click Copilot → Draft Reply.
3.   Choose the tone or intent: Approve, Decline, Request more information or Friendly response
4.   Edit the draft before sending.

This helps you reply quickly while keeping your communication consistent and professional.

V.   SCHEDULING MEETINGS WITH COPILOT

Copilot can help you convert an email conversation into a scheduled meeting.

1.   Open an email where the conversation mentions meeting or timing.
2.   Click Copilot → Schedule a Meeting.
3.   Copilot will:
   »   Scan the email for preferred dates
   »   Check your calendar
   »   Suggest meeting times
4.   Select the option you want, and Copilot creates the meeting invite.

VI.   MANAGING TASKS AND FOLLOW-UPS

Copilot can extract tasks from emails and help you organize follow-up items. For examples:

- Identify tasks in a long conversation
- Create To Do items automatically
- Suggest follow-up reminders
- Highlight deadlines mentioned in the message

Steps:

1.   Open the email.
2.   Click Copilot → Identify Tasks.
3.   Choose which tasks to add to Microsoft To Do.

MASTERING MICROSOFT TEAMS

THE COMPLETE GUIDE TO SEAMLESS COLLABORATION AND COMMUNICATION

CHAPTER 1: GETTING STARTED WITH MICROSOFT TEAMS

I. INSTALLING MICROSOFT TEAMS ON DESKTOP AND MOBILE

Microsoft Teams is available on a wide variety of platforms, ensuring seamless collaboration no matter where you work. This section will walk you through the steps to install Teams.

Installing Microsoft Teams on Desktop

1. **Download Microsoft Teams:** Visit the Microsoft Teams website and click on the "Download for desktop" button.
2. **Installation Steps:**
   » Open the downloaded file and follow the installation prompts.
   » Once installed, launch Teams and log in with your Microsoft account credentials.

Installing Microsoft Teams on Mobile

1. **Download the App:** Open your device's app store and search for "Microsoft Teams" and tap on the official app by Microsoft Corporation.
2. **Installation Steps:**
   » Tap "Install" or "Get" and wait for the app to download.
   » Once installed, open the app and log in with your Microsoft account.

II. SETTING UP MICROSOFT TEAMS

Creating and Configuring an Account

1. **Sign In or Sign Up:** Open Microsoft Teams and sign in with your Microsoft account.
2. **Selecting an Account Type:**
   » **Personal:** Perfect for family use or small groups.
   » **Work or School:** Offers robust collaboration tools tailored to professional or educational needs.

Initial Setup for Businesses, Schools, and Personal Use

1. **Businesses:**
   » Set up your organization's domain if applicable.
   » Add team members by email and assign roles (owner, member, or guest).
2. **Schools:**
   » Link Teams to your institution's Microsoft 365 Education plan.
   » Organize classes with specific Teams for each subject or group.
3. **Personal Use:** Add friends or family to your Teams. Explore fun features like Together Mode for virtual gatherings.

III. NAVIGATING TEAMS

Teams Navigation Buttons

Microsoft Teams features a simple sidebar on the left-hand side of the interface, known as the navigation bar. These buttons help you quickly access core functionalities:

1. **Activity:**
   » View notifications, mentions, and missed calls.
   » Stay updated with a personalized activity feed.

2. **Chat:**
   » Engage in one-on-one or group chats.
   » Access past conversations and send quick messages.

3. **Teams:**
   » View all the Teams you're part of.
   » Access specific channels for focused discussions and file sharing.

4. **Calendar:**
   » Schedule and join meetings.
   » Integrates seamlessly with Outlook to keep all events in one place.

5. **Files:**
   » View and manage all shared documents.
   » Access recent files and upload new ones directly from your device.

Understanding the Teams Interface

1. **Teams and Channels:**
   » **Teams:** Think of Teams as a group workspace for a specific purpose, such as a project, department, or class.
   » **Channels:** Channels are sub-sections within a Team for organizing discussions.

2. **Tabs:**
   » Located at the top of every channel, tabs provide quick access to apps, files, and tools.
   » Default tabs include Posts, Files, and Wiki. You can add more tabs, such as Planner, OneNote, or custom apps, to fit your needs.

3. **Command Bar:**
   » Found at the top of the Teams app, the Command Bar lets you search for messages, files, and people.

IV. CREATING AND JOINING CHANNELS

Creating a Channel and Understanding Channel Types

Channels are the heart of Teams collaboration, organizing discussions and resources for better efficiency.

1. **How to Create a Channel:**
   - » Go to a Team and click the ellipsis (...) next to the Team name.
   - » Select **Add Channel**, then name your channel and add an optional description.
   - » Choose the privacy setting: **Standard** (accessible to all team members) or **Private** (Restricted to invited members only).

2. **Channel Tabs and Tools:**
   - » Customize your channel by adding tabs for files, apps, or resources relevant.

Understanding Channel Types

1. **Standard Channels:**
   - » Open to all members of the Team.
   - » Ideal for general discussions or shared topics.

2. **Private Channels:**
   - » Restricted to selected members.
   - » Use for sensitive topics, such as HR discussions or project-specific tasks.

3. **Shared Channels:**
   - » Allows collaboration with people outside your organization.
   - » Perfect for external partnerships or cross-organization projects.

Joining a Channel: How to Access and Participate

1. **Joining a Channel:**
   - » Team members automatically have access to standard channels.
   - » To join a private channel, you must be invited by a channel owner.

2. **Participating in a Channel:**
   - » Post messages in the **Posts** tab to start or contribute to discussions.
   - » Share files, links, or images directly in the channel for seamless collaboration.

CHAPTER 2: VIDEO CONFERENCING AND MEETINGS

I.   SCHEDULING AND JOINING MEETINGS

Starting an Instant Meeting:

- Click the **Meet Now** button in the **Teams** or **Calendar** tab.
- Choose the meeting's title and invite participants by email or name.

Using the Teams Calendar:

- Navigate to the **Calendar** tab in the left-hand navigation bar. Click **New Meeting** in the top-right corner.
- Fill in the following details:
  » Title: Add a descriptive title (e.g., "Team Weekly Stand-Up").
  » Date and Time: Select the meeting's start and end times.
  » Participants: Enter participant names or email addresses to send invitations.
  » Location: Add a physical location if needed (for hybrid meetings).
  » Description: Include the meeting agenda or notes.
- Click **Save** to share the meeting details with participants.

Scheduling Recurring Meetings:

- While setting up a meeting, select the **Does not repeat** dropdown and choose a recurrence pattern (daily, weekly, or custom).

Configuring Meeting Options

- Meeting Permissions:
  » Once the meeting is scheduled, click the meeting in your calendar and choose **Meeting Options** to configure who can bypass the lobby, whether attendees can present or only view or enabling/disabling meeting chat.
- Audio and Video Settings:

» Before joining, configure your camera, microphone, and speakers in the pre-join screen.

» Use the background effects feature to blur or change your video background.

• **Meeting Links:** Each meeting includes a unique link that can be shared with participants.

Joining Meetings in Microsoft Teams

1. **Joining via Link:**

» Click the meeting link provided in the email invitation, calendar event, or Teams chat.

» The link will open in your Teams app or browser.

2. **Joining from the Calendar:**

» Go to the Calendar tab in Teams and find the scheduled meeting.

» Click on the meeting and select Join to enter.

3. **Joining from a Channel:**

» If the meeting is associated with a channel, navigate to the channel and locate the meeting in the Posts tab. Click Join to participate.

4. **Joining as a Guest:**

» Non-Team members can join meetings using the provided link.

» Guests may need to enter their names before joining.

II. MANAGING MEETINGS

Effectively managing meetings in Microsoft Teams ensures a productive and engaging experience. This section covers tools to help you host meetings smoothly, from recording sessions to using breakout rooms.

Recording Teams Meetings

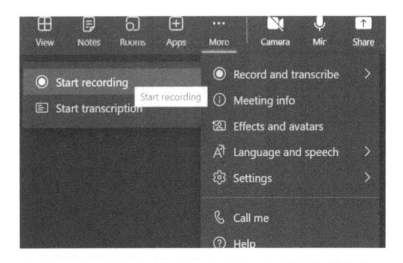

1. **How to Record:**

» Start the meeting and click on the **More (⋯)** menu in the meeting toolbar.

» Select **Record and transcribe > Start recording** to begin capturing the meeting.

» Teams will notify all participants that the meeting is being recorded.

2. **Accessing and Sharing Recordings:**

» After the meeting, recordings are stored in the **Files** tab of the meeting's associated chat or channel.

» Share recordings by copying the link and sending it to others via Teams or email.

Adding Attendees and Managing Roles

1. Inviting Participants During a Meeting: Click Participants in the toolbar, then select Add Participants to invite additional attendees.

2. Managing Roles: Go to the Participants panel, click the ellipsis (...) next to a participant's name, and choose their role: Presenter or Attendee.

3. Locking the Meeting: To prevent disruptions, lock the meeting once all participants have joined. Go to More Actions (⋯) and select Lock Meeting.

Sharing Screens, Files, and Presentations

1. **Sharing Your Screen:**
   - » Click the **Share Content** button (an upward arrow icon) in the toolbar.
   - » Choose what to share:
     - » **Entire Screen:** Share everything on your display.
     - » **Window:** Share a specific app or window.
     - » **PowerPoint Live:** Share a PowerPoint file directly, allowing participants to navigate slides independently.

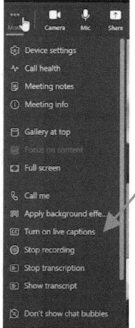

2. **Sharing Files During Meetings:**
   - » Drag and drop files into the meeting chat.
   - » Upload files to the meeting's **Files** tab for quick access.

Using Live Captions and Transcription

1. **Enabling Live Captions:**
   - » Click **More Actions (⋯)** and select **Turn on Live Captions.**
   - » Teams will display real-time captions at the bottom of the screen, enhancing accessibility.

2. **Using Transcriptions:**
   - » Enable transcription during the meeting to create transcription.
   - » Access the transcript in the meeting chat or channel after the meeting ends.

Using Breakout Rooms for Smaller Discussions

1. **Setting Up Breakout Rooms:**
   - » Click the **Breakout Rooms** icon in the toolbar and choose the number of rooms to create.
   - » Assign participants to rooms manually or automatically.

2. **Managing Breakout Rooms:**
   - » Open or close rooms with one click.
   - » Join rooms as the host to facilitate discussions or answer questions.

3. **Rejoining the Main Meeting:**
   - » Participants can return to the main meeting when the breakout session ends, or the host can close all rooms to bring everyone back.

CHAPTER 3:
MANAGING TEAMS AND CHANNELS

I. ADDING AND REMOVING MEMBERS AND OWNERS

Managing your Teams' membership and permissions is a fundamental skill for keeping your workspace organized and efficient.

Adding Members to a Team

1. **Inviting Members:**
    » Navigate to the **Teams** tab on the left-hand menu.
    » Click the ellipsis (...) next to the Team you want to manage and select **Manage Team.**
    » In the **Members** tab, click **Add Member.**
    » Enter the email addresses or names of individuals you want to add.
    » Choose whether they will join as a **Member** or **Guest** (for external users).

2. **Adding Guests:**
    » Guests are external users who don't belong to your organization.
    » They will receive an email invitation to join your Team.
    » Guests have limited access to files and channels, depending on your Team's settings.

Removing Members from a Team

» Go to the **Teams** tab and select **Manage Team** for the relevant Team.
» In the **Members** tab, locate the individual you want to remove.
» Click the Remove button (X) next to their name.

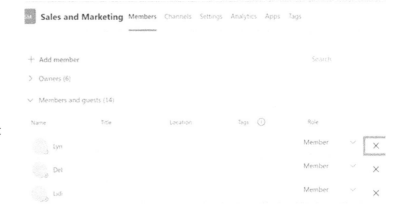

Assigning and Managing Team Owners

1. **Understanding Roles:**
    » **Owners:** Have full control over the Team, including adding/removing members, managing settings, and deleting the Team.
    » **Members:** Can participate in discussions, share files, and use basic features.

2. **How to Assign Ownership:**
    » Navigate to the **Members** tab and locate the member you want to promote.
    » Click the dropdown next to their name to assign Member or Owner.

Note: assign at least two owners to ensure continuity if one owner becomes unavailable, regularly review and update ownership to reflect changes in responsibilities.

II.   MANAGING TEAMS SETTINGS AND PERMISSIONS

Updating Team Details when you are a team owner

1. **Editing Team Name and Description:**
   - » Navigate to the **Teams** tab and locate the Team you want to update.
   - » Click the ellipsis (...) next to the Team name and select **Manage team**.
   - » In the **Settings** tab, expand the **Team details** section and select **Edit.** Change team name and description, then select **Done**.

2. **Changing Team Picture:**
   - » Go to **Manage Team** and select the **Settings** tab.
   - » Expand **Team details** and select **Change picture**. Select **Upload** to upload an image and select **Save**.

Managing Team Permissions

1. **Adjusting Member Permissions:**
   - » Go to **Manage Team** and click the **Settings** tab.
   - » Under **Member Permissions**, enable or disable features such as adding or deleting channels, pinning tabs or managing apps.

2. **Configuring Guest Permissions:**
   - » In the **Settings** tab, navigate to **Guest Permissions.**
   - » Decide whether guests can create, update, or delete channels.

3. **Allowing/Restricting Fun Features:**
   - » In the **Settings** tab, under **Fun Stuff**, enable or disable features like: GIFs, memes, and stickers.
   - » These options can add a playful element to discussions but may need restriction in formal settings.

Advanced Team Settings

1. **Team Code for Joining:**
   - » In the **Settings** tab, enable the **Team Code** feature to generate a unique code.
   - » Share this code with participants to allow them to join without individual invitations.

2. **Tags for Better Organization:**
   - » Use tags to group members for targeted communication. For example: create a tag like **"Design Team"** to message all designers in a Team.
   - » Add tags in **Manage Team > Tags.**

Archiving and Deleting a Team

1. **Archiving a Team:**
   - » Archive Teams that are no longer active but need to be retained for reference.
   - » Navigate to the **Teams** tab, click the ellipsis (...) next to the Team, and select **Archive Team.**
   - » Archived Teams are read-only but can be restored if needed.

2. **Deleting a Team:**

» Only delete Teams that are no longer needed.

» Click the ellipsis (...), select **Delete Team,** and confirm.

» Deleting a Team permanently removes all content, so proceed cautiously.

III.   MANAGING CHANNELS

Channels are where the real collaboration happens in Microsoft Teams. They allow you to organize discussions, files, and tools within a Team, making it easier for members to focus on specific topics or projects. This section covers how to manage channels effectively.

Customizing Channels

1.   **Adding Tabs:**

» At the top of the channel, click the **+** icon to add tabs.

» Tabs provide quick access to apps, files, or tools, such as: Planner for task management, OneNote for shared notes and Power BI for data visualizations.

2.   **Pinning Important Messages:**

» Highlight key announcements or instructions by pinning messages in the channel's **Posts** tab.

3.   **Using Channel Notifications:**

» Click the ellipsis (...) next to a channel and select **Channel Notifications.**

» Choose notification preferences to stay updated on activity.

Managing Channels

1.   **Setting Up Channel Moderation:**

» Go to the channel settings and enable **Channel Moderation.**

» Assign moderators to control who can post messages or manage conversations.

2.   **Renaming or Deleting Channels:**

» Click the ellipsis (...) next to the channel name and select **Edit This Channel** to rename it.

» Select **Delete This Channel** to remove it permanently. Note that all content in a deleted channel will be lost.

3.   **Archiving Channels:**

» Archive channels within a Team for future reference. Archived channels become read-only but retain all their content.

CHAPTER 4: COLLABORATING AND CUSTOMIZING TEAMS

I. USING THE FILES TAB

Microsoft Teams makes file collaboration seamless by integrating file management directly into each channel. The **Files** tab is your go-to location for uploading, organizing, and sharing documents within a Team or channel.

Uploading Files

1. **How to Upload Files:**
   - » Open the desired channel and navigate to the **Files** tab.
   - » Click **Upload** and select files or folders from your device.
   - » Drag-and-drop functionality is also available for quick uploads.

2. **File Types Supported:**
   - » Teams supports most common file formats, including documents, spreadsheets, presentations, images, and PDFs.

3. **File Access Permissions:**
   - » Uploaded files inherit the permissions of the channel.
   - » Private channels restrict file access to approved members only.

Organizing Files

1. **Creating Folders:**
   - » In the **Files** tab, click **New** and select **Folder** to create a folder.
   - » Use folders to group related files (e.g., "Project Plans" or "Marketing Assets").

2. **Renaming or Deleting Files and Folders:**
   - » Hover over a file or folder, click the ellipsis (...), and choose **Rename** or **Delete.**
   - » Deleting files moves them to the recycle bin, where they can be recovered within 93 days.

3. **Sorting and Filtering Files:**
   - » Use the sorting options at the top of the **Files** tab to organize files by name, date, or size.
   - » Apply filters to quickly locate specific files.

Accessing Files Across Teams

1. **Recent Files:** Access your recently used files from the **Files** tab in the Teams navigation bar.
2. **Shared Files:** Files shared during conversations are automatically added to the **Files** tab of the respective channel.
3. **Global File Search:** Use the search bar at the top of the Teams interface to locate files across all Teams and channels.

Using Built-In File Tools

1. **Preview Files in Teams:**
   - » Click on a file in the **Files** tab to open a preview directly in Teams.
   - » This feature supports quick viewing for Word, Excel, PowerPoint, PDFs, and more.

2. **Editing Files in Real Time:**
   - » Open a file and choose **Edit in Teams** or **Edit in [Application]** for advanced editing.
   - » Real-time collaboration allows multiple users to edit simultaneously, with changes saved automatically.

II. SHARING YOUR DOCUMENTS

Microsoft Teams simplifies document sharing, ensuring your team can collaborate efficiently on important files. This section explores how to share files, co-author documents in real time, and utilize OneDrive and SharePoint for seamless collaboration.

Sharing Files in Teams

1. **Sharing Files in a Channel:**
   - » Upload files to the **Files** tab in a channel to make them accessible to all members.
   - » Use the **Posts** tab to announce the file and provide context.

2. **Sharing Files in a Chat:**
   - » In a one-on-one or group chat, click the **Attach** icon (paperclip) to upload a file.
   - » Shared files appear in the chat history and are also saved in the **Files** tab of the chat.

3. **Sharing Links to Existing Files:**
   - » Instead of uploading, share a link to an existing file in OneDrive or SharePoint.
   - » Click **Attach**, select **OneDrive**, and choose the file you want to share.

Co-Authoring Documents in Real Time

1. **How Co-Authoring Works:**
   - » Open a shared Word, Excel, or PowerPoint document directly in Teams.
   - » Multiple users can edit the document simultaneously, with changes saved automatically.

2. **Identifying Collaborators:**
   - » See who is currently working on the document by viewing their initials or profile pictures in the top-right corner of the file.

3. **Comments and Suggestions:**
   - » Use the **Review** tools to leave comments, suggest edits, or resolve feedback during collaboration.

Using OneDrive for File Sharing

1. **Sharing Files from OneDrive:**
   - » Click **Attach** in a channel or chat and select **OneDrive.**
   - » Choose the file, configure permissions (view or edit), and share the link.

2. **Advantages of OneDrive Integration:**
   - » Files are stored securely in the cloud.

» You can update permissions or remove access at any time.

Sharing Files Externally

1. **Sharing Files with Guests:**
   » Guests added to a Team or channel can view shared files based on their permissions.
   » Ensure external sharing is enabled in your organization's Teams settings.

2. **Sharing via Links:**
   » Generate a sharable link from OneDrive or SharePoint and set expiration dates or passwords for added security.

III. CUSTOMIZING AND ENHANCING TEAMS

Customizing Microsoft Teams allows you to create a personalized workspace that aligns with your workflow and preferences.

Personalizing Settings and Themes

1. **Accessing Settings:**
   » Click on your profile picture in the top-right corner of Teams.
   » Select **Settings** from the dropdown menu.

2. **Changing Themes:** In the **General** tab, choose from:
   » **Default (Light):** A bright interface for well-lit environments.
   » **Dark:** Reduces eye strain in low-light settings.
   » **High Contrast:** Improves visibility for users with visual impairments.

3. **Adjusting Layout:**
   » Use the compact layout option to display more messages and reduce scrolling.

Customizing Notifications

1. **Managing Notifications:** Navigate to **Settings > Notifications,** customize alerts for:
   » **Mentions:** Alerts when you're tagged in messages.
   » **Messages:** Notifications for chats, replies, or reactions.
   » **Teams and Channels:** Set notifications for activity within specific Teams or channels.

2. **Setting Quiet Hours:**
   » For mobile users, set **Quiet Hours** in the Teams app to mute notifications during specific times.

CHAPTER 5: USING COPILOT IN TEAMS

Copilot is an AI-powered assistant built directly into Microsoft Teams. It helps you summarize meetings, manage conversations, extract action items, and prepare responses without manually reviewing long messages or recordings. Copilot works inside chats, meetings, and channels to improve communication and productivity.

I.   SUMMARIZING MEETINGS

Copilot can summarize meetings automatically using transcripts and recordings.

1.   Open the meeting in Teams after it ends.
2.   Click Copilot.
3.   Select Summarize Meeting.

II.   GENERATING RECAP NOTES AND ACTION ITEMS

Copilot identifies follow-up tasks discussed during meetings and suggests action items.

1.   Open Copilot after the meeting.
2.   Select Generate Action Items.

Copilot produces a task list, who is responsible, what was decided and next steps. You can copy these directly into chat or task tools.

III.   SUMMARIZING CHATS AND CHANNELS

Copilot can summarize long chats so you don't need to scroll through hundreds of messages.

1.   Open a chat or channel.
2.   Click Copilot.
3.   Select Summarize conversation.

IV.   DRAFTING MESSAGES WITH COPILOT

Copilot assists with writing replies and new messages.

Example:

1.   Click inside the message box.
2.   Select Copilot.
3.   Enter a prompt such as: "Write a polite update requesting project status."

You can revise or rewrite before sending.

MASTERING MICROSOFT ONENOTE

ORGANIZE, COLLABORATE, AND ACHIEVE MORE

CHAPTER 1: GETTING STARTED

I. WHAT IS ONENOTE?

Microsoft OneNote is a digital notebook designed for capturing, organizing, and sharing information in a way that feels intuitive and accessible. Unlike traditional notebooks, OneNote is dynamic—it can include typed notes, handwritten content, images, audio recordings, and even web clippings, all in one place. OneNote's flexibility, real-time collaboration features, and seamless integration with Microsoft Office make it a favorite for millions.

At its core, OneNote organizes information in a familiar, hierarchical format:

- Notebooks: Think of these as individual binders.
- Sections: These are like the dividers within a binder.
- Pages: The content within each section is stored on pages.

This structure provides the freedom to create, rearrange, and customize information in a way that mirrors how you think.

II. INSTALLING AND SETTING UP ONENOTE

Getting started with OneNote begins with installing the app on your preferred platform and setting it up for your needs. Follow these simple steps to ensure a smooth start.

Step 1: Downloading OneNote

Microsoft OneNote is available on Windows, Mac, iOS, Android, and the web.

- Windows or Mac:
  - » Go to the Microsoft OneNote website or use the Microsoft Store (Windows) or Mac App Store.
  - » Click "Download" or "Get the App" and follow the prompts.
- Mobile Devices (iOS or Android):
  - » Open the App Store or Google Play Store.
  - » Search for "Microsoft OneNote" and tap "Install."
- Web Version:
  - » Access OneNote directly from your browser at https://www.onenote.com.

Step 2: Signing In and Setting Up

After downloading OneNote, follow these steps to get started:

1. Sign In: Open the app and log in with your Microsoft account. If you don't have one, you can create it for free.
2. Choose Your Default Notebook: By default, OneNote will create a notebook for you. You can rename it or start fresh with a new notebook.
3. Sync Your Notebooks: Ensure your notebooks are connected to OneDrive to enable syncing across devices. This allows you to access your notes anywhere.

Step 3: Configuring Your Settings

Once OneNote is installed, take a moment to customize the app for your preferences:

1. Default Location: Choose where new notebooks will be stored—locally or in the cloud.
2. Language and Proofing: Set your preferred language and enable spell check or grammar tools.
3. Automatic Sync: Ensure the "Auto Sync" is enabled to keep your notes up to date on all devices.

III.   NAVIGATING THE INTERFACE

Microsoft OneNote's interface is designed to be intuitive and user-friendly, but mastering its layout will unlock its full potential. Here's a detailed walkthrough of the key components to help you navigate with confidence.

The Ribbon Toolbar

The Ribbon Toolbar at the top of the OneNote window provides quick access to essential features and tools.

1. Tabs: Organized into categories like Home, Insert, Draw, View, and more. Each tab contains groups of related tools.
   » Home Tab: Formatting options, text styles, and basic organization tools.
   » Insert Tab: Add images, tables, audio recordings, or files.
   » Draw Tab: Tools for handwriting, highlighting, and shapes.
   » View Tab: Adjust page views, switch to dark mode, and enable rule lines or gridlines.
2. Quick Access Toolbar: Located above or below the ribbon, this customizable bar allows you to pin frequently used tools.

The Navigation Pane

The Navigation Pane is your roadmap to organizing and accessing your notes efficiently. It's divided into three main sections:

1. Notebook List: Shows all the notebooks linked to your Microsoft account. Click on a notebook to open it.
2. Section Tabs: Located horizontally, these tabs represent sections within the active notebook. Think of them as dividers in a binder.
3. Page List: Displayed vertically, this shows all pages within the selected section. Click on a page to view or edit it.

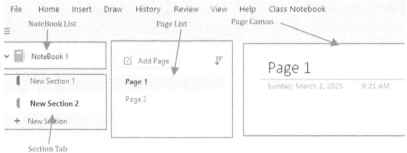

Pro Tip: Collapse or expand the navigation pane to maximize your workspace.

The Page Canvas

The Page Canvas is where all your note-taking magic happens. It's a blank canvas, allowing for text, images, tables, and more.

1. Typing and Writing: Click anywhere on the canvas to start typing. Use the Draw Tab for handwriting.
2. Freeform Layout: Unlike traditional word processors, OneNote lets you move and arrange content boxes freely.
3. Infinite Scroll: Pages automatically expand as you add more content—no need to worry about running out of space.

Search Bar

The Search Bar is a powerful tool to find what you need quickly. Located at the top of the interface:

1. Search by Keywords: Enter a word or phrase to search across all notebooks, sections, and pages.
2. Filter Options: Narrow your search by specifying notebooks, sections, or tags.
3. Highlight Results: The results will be highlighted on the relevant pages for easy navigation.

Other Interface Features

1. Tags: Found in the Home Tab, tags help you organize and prioritize notes (e.g., To-Do, Important, Question).
2. OneNote Badge: On mobile versions, the OneNote badge floats on your screen, allowing quick note-taking without opening the full app.
3. View Modes: Switch between normal view and full-screen mode to focus on your notes.

IV.   CREATING AND MANAGING NOTEBOOKS

Microsoft OneNote's strength lies in its ability to organize information seamlessly through notebooks, sections, and pages. In this section, you'll learn how to create and manage notebooks to keep your ideas structured and accessible.

Creating a New Notebook

1. Desktop Version:
   » Open OneNote and navigate to the File menu.
   » Click New and select where you want to save it (e.g., OneDrive or your computer).
   » Name your notebook and click Create.

2. Mobile Version:
   » Open the OneNote app and tap the Notebooks icon. Tap + Add Notebook, name it, and save it to OneDrive.

Adding Sections and Pages

Once your notebook is ready, you can divide it into sections and pages for better organization.

1. Adding Sections:
   » Click + Section in the navigation pane.
   » Name the section and press Enter. Each section can house multiple pages.

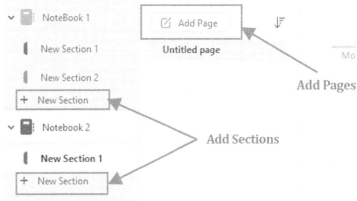

2. Adding Pages:
   » Click + Page under the section tabs.
   » Give the page a title in the header area, which will also serve as its name in the navigation pane.

Pro Tip: Use subpages for additional layers of organization. Right-click on a page and select Make Subpage to nest it under another page.

Renaming and Deleting Notebooks, Sections, or Pages

1. Renaming:
   » Right-click on the notebook, section, or page you want to rename and select Rename.
   » Enter the new name and press Enter.
2. Deleting:
   » Right-click and select Delete. Be cautious—deleted items may not always be recoverable if they aren't synced or stored in the Recycle Bin.

Rearranging Sections and Pages

To keep your notebook organized, you can easily rearrange sections and pages:

1. Sections: Drag and drop section tabs to rearrange them.
2. Pages: Drag a page in the navigation pane to reorder it. For subpages, you can also indent or outdent them by right-clicking and selecting the appropriate option.

Syncing Notebooks with OneDrive

Syncing ensures your notes are accessible across all your devices.

1. Automatic Sync: By default, notebooks saved to OneDrive sync automatically. Check your sync status by clicking File > Info > View Sync Status.
2. Manual Sync: If syncing fails, right-click on the notebook in the navigation pane and select Sync This Notebook Now.

Troubleshooting Tip: Ensure you have an active internet connection and that your OneDrive storage isn't full.

Managing Multiple Notebooks

1. Switching Between Notebooks: Click the Notebooks dropdown menu in the navigation pane to see a list of all your notebooks. Select one to open it.
2. Closing Notebooks: Right-click on the notebook name and select Close This Notebook. You can reopen it later via the File > Open menu.

Backup and Restore

1. Backing Up: Go to File > Options > Save & Backup and choose a location for backups. For manual backups, click Back Up All Notebooks Now.
2. Restoring: Navigate to the backup location, open the file, and copy the contents to your active notebook.

CHAPTER 2: TYPING, WRITING, AND FORMATTING

I. ADDING CONTENT

OneNote allows you to capture ideas in various forms, whether you prefer typing, handwriting, or annotating over existing content. This section covers how to add and manage these elements effectively.

Adding Typed Text

Typing is the most straightforward way to capture notes in OneNote. Here's how to get started:

1. Create a Text Container:
   » Click anywhere on the page to create a text container.
   » Start typing, and OneNote will automatically save your text.

2. Formatting Options: Use the Home tab to change fonts, sizes, and colors or apply styles like bold, italics, underline, or highlight.

3. Organizing Text:
   » Drag text containers to reposition them on the page.
   » Use bullet points, numbered lists, or checkboxes for structured notes.

Adding Handwriting

Handwriting is a great option for tablet users or those prefer a natural note-taking experience.

1. Using the Draw Tab:
   » Open the Draw tab and select a pen, pencil, or highlighter.
   » Choose ink color and thickness to customize your handwriting.

2. Handwriting Conversion: Convert handwriting to typed text by selecting the written content and clicking Ink to Text in the Draw tab.

Adding Annotations

Annotations allow you to add emphasis or context to existing content, such as images, documents, or text.

1. Annotating Text:

» Use the Highlight tool in the Draw tab to emphasize key points.

» Add comments by typing next to the content you want to annotate.

2. Annotating Images and PDFs:

» Insert an image or PDF using the Insert tab.

» Use the drawing tools to write or draw directly on the image or document.

3. Sticky Notes:

» Add virtual sticky notes to your pages for quick reminders or annotations.

» These can be resized, repositioned, and formatted as needed.

II. USING TAGS

Tags are visual markers that you can add to your notes to provide context or signify importance. Common uses for tags include:

- Highlighting key information with tags like Important or Remember for Later.
- Categorizing questions, ideas, or follow-up actions.

How to Add Tags

1. Using the Ribbon Toolbar:

» Navigate to the Home tab.

» In the Tags section, choose from a variety of predefined tags such as To-Do, Important, Question.

2. Applying Tags to Content:

» Place your cursor on the text or object you want to tag.

» Click the desired tag in the ribbon to apply it.

3. Prioritizing Tasks:

» Combine the To-Do tag with additional tags like Important to signify high-priority items.

» Mark completed tasks by clicking the checkbox next to the tagged item.

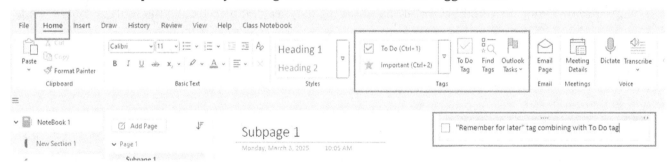

Customizing Tags: OneNote lets you create custom tags to suit your unique needs.

1. Creating a Custom Tag:

» In the Tags section, click the dropdown menu and select Customize Tags. Click New Tag, give it a name, and choose an icon.

2. Editing or Deleting Tags: Open the Customize Tags menu to modify or delete existing tags.

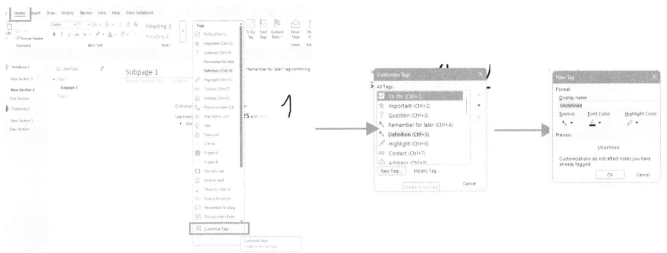

3. Reordering Tags: Drag and drop tags within the Customize Tags menu to rearrange their order for quicker access.

Organizing with Tags

1. Go to the Home tab and click Find Tags. The summary pane displays all tags across your notebook, grouped by type or location.
2. Use the search bar to filter tags by keywords.

III.   ADDING GRIDS AND TABLES

Adding and Formatting Tables

1. Inserting a Table:
   » Go to the Insert tab and click Table. Drag your cursor across the grid to choose the number of rows and columns, then release to insert the table.

2. Adding or Removing Rows and Columns:
   » Right-click on a cell and select Insert Rows Above/Below or Insert Columns Left/Right.
   » To delete, right-click on a row or column and choose Delete Rows or Delete Columns.

3. Formatting Tables: Use the Table Tools in the toolbar to apply shading for better visibility, adjust border styles and align text within cells.

4. Merging and Splitting Cells:
   » Select the cells you want to merge, right-click, and choose Merge Cells.
   » To split a cell, right-click and select Split Cells.

Adding Grids

1. Enable Gridlines:
   » Go to the View tab and select Rule Lines or Grid Lines from the options.
   » Choose the desired grid size for your page.

2. Customizing Grids:
   » Use the Draw tab to overlay shapes or annotations on the grid for better visualization.
   » Combine gridlines with tables to create structured layouts.

CHAPTER 3: ADVANCED FEATURES

I.   ADDING MULTIMEDIA

Adding Images

Images can visually enhance your notes and make them more memorable.

1.   Insert an Image:
   » Go to the Insert tab and select Pictures.
   » Choose From File to upload an image from your device or From Online to search and insert images.

2.   Drag and Drop: Drag images from your desktop or file explorer directly into your OneNote page.

3.   Resizing and Positioning: Drag the corners of the image to resize it or reposition it on the page.

Adding Audio Recordings

1.   Record Audio:
   » Navigate to the Insert tab and select Transcribe > Record Audio.
   » OneNote will start recording immediately and embed the audio file on the page.

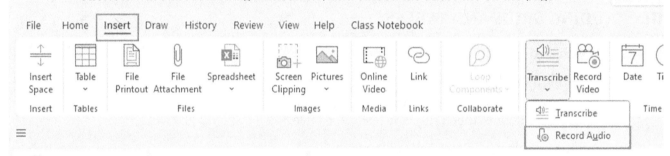

2.   Playback Options:
   » Click the embedded audio file to play it back.
   » Use playback controls to pause, rewind, or fast-forward.

3.   Annotate During Recording: While recording, you can take notes on the same page. OneNote timestamps these notes, linking them to specific points in the recording.

Voice-to-Text Integration

1.   Using Voice-to-Text:

   » Open the Draw or Home tab, depending on your version.
   » Click the Dictate button (a microphone icon) to start.

» Speak clearly, and OneNote will transcribe your speech into typed text.

2. Best Practices for Accurate Transcription:
   » Ensure minimal background noise for better accuracy.
   » Speak slowly and clearly.
   » Use punctuation commands like "period" or "comma" to format your text.

3. Editing Transcriptions:
   » Review the transcribed text and manually edit any errors.
   » Combine transcription with tags or headings for better organization.

Adding Videos

1. Insert a Video:
   » Copy the URL of the video (e.g., from YouTube or Microsoft Stream).
   » Paste the URL into OneNote. If supported, the video will embed automatically.

2. Upload Local Video Files:
   » Go to the Insert tab, choose File Attachment, and upload a video file from your device.
   » The file will be embedded, ready for playback.

3. Annotating Videos:
   » Add notes or summaries next to the video to provide context or highlight key points.

II. OPTICAL CHARACTER RECOGNITION: EXTRACTING TEXT FROM IMAGES

OCR is a technology that recognizes text within images and transforms it into digital text. You can:

- Copy text from images to edit or reuse it.
- Search for specific words within an image.
- Extract handwritten notes and turn them into typed text.

Extracting Text from Images

1. Insert the Image:
   » Go to the Insert tab and select Pictures.
   » Upload the image or screenshot containing the text.

2. Copy Text from the Image:
   » Right-click on the image and select Copy Text from Picture.
   » Paste the copied text anywhere in your OneNote notebook.

3. Extract Text from a Scanned File:
   » Insert a scanned document or PDF as an image.
   » Use the same steps to extract text.

Searching for Text in Images

OneNote's OCR also enables you to search for words embedded within images.

1. Search Across Notebooks:
    »   Use the search bar (top-right corner) to type a keyword.
    »   OneNote will display results, including matches found in images.

2. Enable OCR for Images: Ensure your images are synced to the cloud, as OCR works best when processed on Microsoft's servers.

Editing Extracted Text

After extracting text, you may need to clean up formatting or fix recognition errors:

- Proofread the extracted text for accuracy, especially with handwritten notes or unusual fonts.
- Format the text using tools in the Home tab.

OCR for Handwriting

OneNote's OCR can also convert handwritten notes into typed text, depending on the clarity of the handwriting.

1. Insert Handwritten Notes: Use a stylus or scan handwritten notes into OneNote.
2. Convert Handwriting to Text: Select the handwritten content and choose Ink to Text from the Draw tab.

MASTERING MICROSOFT ACCESS

BUILD, MANAGE, AND ANALYZE DATABASES LIKE A PRO

CHAPTER 1: GETTING STARTED WITH MICROSOFT ACCESS

I. INTRODUCTION TO THE ACCESS DATABASE

Microsoft Access is a robust database management system (DBMS) that enables users to organize, store, and retrieve information effectively. Unlike simple spreadsheet tools, Access provides a structured way to manage data across multiple tables while maintaining relationships between them.

What Is a Database?

At its core, a database is a collection of data organized for easy access, management, and updating. Think of it as a digital filing cabinet where data is stored systematically, making it easier to locate specific pieces of information when needed.

In Microsoft Access, databases are built using various objects, each serving a unique purpose:

- Tables: Store raw data in rows and columns, similar to a spreadsheet.
- Queries: Allow you to extract, analyze, and manipulate data.
- Forms: Provide a user-friendly interface for data entry and navigation.
- Reports: Enable you to present data in an organized and printable format.

Launching the Microsoft Access Application

1. From the Start Menu:
   » Click the Start button or press the Windows key. Type Microsoft Access into the search bar.
   » Select Microsoft Access from the search results.
2. From the Desktop Shortcut: If you've created a shortcut on your desktop, double-click the Access icon to open the application.
3. From the Office Hub:
   » Open the Office app on your desktop or online.
   » Navigate to Access and click on it to start.

II. WORKING WITH THE ACCESS OPENING SCREEN

Key Components of the Opening Screen

1. Blank Database:
   » This option lets you start from scratch with an empty database. Ideal for projects requiring full customization. Selecting this opens a new database file with a default table.
2. Templates:
   » Microsoft Access offers a variety of preformatted database templates for common cases.
   » Templates come with prebuilt tables, queries, forms, and reports.
3. Recent Files:

» A list of databases you've recently worked on, displayed for quick access.

» Hover over a file to view its location or click to open it directly.

4. Search Online Templates: Use this feature to find more templates by entering keywords in the search bar.

5. Account Information:

» Located in the top-right corner, this section shows the logged-in Microsoft account.

» Options include signing in, switching accounts, or managing Office settings.

6. Options Menu: Access settings to customize your workspace and preferences via File > Options.

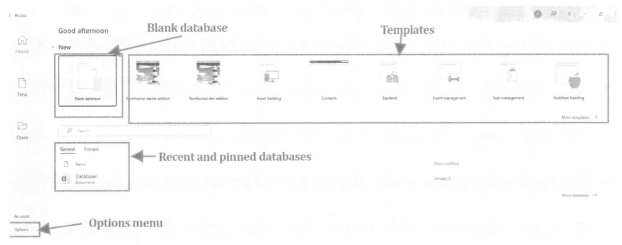

III. CREATING YOUR FIRST DATABASE: A STEP-BY-STEP GUIDE

1. Starting from a Blank Database:

» Click Blank Database.

» Name your database in the File Name field.

» Choose a location to save the file by clicking the folder icon.

» Click Create to open your new database file.

2. Using a Template:

» Browse the available templates or search online for one that suits your needs.

» Preview the template by clicking on it.

» Click Create to download and open the selected template.

» Modify the template as needed to fit your project.

CHAPTER 2: NAVIGATING THE WORKSPACE IN ACCESS

I. STARTING WITH THE WORKSPACE IN ACCESS

1. KEY COMPONENTS OF THE ACCESS WORKSPACE

The Ribbon:

- The ribbon is a toolbar at the top of the workspace, organized into tabs such as **Home**, **Create**, **External Data**, and **Database Tools**.
- Each tab contains groups of commands relevant to specific tasks, such as creating tables, designing forms, or running queries.
- The **Home** tab offers commonly used actions like formatting and filtering data.

Quick Access Toolbar:

- A small toolbar above the ribbon with frequently used commands like **Undo**, and **Redo**.
- Customizable to include other commands you use often.

Context-Sensitive Panels:

- Panels like **Field List** or **Property Sheet** appear when editing specific objects.
- These provide options tailored to the object you're working on.

Navigation Pane:

- Located on the left side of the workspace, the navigation pane lists all the objects in your database (tables, queries, forms, reports, macros, and modules).
- Use it to open, rename, or manage your database objects.
- Objects can be grouped into predefined categories (e.g., Object Type or Tables).

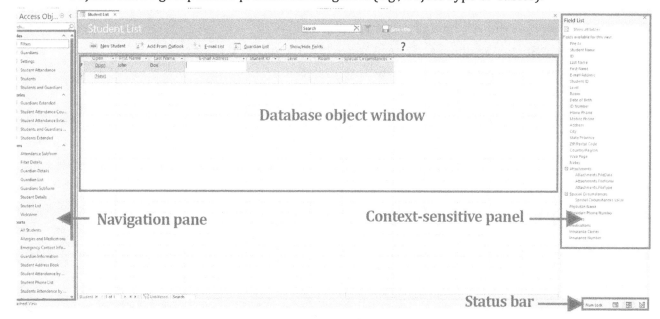

Database Object Window:

- The central part of the workspace where database objects (like tables and forms) open for editing and interaction.
- Multiple objects can be opened simultaneously in tabs for easy switching.

Status Bar:

- Found at the bottom of the workspace, the status bar provides information about the current view (e.g., Datasheet View or Design View).
- It includes quick toggles for changing views and navigating records.

2. NAVIGATING THE WORKSPACE

Switching Between Tabs and Objects:

- Use the navigation pane to open and switch between database objects.
- Tabs at the top of the object window let you toggle between open objects.

Changing Views:

- Each database object has multiple views:
  - » **Tables**: Datasheet View, Design View.
  - » **Forms**: Form View, Layout View, Design View.
  - » **Reports**: Report View, Print Preview.
- Use the **View** button on the ribbon or the status bar to switch between these views.

Using Panels and Panes:

- Open or close panels like the **Navigation Pane** by clicking the **Pane Toggle Button** on the left.
- Resize panes by dragging their edges to customize your workspace.

II. CUSTOMIZING THE WORKSPACE

Adding Tools to the Quick Access Toolbar

1. Click the drop-down arrow next to the Quick Access Toolbar.
2. Select a command from the list, such as **Print Preview** or **Open**.
3. For additional commands:
   - » Select **More Commands** from the drop-down menu.
   - » In the **Access Options** dialog box, choose a command from the list on the left and click **Add**. Click **OK** to save changes.

Removing Tools from the Quick Access Toolbar

1. Right-click the tool you want to remove from the toolbar.
2. Select **Remove from Quick Access Toolbar**.

Changing the Location of the Toolbar

1. Click the drop-down arrow on the toolbar.
2. Select **Show Below the Ribbon** to move it below the ribbon or **Show Above the Ribbon** to return it to its default position.

Minimizing and Maximizing the Ribbon

1. To minimize the ribbon, click the small arrow at the top-right corner of the ribbon. Alternatively, press **Ctrl + F1**.
2. To maximize the ribbon, click the arrow again or press **Ctrl + F1**.

Adding or Removing Ribbon Tabs

1. Go to **File > Options > Customize Ribbon**.
2. Use the **Customize the Ribbon** section to:
   » Add new tabs by clicking **New Tab**.
   » Remove tabs by unchecking their boxes.
3. Click **OK** to save changes.

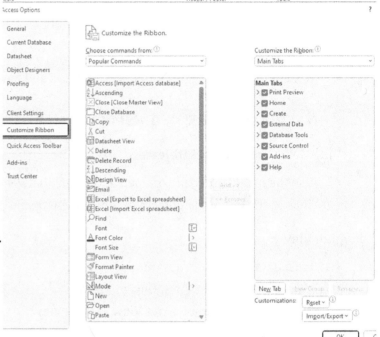

Using ScreenTips

ScreenTips are small pop-up descriptions that appear when you hover over a button or tool in Access. These tips can help you understand the function of tools and commands.

In the **User Interface Options** section, adjust the ScreenTip style:

1. Show Feature Descriptions in ScreenTips: Displays detailed tips.
2. Don't Show Feature Descriptions in ScreenTips: Displays the tool name only.
3. Don't Show ScreenTips: Disables tips entirely.

CHAPTER 3:
TABLES AND DATABASE BASICS

I. TABLES OVERVIEW

A table is where all the data in a database is stored. Each table consists of:

- Rows (Records): Individual entries in the database (e.g., a single customer or product).
- Columns (Fields): Categories of data stored in the table (e.g., customer name, phone number, email address).

Understanding Table Design

In Access, tables are more than just grids for data entry. Each table should be designed with clear rules to ensure data consistency.

- Field Name: A unique name for each column.
- Data Type: Defines the kind of data stored in the field (e.g., text, number, date/ time).
- Field Properties: Additional settings, such as default values, required fields, or input masks.

Adding and Deleting Fields:

- To add a field, use the Click to Add header in Datasheet View or insert a field in Design View.
- To delete a field, select it, right-click, and choose Delete Field.

Insert Field Name and data type

Renaming Fields:

- Right-click the field header and select Rename Field.
- Type the new name and press Enter.

Sorting and Filtering Data:

- Sort records by clicking the drop-down arrow in the field header and selecting Sort A-Z or Sort Z-A.
- Filter records using criteria by selecting Text Filters or Number Filters from the same menu.

II.   CREATING A DATABASE TABLE FROM SCRATCH

Building a table from scratch in Microsoft Access gives you complete control over its structure, ensuring it meets the specific needs of your database. This section walks you through the process of creating a table manually and tailoring it to your project.

Why Create a Table from Scratch?

Starting with a blank table allows you to:

- Customize the structure and field types to align with your data requirements.
- Avoid unnecessary fields or predefined layouts included in templates.
- Build a database with efficiency and accuracy in mind.

Steps to Create a Blank Table

1.   Open Your Database:
   »   Open an existing database or create a new blank database.

2.   Navigate to Table Creation:
   »   Go to the Create tab on the ribbon.
   »   Click Table in the Tables group. A blank table will open in Datasheet View.

3.   Define Table Fields:
   »   Click on the Click to Add header to create a new field.
   »   Select a data type for the field (e.g., Short Text, Number, Date/Time) from the dropdown menu.
   »   Enter a descriptive name for the field.

4.   Save the Table:
   »   Press Ctrl + S or go to File > Save.
   »   Enter a descriptive name for the table (e.g., "Products" or "Orders") and click OK.

ID	Product ID	Product Name	Unit Price	Quantity	Click to Add
1	1001	Product 1	$1.50	200	
2	1002	Product 2	$2.00	400	
3	1003	Product 3	$4.00	800	
* (New)	0		$0.00	0	

Field Naming Best Practices

- Use descriptive names, such as "Product Name" instead of "Field1."
- Avoid spaces or special characters; use underscores if necessary (e.g., "Order_Date").
- Keep field names consistent across related tables for clarity.

III.   CREATING A DATABASE TABLE USING A BUILT-IN TEMPLATE

Why Use a Template?

Templates are ideal for:

- Quick database setup without starting from scratch.
- Ensuring a standard structure for common database tasks.
- Reducing design errors by using preconfigured fields and settings.

Examples of Built-In Templates:

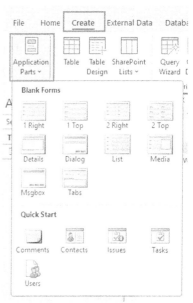

- Contacts: Manage customer or personal contact information.
- Tasks: Track project assignments or to-do lists.
- Issues: Record and monitor problems or bug reports.

Steps to Create a Table Using a Template

1. Open Your Database:
   - » Open an existing database or create a new blank database.

2. Access the Templates:
   - » Navigate to the Create tab on the ribbon.
   - » In the Templates group, click Application Parts.

3. Select a Template:
   - » Choose a template from the list, such as Contacts or Tasks.
   - » The selected template will add a pre-designed table to your database, along with related objects like forms and queries (if applicable).

4. Customize the Table:
   - » Open the table in Design View to modify field names, data types, or properties.
   - » Add or remove fields as needed to tailor the table to your project.

Modifying a Template-Based Table

Even with a pre-designed template, it's important to adjust it to fit your specific requirements.

1. Rename Fields: Use descriptive names that align with your data.
2. Add Fields: Insert additional fields by selecting Click to Add in Datasheet View or using the Field Name column in Design View.
3. Delete Unnecessary Fields: Remove fields that don't apply to your project by right-clicking the field header and selecting Delete Field.

IV.   IMPORTING TABLES FROM OTHER SOURCES

Importing tables is beneficial when you have data stored in external applications like Excel or another database system, you want to combine multiple datasets into a single Access database or you need to migrate data from an old system to Access.

Access supports importing tables from various file formats and systems, including:

- Microsoft Excel: XLS, XLSX files.
- Text Files: CSV, TXT files with delimited or fixed-width formats.
- Access Databases: Tables from other Access databases.

- SQL Databases: Tables or views from SQL Server or other relational databases.
- SharePoint Lists: Data stored in SharePoint.

Steps to Import a Table

1. Open Your Database: Open the database where you want to import the table.
2. Launch the Import Wizard:
   » Go to the External Data tab on the ribbon.
   » Select the appropriate source type in the Import & Link group (e.g., Excel, Text File).
3. Choose the File:
   » Browse to locate the source file or database. Select the file and click Open.
4. Follow the Wizard Instructions:
   » For Excel or Text Files: select the worksheet or specify the delimiter (e.g., comma for CSV files), define whether the first row contains column headings.
   » For Access Databases: choose the table or query you want to import.
   » For SQL Databases: provide the server name, database name, and authentication details.
5. Select Import Options: Choose whether to import the data into a new table or append it to an existing table. Specify data types and field names, if needed.
6. Finish and Save the Import: Review the summary and click Finish.

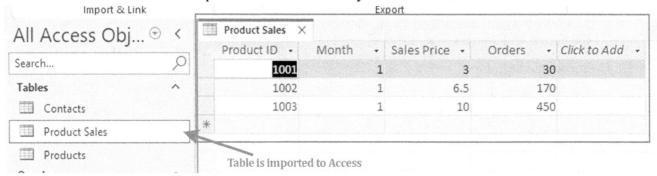

Table is imported to Access

V. TWO WAYS TO OPEN A DATABASE TABLE

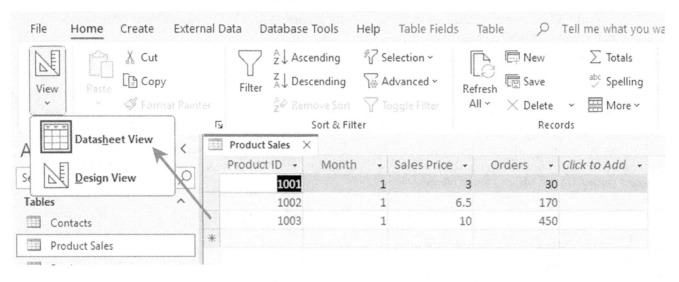

216

1. OPENING A TABLE IN DATASHEET VIEW

The Datasheet View displays table data in a grid format, similar to a spreadsheet. This view is ideal for entering, editing, and viewing data.

Steps to Open a Table in Datasheet View:

1. Locate the table in the Navigation Pane on the left side of the Access workspace. Double-click the table name to open it in Datasheet View.
2. Use the grid to add, edit, or delete data as needed.

Features of Datasheet View:

- Add Records: Use the blank row at the bottom of the table to add new records.
- Edit Records: Click any cell and type to update its value.
- Sort and Filter: Right-click on a column header to sort records or apply filters.

2. OPENING A TABLE IN DESIGN VIEW

The Design View lets you modify the structure of a table, such as field names, data types, and field properties. This view focuses on the table's setup rather than its data.

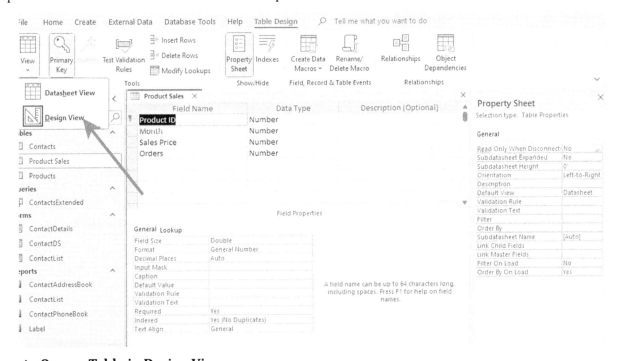

Steps to Open a Table in Design View:

1. Locate the table in the Navigation Pane. Right-click the table name and select Design View.
2. The table structure will open, displaying Field Name column, Data Type column and Field Properties panel.

Features of Design View:

- Add or Delete Fields: Insert new fields or remove unused ones.
- Modify Data Types: Change the type of data a field can store (e.g., Short Text, Number).

- Set Field Properties: Customize properties like default values, validation rules, and input masks.

You can switch between Datasheet View and Design View at any time while working with a table.

1. Open the table in either Datasheet or Design View.
2. Click the View button on the Home tab or the View dropdown in the top-left corner of the Access workspace. Select the desired view (Datasheet View or Design View).

VI.   DETERMINING AND ASSIGNING DATA TYPES

A data type specifies the format of data that a field can hold, such as text, numbers, dates, or currency. Selecting the correct data type helps:

- Prevent invalid data entry (e.g., entering text in a numeric field).
- Optimize database performance by using appropriate storage formats.
- Enable specific functionalities, such as calculations or date-based sorting.

Common Data Types in Microsoft Access

Data Type	Description	Example
Short Text	Alphanumeric data up to 255 characters	Names, addresses
Long Text	Longer text for extended descriptions or notes	Product descriptions
Number	Numeric data for calculations	Quantities, prices
Date/Time	Dates and times	Order dates, birthdates
Currency	Monetary values	Product prices
Yes/No	Boolean data for true/false values	In stock (Yes/No)
AutoNumber	Automatically generates unique numbers for each record	Customer IDs, order numbers
Hyperlink	Links to websites, files, or email addresses	https://example.com
Attachment	Stores files, such as images or documents	Product images

Steps to Assign Data Types

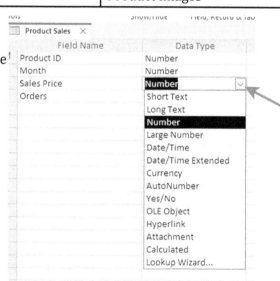

1. Open the Table in Design View: Right-click the table in the Navigation Pane and select Design View.
2. Select a Field: Click the field you want to define or modify.
3. Choose a Data Type: In the Data Type column, select the appropriate type from the dropdown menu.
4. Adjust Field Properties: Use the Field Properties panel to customize settings.

Tips for Selecting the Right Data Type

- Text or Long Text: Use for names, addresses, or other non-numeric data.

218

- Number: Use for fields that require calculations, such as quantities or percentages.
- Date/Time: Use for fields that involve calendar-based operations.
- Currency: Use for financial data to ensure proper formatting and avoid rounding errors.
- Yes/No: Use for binary choices like "In Stock" (Yes/No) or "Active" (True/False).
- AutoNumber: Use for unique identifiers that don't require user input, such as primary keys.

VII. DATA ENTRY APPROACHES

Once your tables are created and structured, entering data is the next crucial step. Microsoft Access provides multiple methods for adding data, allowing you to choose the approach that best suits your workflow.

Entering Data Directly in Datasheet View: This method involves manually typing data into the table's grid format like a spreadsheet.

1. Open the table in Datasheet View by double-clicking it in the Navigation Pane.
2. Click in the first empty cell of a field and type your data.
3. Use the Tab key to move to the next field in the row.
4. Use the Enter key to move to the next row when a record is complete.

Entering Data Using a Form: Forms offer a more user-friendly interface for data entry, especially for complex tables with many fields.

1. Open the form linked to the table by double-clicking it in the Navigation Pane.
2. Fill out the fields on the form.
3. Click the Save button (or move to a new record) to save the data.

Tips for Efficient Data Entry

- Use Defaults: Define default values for fields to speed up repetitive entries.
- Validate Data: Set validation rules and input masks to ensure data accuracy.
- Minimize Errors: Use drop-down lists (combo boxes) for fields with predefined options.

VIII. AMENDING THE LOOK OF THE DATASHEET

Customizing the appearance of your table in Datasheet View improves readability and usability, especially when working with large datasets.

Resizing Columns and Rows

- Adjust Column Width: Hover over the border of a column header until the resize cursor appears. Drag to resize or double-click the border to auto-fit the content.
- Adjust Row Height: Right-click a row header and select Row Height. Enter the desired height and click OK.

Freezing Columns

Freezing a column keeps it visible while scrolling through the datasheet.

- Right-click the column header. Select Freeze Fields.
- To unfreeze, select Unfreeze All Fields from the same menu.

Hiding and Unhiding Columns

Hide fields that are not immediately relevant to declutter the datasheet.

- Hide a Column: Right-click the column header and select Hide Fields.
- Unhide Columns: Right-click any column header, select Unhide Fields, and check the boxes for the columns to display.

Changing Font and Gridline Settings

- Modify Font: Go to the Home tab and use the font options in the Text Formatting group to change font type, size, or color.
- Adjust Gridlines: Click Gridlines or Datasheet Formatting in the Home tab, customize the style, color, and visibility of gridlines.

Adjusting Alternating Row Colors

Alternating row colors improve readability by visually separating rows.

1. Go to the Home tab.
2. Select Datasheet Formatting and choose a new color for alternating rows.

IX. OTHER DATABASE BASICS WHEN WORKING WITH TABLES

1. FORMS

A form is a graphical representation of the data stored in your tables. It acts as a bridge between the user and the database, ensuring data is entered accurately and efficiently.

Key Advantages of Using Forms:

- Simplified Data Entry: Users interact with fields one at a time, reducing errors.
- Custom Layouts: Forms can be tailored to display specific fields in a logical order.
- Enhanced Usability: Add buttons, drop-down lists, other controls to streamline tasks.
- Data Security: Limit user access to specific fields or tables.

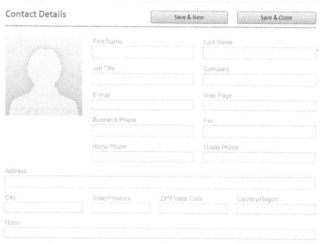

2. QUERIES

A query is a request for information from one or more tables or other queries in your database. It allows you to retrieve only the data you need, analyze data by performing calculations or aggregations, update, append, or delete data in bulk.

Examples of Queries:

- Retrieve all customers who made purchases in the last month.
- Calculate the total sales for each product category.
- Update the stock quantity for a list of imported products.

Types of Queries in Access

1. Select Query:
    » Retrieves specific data from tables or other queries.
    » Example: Find all orders placed in December.

2. Action Queries: modify data in tables. These include:
    » Update Query: Changes existing data.
    » Append Query: Adds new records to a table.
    » Delete Query: Removes records that meet specific criteria.
    » Make-Table Query: Creates a new table with the results of the query.

3. Parameter Query:
    » Prompts the user to enter criteria when the query runs.
    » Example: Ask for a date range to display orders from that period.

4. Crosstab Query:
    » Summarizes data in a table format with rows, columns, and values.
    » Example: Show total sales by product (rows) and month (columns).

5. SQL-Specific Queries:
    » Written directly in SQL for advanced functionality.
    » Example: UNION queries to combine results from multiple queries.

Why Use Queries?

- Efficiency: Queries extract only the necessary data, speeding up analysis.
- Flexibility: Use criteria to customize data retrieval and focus on specific records.
- Automation: Save queries to reuse them for recurring tasks, like generating monthly reports.
- Data Integrity: Use queries to verify and clean data, such as duplicates or invalid entries.

3. PRIMARY KEYS AND RELATIONSHIPS

What Is a Primary Key?

The primary key is a field (or combination of fields) that uniquely identifies each record in a table. For example:

- In a Customer Table, the primary key might be Customer ID.
- In an Orders Table, it might be Order ID.

Key Features of a Primary Key:

- Uniqueness: No two records can have the same value in the primary key field.
- Mandatory: Every record must have a value in the primary key field (it cannot be null).

Primary Keys and Foreign Keys

Keys are essential for linking tables and ensuring data integrity. Every table has a primary key. To connect and refer between tables, a primary key from a table must reference another field (which is called foreign key) of another table. For example:

- In a Customer Table, the primary key might be Customer ID.
- In an Orders Table, the Customer ID field links to the primary key in the Customer Table. In the Orders Table, Customer ID is a foreign key.

Best Practices for Choosing a Primary Key

- Use a Single Field When Possible: It's simpler and more efficient.
- Avoid Changing Primary Key Values: Choose a field that won't need frequent updates (e.g., avoid using phone numbers or names).
- Ensure Field Consistency: Make sure the primary key field is consistent across related tables.

What Are Relationships in Access?

A relationship connects two tables by linking a primary key in one table to a corresponding foreign key in another. These relationships are crucial for maintaining data consistency and enabling efficient data retrieval.

Types of Relationships:

- One-to-One: Each record in Table A matches one record in Table B.
- One-to-Many: A single record in Table A can match multiple records in Table B.
- Many-to-Many: Records in Table A can match multiple records in Table B, and vice versa.

Examples:

- One-to-One relationship: A table of employees and a table of their assigned workstations.
- One-to-Many: A Customer Table and an Orders Table, where each customer can place multiple orders.
- Many-to-Many: A Students Table and a Classes Table (students can enroll in multiple classes, and classes can have multiple students).

X. EDITING, UPDATING, AND DELETING RECORDS IN A TABLE

Once your data is entered into Microsoft Access, you may need to update, edit, or delete records to keep your database accurate and up to date. Access provides tools to manage these tasks efficiently.

Editing Records

1. Open the table in Datasheet View or the associated form.
2. Click on the field you want to edit.
3. Type the new data and press Enter or Tab to save the changes.

Tips for Editing Records:

- Undo Changes: Press Ctrl + Z to revert recent edits.
- Spell Check: Use the Spell Check tool in the Review tab to correct text fields.
- Batch Edits: Use queries to update multiple records simultaneously for efficiency.

Updating Records

For bulk updates, create an Update Query to modify multiple records at once.

1. Create the Query:
   » Go to the Create tab and click Query Design.

   » Add the table containing the records you want to update.

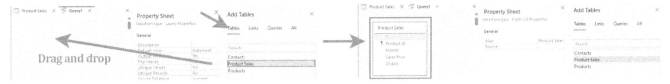

2. Change Query Type: Click Update in the Query Type group of the ribbon.

3. Set the Update Fields:
   » In the query design grid, select the field to update.
   » Enter the new value or an expression in the Update To row.

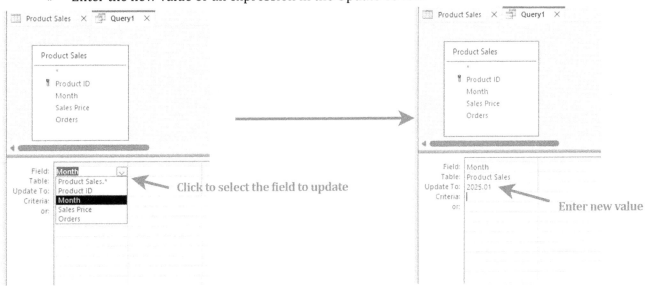

4. Run the Query:
   » Click Run on the ribbon.
   » Review the warning and confirm the changes.

Deleting Records Manually:

1. Open the table in Datasheet View.
2. Select the record you want to delete by clicking the row selector on the left.
3. Press Delete on your keyboard or click Delete Record in the Home tab.

Using a Delete Query:

To remove entire records (rows) from a table or from two related tables simultaneously, use a Delete Query.

1. Create the Query:
   » Go to the Create tab and click Query Design.
   » Add the table containing the records you want to delete.

2. Change Query Type:
   » Click Delete in the Query Type group of the ribbon.

3. Set the Criteria:
   » Add the fields to the query grid.
   » Specify the criteria for the records to delete in the Criteria row.

4. Run the Query:
   » Click Run on the ribbon.
   » Review the warning and confirm the deletion.

If the records reside on the "one" side of a one-to-many relationship, you might need to change the relationship before you run the delete query.

CHAPTER 4: PLANNING AND CONSTRUCTING A DATABASE

I. PLANNING FOR DATABASE

Before creating a database, it's essential to carefully plan what information you need to collect, store, and analyze. This foundational step ensures that your database is efficient, organized, and tailored to meet your specific requirements.

1. UNDERSTANDING THE PURPOSE OF YOUR DATABASE

Start by clearly defining the purpose of your database. Ask yourself:

- What problems will this database solve?
- Who will use the database, and how will they interact with it?
- What types of information need to be stored and accessed?

2. IDENTIFYING KEY DATA CATEGORIES

Next, determine the main categories of information your database needs to handle. These categories will guide the structure of your tables. Examples:

- Customer Database: Customer name, contact information, purchase history.
- Inventory Database: Product ID, description, quantity in stock, supplier information.

For each category, consider:

- Attributes: What details should be included? For example, a "Customer" category might include attributes like name, phone number, and email address.
- Relationships: How do categories relate to each other? For example, customers might be linked to orders they place.

3. ANTICIPATING DATA USAGE

Think about how you'll use the data in your database. This will help you design tables, queries, forms, and reports effectively. Questions to consider:

1. What kinds of reports will you need (e.g., monthly sales reports, inventory summaries)?
2. What types of analysis will you perform (e.g., identifying top-performing products)?
3. How will users interact with the database (e.g., entering data, generating invoices)?

4. DRAFTING YOUR DATABASE PLAN

Before diving into Access, sketch out a plan for your database on paper or using diagramming tools. This step will save you time and effort later.

Steps for Drafting a Plan:

- List Data Categories: Write down all the main categories of information.
- Define Fields: For each category, list the fields you'll need (e.g., Customer Name, Order Date).
- Map Relationships: Draw connections between related categories (e.g., link customers to their orders, products to their suppliers).

II.   DISTRIBUTING INFORMATION ACROSS DATABASE TABLES

Why Split Information Into Multiple Tables?

Instead of storing all your data in a single table, dividing it into multiple related tables reduces duplicate data entries, saving storage space and makes it easier to update and manage specific data points.

Steps to Distribute Information

   1.   **Identify Data Categories**:

Group data into categories that naturally belong together (e.g., Customers, Products, Orders) as explained in above section.

   2.   **Define Tables for Each Category**:

Each category should have its own table. For example:

- Customers Table: Stores customer details.
- Products Table: Stores product information.
- Orders Table: Stores information about each order.

   3.   **Create Tables:** Follow steps in Chapter 3 to create relevant tables.

III.   ASSIGNING FIELDS TO DATABASE TABLES

Once you've distributed your information across tables, the next step is to assign fields to each table. Fields represent the individual pieces of data you want to store in a table, such as names, dates, or numbers.

Steps for Assigning Fields

   1.   **Identify the Attributes of Each Table**:

- For every table, list the attributes you need to store.
- Example for a Products Table: Product ID, Product Name, Description, Price, Stock Quantity.

   2.   Determine the Data Type for Each Field: Each field in Access must have a defined data type that matches the kind of information it will store.

Set Field Properties

- Customize fields to improve data accuracy and consistency. Examples:
   » Field Size: Limits the number of characters in text fields.
   » Default Value: Automatically fills in a value for new records (e.g., "0" for quantity).
   » Validation Rule: Ensures data meets specific criteria (e.g., price must be greater than 0).

IV.   SELECT A PRIMARY KEY

Steps to Select a Primary Key

1. Identify the Field That Best Represents Uniqueness:
    »   Look for a field that contains unique values for each record.
    »   Examples: Customer ID for customers, Product ID for products, Order Number for orders.

2. Use AutoNumber for System-Generated IDs:
    »   If your table doesn't have a natural unique identifier (e.g., Social Security Number, ISBN), use the AutoNumber data type.
    »   Access will automatically generate a unique number for each record.

3. Consider Composite Keys for Multi-Field Uniqueness:
    »   If no single field is unique, combine two or more fields to create a composite key.
    »   Example: In a Sales Table, you might use a combination of Salesperson ID and Sale Date as the primary key.

Steps to set the primary keys

To designate a field as the primary key:

*   Open the table, click Design View.
*   Select the field you want to use as primary key. Click Primary Key in the Table Design tab.

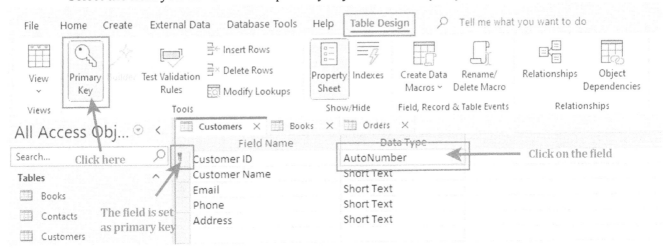

V.   ESTABLISHING RELATIONSHIPS BETWEEN DATABASE TABLES

Once your tables are structured and primary keys are defined, the next step is to establish relationships between them. Relationships enable you to link tables, ensuring data integrity and making it easier to extract meaningful information through queries, forms, and reports.

Steps to Establish Relationships in Access

1. Open the Relationships Window: Go to the Database Tools tab on the ribbon. Click Relationships.
2. Add Tables to the Relationship Diagram: In the Relationships window, select the tables you want to connect and click Add.
3. Link Fields to Define Relationships: Drag the primary key field from one table to the corresponding foreign key field in another table. The Edit Relationships dialog box will appear.
4. Set Relationship Options:

- » Enforce Referential Integrity: Ensures that records in the related table always match a valid record in the primary table.
- » Cascade Update Related Fields: Automatically updates foreign key values when the primary key value changes.
- » Cascade Delete Related Records: Deletes related records in other tables when a record is removed from the primary table.

5. Save the Relationship: Click Create to finalize the relationship.

Viewing and Managing Relationships

Use the Relationships window to view all table connections at a glance.

- To modify a relationship: Double-click the relationship line in the diagram to open the Edit Relationships dialog box.
- To delete a relationship: Select the relationship line and press Delete.

VI.   REAL-LIFE EXAMPLE

Example: create a database for an online bookstore.

1.   PLANNING

STEP 1: UNDERSTANDING THE PURPOSE

- Purpose: An online bookstore needs a database to manage book inventory, customer information, and customer orders.

STEP 2: IDENTIFYING KEY DATA CATEGORIES

- Customers: Customer ID, Name, Email, Phone, Address
- Books (Products): Book ID, Title, Author, Genre, Price, Quantity in Stock
- Orders: Order ID, Order Date, Customer ID, Book ID, Quantity Ordered, Total Price

STEP 3: ANTICIPATING DATA USAGE

- Reports Needed: Monthly sales, Inventory stock levels, Customer purchase history.
- User Interaction: Employees entering customer orders, Managers updating inventory data, customer service staff reviewing orders and customer info.

STEP 4: DRAFTING YOUR DATABASE PLAN

Customers Table	Books Table	Orders Table
Customer ID (Primary Key)	Book ID (Primary Key)	Order ID (Primary Key)
Customer Name	Title	Order Date
Email	Author	Customer ID (Foreign Key)
Phone	Genre	Book ID (Foreign Key)
Address	Price	Quantity Ordered
	Quantity in Stock	Total Price

2. DISTRIBUTING INFORMATION ACROSS TABLES

We create 3 tables as in Step 2 of Planning.

Order ID	Order Date	Customer II	Book ID	Quantity Or	Total Price	Click to Add
1001	1/15/2025	1	101	2	$25.98	
1002	1/16/2025	2	103	1	$9.99	
1003	1/17/2025	3	104	3	$44.97	
1004	1/18/2025	1	102	1	$15.99	
(New)				0	$0.00	

3. ASSIGNING FIELDS AND DATA TYPES

Field Name	Data Type	Description
Customer ID	AutoNumber (Primary Key)	Unique ID for each customer
Customer Name	Short Text	Customer's full name
Email	Short Text	Customer email address
Phone	Short Text	Contact phone number
Address	Short Text	Delivery address
Book ID	AutoNumber (Primary Key)	Unique ID for each book
Title	Short Text	Book's title
Author	Short Text	Book's author
Genre	Short Text	Genre category
Price	Currency	Book selling price
Quantity in Stock	Number	Quantity available
Order ID	AutoNumber (Primary Key)	Unique order identifier
Order Date	Date/Time	Date of customer's order
Quantity Ordered	Number	Number of copies ordered
Total Price	Currency	Total order amount

4. ESTABLISHING RELATIONSHIPS BETWEEN TABLES

Relationship Types: One-to-Many:

- Customers → Orders (Each customer can have many orders; each order belongs to one customer).
- Books → Orders (Each book can appear in many orders; each order entry references one book).

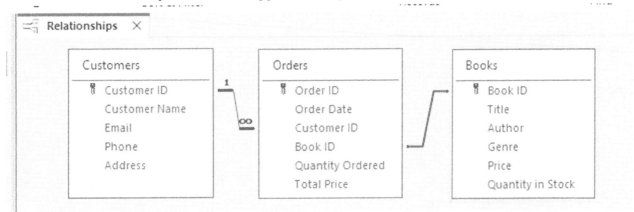

CHAPTER 5: QUERYING DATA

Queries are at the heart of Microsoft Access, providing powerful tools to filter, retrieve, and analyze data from your database. With queries, you can ask specific questions about your data and get precise answers, enabling better decision-making and insights.

I. CREATING AND RUNNING QUERIES

Creating and Running Select Queries

A Select Query is the most commonly used query type in Microsoft Access. It retrieves data from one or more tables or queries based on specified criteria and displays the results in a datasheet format.

1. Open the Query Design Tool
   » Go to the Create tab on the ribbon. Click Query Design.
   » Add or drag and drop the tables or queries you want to include in your query into the database object window.

2. Select the Fields
   » Drag fields from the table(s) in the upper pane to the query design grid below.
   » Alternatively, double-click a field in the table to add it to the grid.

3. Set Criteria
   » In the Criteria row of the design grid, enter conditions to filter the results.
   » Use logical operators like AND, OR, and comparison operators (>, <, >=, etc.) for more complex criteria.

4. Run the Query
   » Click Run in the Design tab or press Ctrl + R. The results will appear in Datasheet View.

5. Save the Query: Click Save or press Ctrl + S.

Example 1: Simple Select Query

Using the Books table in Chapter 4's real-life example, retrieve a list of all books priced above $10.

1. Open Query Design & add table to Query
2. Select Fields to Display: double-click the fields in the table.

3. Apply Criteria to Filter Results

4. Run the Query and review the Results.

Book ID	Title	Author	Price
101	The Great Gat	F. Scott Fitzge	$12.99
102	A Brief History	Stephen Hawk	$15.99
104	1984	George Orwel	$14.99
* (New)			$0.00

II.   USING CRITERIA, WILDCARDS, AND EXPRESSIONS IN QUERIES

Using Criteria to Filter Data: Criteria are conditions you apply to a query to filter the data returned.

- **Text Criteria:**
  » Example: ="New York" retrieves records where the field value is "New York."
  » Example: <> "California" excludes records where the field value is "California."

- **Numeric Criteria:**
  » Example: >100 retrieves values greater than 100.

- **Date/Time Criteria:**
  » Example: #01/01/2025# retrieves records with the exact date.

- **Logical Operators:**
  » Example: AND: City = "New York" AND State = "NY"

Using Wildcards for Partial Matches:

Wildcards allow you to search for patterns in text fields, making it easier to locate records when the exact value is unknown.

Wildcard	Function	Example	Result
*	Matches any number of characters	"Jo*"	Retrieves "John," "Joseph," "Jordan"
?	Matches a single character	"J?ne"	Retrieves "Jane" and "June"
#	Matches a single digit	"123#"	Retrieves "1234" and "1239"
[ ]	Matches characters in brackets	"J[ao]hn"	Retrieves "John" and "Jahn"
[!]	Excludes characters in brackets	"J[!o]hn"	Retrieves "Jahn" but not "John"

Example: Find customers whose names start with "Jo".

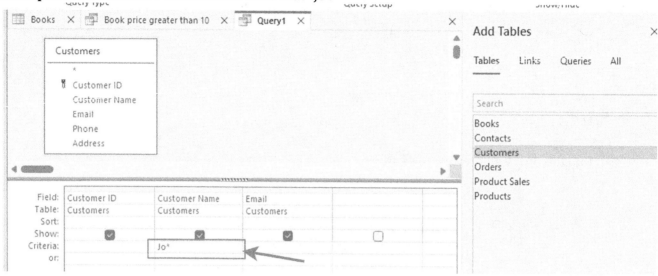

Creating a Calculated Field:

1. Open your query in Design View.
2. In the query grid, type your expression followed by a colon (:) and the formula. Example: Discounted Price: [Total Price] * 0.9

Common Expressions:

- Mathematical Calculations: Example: Total Sales: [Quantity] * [Unit Price]
- Text Manipulation: Example: Full Name: [First Name] & " " & [Last Name]
- Conditional Logic: Example: Bonus Eligibility: IIf([Sales] > 10000, "Yes", "No")

Example: Display each order with a new calculated field showing a 10% discounted price.

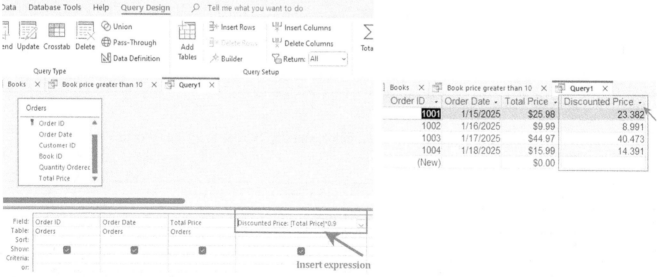

III. JOINING TABLES IN QUERIES

A join connects two or more tables by linking a common field, typically the primary key from one table and the foreign key in another. Joins allow you to:

- Retrieve related data from different tables.
- Avoid redundant data by splitting information into separate, related tables.
- Analyze relationships between data points.

Types of Joins in Access

1. Inner Join:
    - » Retrieves only the records that have matching values in both tables.

2. Left Outer Join:
    - » Retrieves all records from the first (left) table and matching records from the second (right) table. If there's no match, the result includes null values for the second table.

3. Right Outer Join:
    - » Retrieves all records from the second (right) table and matching records from the first (left) table. If there's no match, the result includes null values for the first table.

4. Cross Join (Cartesian Product):
    - » Combines all records from the first table with all records from the second table.

Creating Joins in Access

1. Open Query Design View: Go to the Create tab and click Query Design.
2. Add Tables: Add the tables you want to join.
3. Define Relationship: Drag the common field from one table to the related field in the other table.
4. Select Join Type: Double-click the line connecting the two tables to open the Join Properties dialog box. Choose the appropriate join type.
5. Add Fields to Query Grid: Drag the fields you want to include in the results to query design grid.
6. Run the Query: Click Run to view the results in Datasheet View.

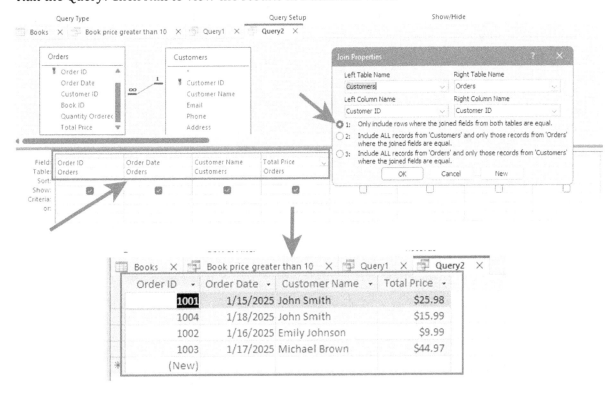

IV.   TOTAL IN QUERIES

Totals allow you to perform aggregate calculations like sums, averages, counts for grouped data.

1. Open Query Design View: Go to the Create tab and select Query Design.

2. Add Tables or Queries: Add the relevant table(s) or query(s) to the design grid.

3. Enable Totals: Click Totals in the Query Design tab. A Total row will appear in the query design grid.

4. Select Aggregate Functions: In the Total row, choose an aggregate function (e.g., Sum, Count, Average) for the field you want to summarize.

5. Run the Query: Click Run to view the grouped and aggregated data.

Example: Find the total quantity ordered of each customer.

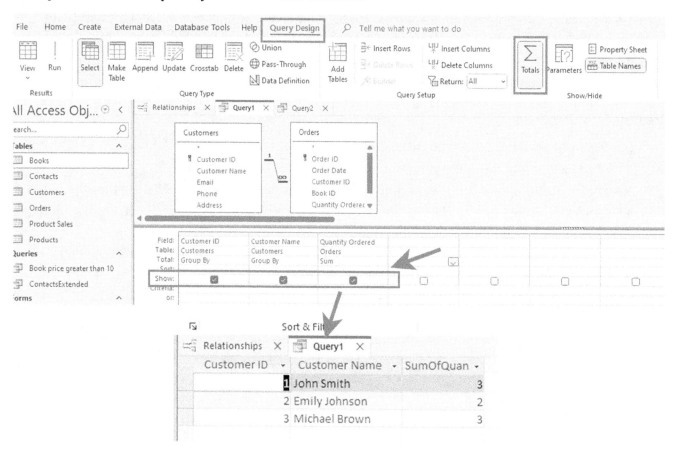

CHAPTER 6: FINDING, FILTERING, AND SORTING DATA

I. CREATING A SIMPLE FILTER

A filter temporarily limits the records displayed in a table, query, or form based on specified conditions. Filters are ideal for:

- Narrowing down large datasets.
- Locating specific records quickly.
- Conducting preliminary analysis without creating a separate query.

Steps to Apply a Simple Filter

1. Open the Table, Query, or Form: Navigate to the table, query, or form you want to filter.
2. Select the Field to Filter: Click the drop-down arrow in the column header (Datasheet View) or right-click a field in a form.
3. Apply a Filter: Choose a predefined filter option:
   » For text fields: Equals, Does Not Equal, Contains.
   » For numeric fields: Greater Than, Less Than, Between.
   » For date fields: Today, This Month, This Year.
4. View the Filtered Results: Access displays only the records that match your selected criteria.
5. Remove the Filter: Click the Toggle Filter button in the Home tab to remove the filter and display all records.

II. CREATING A FILTER FROM A SELECTION

A filter from a selection uses the value of a selected field to display only matching records. For example, selecting a customer name and applying this filter will show only records associated with that customer.

Steps to Create a Filter from a Selection

1. Open the Table, Query, or Form: Navigate to the table, query, or form where you want to use filter.
2. Select a Value: Click a field in the record that contains the value you want to filter by.
3. Apply the Filter: Choose Selection in the Sort & Filter group.
4. View the Results: Access displays only records where the selected field matches the chosen value.

Editing or Removing a Selection-Based Filter

1. Edit the Filter:
   » Open the Filter by Form view to adjust the criteria.
   » Access the filter settings in the Sort & Filter group of the Home tab.
2. Remove the Filter: Click Toggle Filter in the Home tab to remove all applied filters.

III. CREATING A FILTER FROM A SEARCH ITEM

A filter from a search item involves entering specific text, numbers, or dates into a search box to display only the records that match the input. This method is ideal for quick and focused searches.

Steps to Create a Filter from a Search Item

1. Open the Table, Query, or Form: Navigate to the table, query, or form you want to filter.

2. Use the Search Box: Locate the Search Box in the bottom-left corner of the Datasheet View or Form View.

3. Enter the Search Item:

   » Type the specific value you're looking for (e.g., a name, number, or date).

   » As you type, Access highlights the first matching record in real-time.

4. Apply the Filter: Once you locate the record, right-click the matching field and select Filter by Selection to filter all records that match the search item.

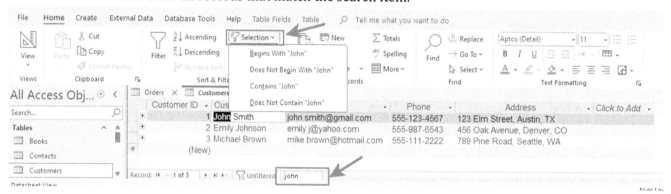

IV. USING THE FIND COMMAND

The **Find Command** searches for records containing specific text, numbers, or dates within a selected field or across the entire table or form. Unlike filters, the Find Command doesn't hide non-matching records but highlights the matching ones.

Steps to Use the Find Command

1. Open the Table, Query, or Form: Navigate to the data source you want to search.

2. Access the Find Command: Click Find in the Home tab or press Ctrl + F to open the Find and Replace dialog box.

3. Enter the Search Criteria: In the Find What box, type the value you're searching for. Example: Enter "John" to search for all records containing "John."

4. Select Search Options:

   » Look In: Select the current field or the entire table/query.

   » Match: Choose Any Part of Field for partial matches, Whole Field for exact matches, or Start of Field for prefix matches.

   » Search: Specify the search direction: Up, Down, or All.

5. Execute the Search:

   » Click Find Next to locate the first matching record.

   » Continue clicking Find Next to navigate through all matches.

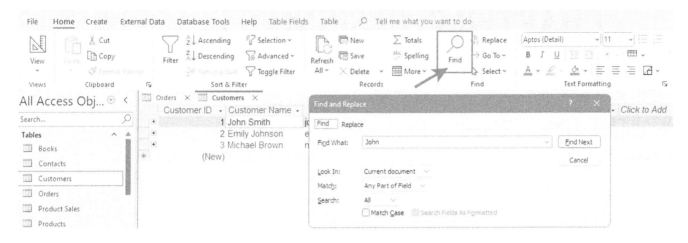

V.   SORTING YOUR RECORDS IN MICROSOFT ACCESS

Sorting records in Microsoft Access allows you to organize your data in a meaningful order, making it easier to analyze and navigate. You can sort records alphabetically, numerically, or by date, depending on the field type.

Steps to Sort Records

1.   Open the Table, Query, or Form: Navigate to the data source where you want to apply sorting.
2.   Select the Field to Sort: Click the column header (in Datasheet View) or select the field in Form View.
3.   Apply Sorting: In the Home tab, click Ascending or Descending in the Sort & Filter group.
    »   Ascending: A to Z for text, smallest to largest for numbers, and oldest to newest for dates.
    »   Descending: Z to A for text, largest to smallest for numbers, and newest to oldest for dates.
4.   View the Sorted Results: Access rearranges the records based on the selected sort order.

Sorting on Multiple Fields

When sorting on multiple fields, the sort order is applied hierarchically.

1.   Open the table or query in Design View.
2.   Add the fields to the query grid in the order of priority for sorting.
3.   In the Sort row, select Ascending or Descending for each field.
4.   Run the query to view the sorted results.

Example:

• Fields: Last Name (Primary Sort), First Name (Secondary Sort).
• Result: Records sorted alphabetically by last name, and within each last name, sorted by first name.

CHAPTER 7: DESIGNING FORMS & REPORTS AND AUTOMATION

I.   CREATING A SIMPLE FORM

Using the Form Wizard:

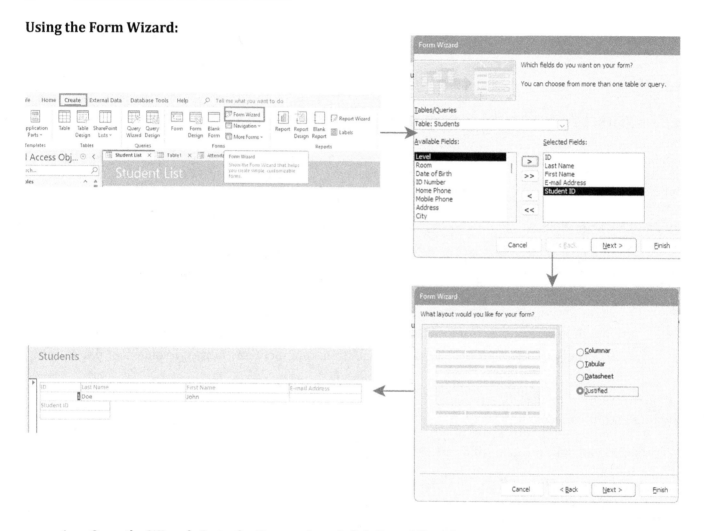

1.   Open the Wizard: Go to the Create tab and click Form Wizard.
2.   Select the Data Source: Choose the table or query to base the form on.
3.   Pick the Fields: Add the fields you want to include in the form.
4.   Select a Layout: Choose a format, such as columnar or tabular.
5.   Name the form: Insert name for your form.
6.   Generate the Form: Click Finish to create the form.

Creating a Quick Form:

1.   Select the table or query in the Navigation Pane.
2.   Go to the Create tab and click Form. Access generates a basic form automatically.

Basic Controls for Forms

Forms can include various controls to facilitate data entry and navigation:

- Text Boxes: Allow users to type or edit data in a field.
- Labels: Display field names or instructions.
- Combo Boxes: Provide dropdown lists of predefined options.
- Buttons: Perform actions like saving records or opening other forms.

Adding Controls:

- Use the Field List Pane to drag fields onto the form.
- Add buttons or dropdowns from the Design tab for enhanced functionality.

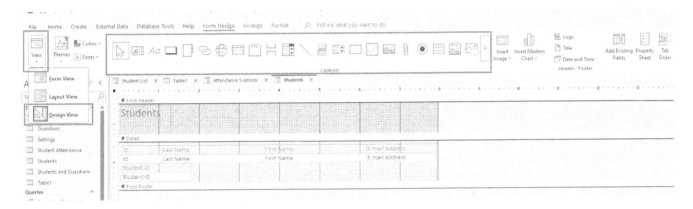

Managing Data Using Forms

Forms not only simplify data entry but also make it easier to navigate and update records.

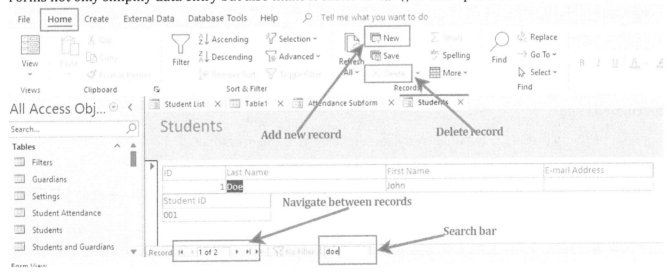

Navigating Records:

- Use the navigation buttons at the bottom of the form to move between records.
- Add new records by clicking the New (blank) record button.

Editing and Deleting Data:

- Select a field and update its content directly.
- To delete a record, use the Delete Record button in the Home tab.

Search and Filter:

- Use the search bar at the bottom of the form to find specific records.
- Apply filters by right-clicking on a field and selecting a filter option.

II.   ADVANCED TECHNIQUES FOR DESIGNING FORMS

After learning the basics of creating forms, this section focuses on advanced techniques for designing forms that are both functional and visually appealing. Advanced design helps improve usability, streamlines workflows, and supports specific database tasks.

Use Design View for Precision

- Switch to Design View for greater control over the form's structure and layout.
- Access the Property Sheet to fine-tune the settings for each field and control.

Add Form Sections: Divide your form into logical sections to improve readability:

- Form Header and Footer: Add titles, instructions, or summary fields.
- Detail Section: Display the main fields for data entry or viewing.

Incorporate Navigation Tools: Add navigation buttons to simplify movement between records or forms:

- Use the Button Wizard to create buttons for saving, deleting, or navigating records.
- Include Next Record and Previous Record buttons for easier data review.

Optimize for Multiple Users

- Use tabs or subforms to prevent clutter while displaying related data. Example: Create a tab for customer information and another for orders.
- Add conditional formatting to highlight fields that require attention.

Calculated Fields

- Add calculated fields to display dynamic results based on user inputs.
- Example: Display total order cost by calculating [Quantity] * [Unit Price].

Subforms

- Embed subforms to display related data.
- Example: In a customer form, include a subform that lists all orders for that customer.

Interactive Charts

- Add charts to visualize data trends directly in the form.
- Example: Show monthly sales performance in a bar or line chart.

Dynamic Dropdowns

- Create combo boxes that filter options based on other fields. Example: A "City" dropdown that updates based on the selected "State."
- Use queries as the row source for dynamic control behavior.

Interactive Buttons

- Add buttons for advanced actions. Example: Create a "Print Report" button that opens a linked report for the current record.
- Use macros or Visual Basic for Applications (VBA) for customized button functionality.

Custom Navigation Menus

- Replace standard navigation buttons with a custom menu using buttons or hyperlinks. Example: Add buttons labeled "Next Customer" or "Previous Order."

III. ADVANCED CUSTOMIZATION OF FORM LAYOUTS

Customizing the layout of a form allows you to optimize its functionality and visual appeal for specific tasks. To customize form layout, you can:

1. Use Grids and Guides for Precision
   » Enable the grid in Design View for better alignment of fields and controls. Go to Arrange > Align to Grid to snap controls into place.
   » Adjust spacing between controls with the Size/Space options in the Arrange tab.

2. Group and Align Controls
   » Group related fields for clarity: use the Control Layout feature to create stacked or tabular layouts.
   » Align controls precisely: use the Align tool to ensure vertical or horizontal consistency.

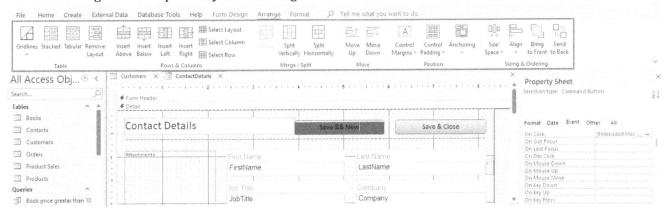

3. Add Tabs for Organized Data
   » Divide fields into tabs for a cleaner layout. Example: Create separate tabs for "Personal Information" and "Order History."
   » Use the Tab Control from the Design tab to add dynamic tabbed sections.

4. Incorporate Subforms
   » Use subforms to display related data without overcrowding the main form. Example: Show customer details in the main form and their orders in a subform.

» Link the subform to the main form using **Parent/Child Fields** to maintain data relationships.

IV.   GENERATING REPORTS FOR DATA ANALYSIS

A report is a formatted output of data from your tables or queries. Reports can display data in a way that is easy to interpret, with options for grouping, sorting, and summarizing information.

Key Uses of Reports:

- Data Summaries: Generate summaries such as sales totals, inventory counts, or attendance logs.
- Professional Documentation: Create polished outputs like invoices, or financial statements.
- Data Insights: Highlight trends or patterns using charts and calculated fields.

1.   CREATING A BASIC REPORT

You can quickly create a report based on a table or query using Access's built-in tools.

Steps to Create a Report Automatically:

1. Open the table or query you want the report to be based on.
2. Go to the **Create** tab on the ribbon.
3. Click **Report** in the Reports group.
4. Access generates a report that includes all the fields in the selected table or query.

Create a Basic Report using the Report Wizard:

1. Navigate to the **Create** tab and click **Report Wizard**.
2. Select the table or query to base the report on.
3. Choose the fields to include in the report.
4. Define grouping levels (e.g., group sales data by region).
5. Select a layout and style.
6. Click **Finish** to generate the report.

Start with a Blank Report

1. Go to the **Create** tab and click **Blank Report**.
2. Use the **Field List Pane** to add fields manually.
3. Adjust the layout and formatting in Design View.

2.   CUSTOMIZING REPORTS

Reports can be fully customized to match your specific needs and preferences.

Designing the Layout:

- Use Layout View to rearrange fields, adjust sizes, and modify the report structure.
- In Design View, access more advanced customization options like adding headers, footers, and control properties.

Grouping and Sorting:

- In Design View, click Group & Sort in the Design tab.
- Add grouping levels (e.g., group sales data by region).
- Define sorting order (e.g., sort within groups by date or amount).

Adding Charts:

- Go to the Design tab and select Insert Modern Chart.
- Choose a chart type and configure its data source.

Incorporating Calculated Fields:

- Add calculated fields to perform operations directly in the report.

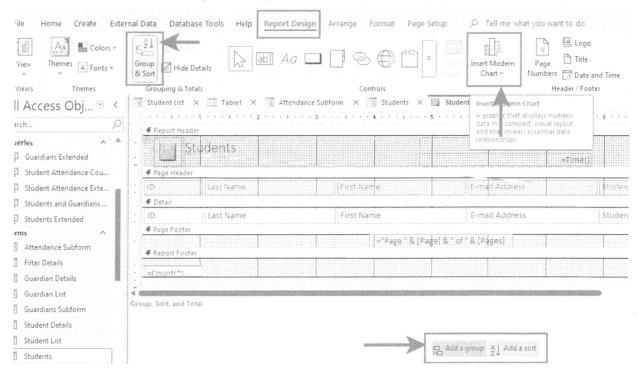

Advanced Reporting Features

1. Subreports
   - » Embed subreports to display related data.
   - » Example: A sales report with a subreport showing order details for each region.

2. Dynamic Filtering
   - » Enable users to filter data directly in the report.
   - » Example: Add dropdown menus for filtering by date or category.

3. FORMATTING REPORTS

Formatting Options:

- Use themes from the Design tab to apply consistent styling.
- Adjust page setup (margins, orientation) under File > Print > Page Setup.

Applying Conditional Formatting

1. Open the report in Layout View, go to the Format tab and select Conditional Formatting.
2. Select the fields you want to set conditional formatting.
3. Click New Rule in the Conditional Formatting Rules Manager.
4. Define the rule and formatting (e.g., highlight orders over $1,000 in bold red text).
5. Click OK to apply the rule.

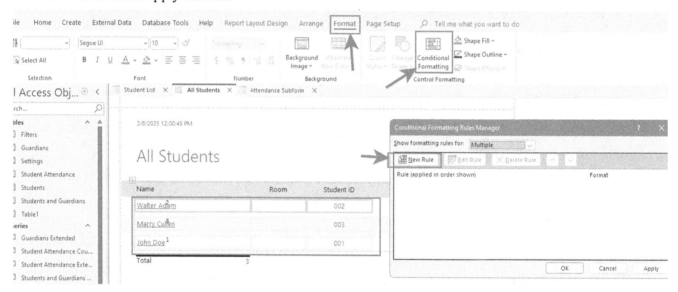

V. INTRODUCTION TO MACROS AND MODULES

1. WHAT ARE MACROS IN ACCESS?

A **macro** is a predefined set of actions that Access executes in sequence. Think of it as a simple form of programming that allows you to automate tasks without needing advanced coding skills.

Key Uses of Macros:

- Automating repetitive actions, such as opening forms or running queries.
- Validating data input to ensure consistency and accuracy.
- Triggering specific actions based on user interactions, such as clicking a button.

Creating a Macro:

1. Go to the **Create** tab on the ribbon.
2. Click **Macro** in the Macros & Code group.

3. Use the **Macro Builder** to add actions:

   » Select an action (e.g., OpenForm, RunQuery) from the dropdown menu.

   » Specify parameters for each action, such as the name of the form or query.

4. Save the macro with a descriptive name.

5. Test the macro by right-clicking and running it from the navigation pane or attaching it to a control, like a button.

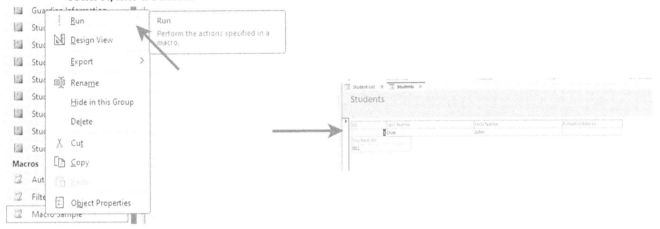

2. WHAT ARE MODULES IN ACCESS?

Modules are containers for Visual Basic for Applications (VBA) code. VBA is a programming language that allows you to create more advanced functionalities and customize database behavior.

Key Uses of Modules:

- Creating complex automation that goes beyond what macros can achieve.
- Writing custom functions for calculations or data manipulation.
- Integrating Access with external applications or databases.

Creating a Module:

1. Go to the **Create** tab on the ribbon.
2. Click **Module** in the Macros & Code group. The **VBA Editor** will open.
3. Write your VBA code in the editor and save the module with a descriptive name.

Comparing Macros and Modules

Feature	Macros	Modules (VBA)
Ease of Use	Beginner-friendly; no coding required	Requires knowledge of VBA
Flexibility	Limited to predefined actions	Fully customizable
Complexity	Ideal for simple automation	Best for advanced functionalities

3. ATTACHING MACROS OR VBA TO OBJECTS

Both macros and modules can be attached to database objects like forms, reports, and buttons to trigger actions.

Attaching a Macro:

1. Open the object in **Design View**. Select the control (e.g., a button).
2. Open the **Property Sheet** and find the **Event** tab.
3. Choose the macro to attach under the desired event (e.g., On Click).

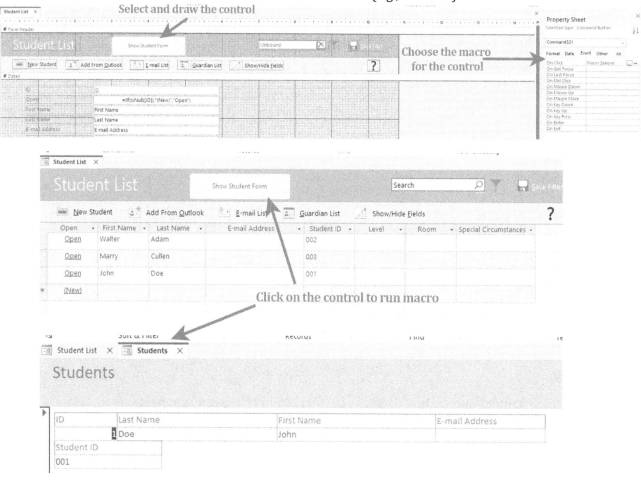

Attaching VBA Code:

1. Open the object in **Design View**.
2. Select the control (e.g., a button).
3. In the Property Sheet, click the **Build** button next to the event you want to customize.
4. Write the VBA code in the editor and save.

MASTERING MICROSOFT DESIGNER

CREATE YOUR OWN VISUAL CONTENT WITH A CLOUD-BASED APPLICATION

CHAPTER 1: GETTING STARTED

Microsoft Designer is a cloud-based design application that helps you create visual content such as flyers, posters, social graphics, and digital announcements using templates and AI assistance. Unlike Publisher (which will be retiring in October 2026), Designer runs entirely online and does not require installation.

Microsoft Designer is best suited for flyers, social graphics, posters and digital announcements. It is not designed for long documents, book layouts, or multi-page publications with complex formatting.

Designer replaces traditional desktop publishing with cloud-based design:

- Use templates or prompts to design faster.
- Edit layouts visually instead of manually positioning every element.
- Export instantly for print or digital use.
- Design from anywhere using a browser.

You can start designing from a prompt, a template, or a blank canvas.

I.   GETTING STARTED WITH MICROSOFT DESIGNER

1.   ACCESSING MICROSOFT DESIGNER

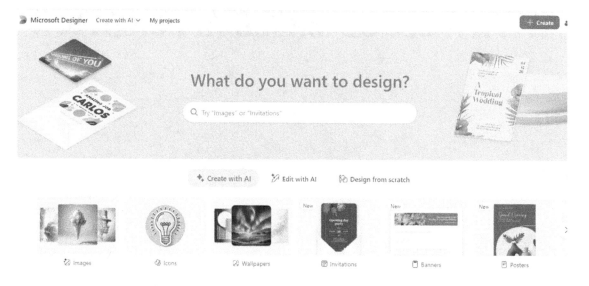

Microsoft Designer runs entirely in your browser.

1. Open your web browser.
2. Go to designer.microsoft.com.
3. Sign in using a Microsoft account (free or Microsoft 365 account).

Once signed in, you will see the Designer home screen where you can begin creating a new design.

2.   STARTING A NEW DESIGN

Microsoft Designer gives you three different entry points to start a project. The option you choose depends on whether you want AI assistance, editing help, or full manual control. Instead of one single prompt box that controls everything, Designer now separates design creation into clear modes.

i.   Create with AI

This option guides you through content-based creation using AI.

1.   On the home screen, click Create with AI.

2.   Designer first asks what type of project you want to create before generating any designs. For example: Poster, Flyer, Invitation, Greeting card, Social post, Banner, Image.

3.   After selecting your content type, you'll be taken to a design screen where you can:

» Type your prompt or description

» Upload an image (optional)

» Choose size and layout

» Click Create

4.   Designer then generates layout suggestions based on your description and format selection. You can open any design and edit it fully.

Choose Create with AI when:

• You want layouts generated from written instructions

• You already know what you want to design

• You want creative direction from AI

• You want quick results without starting from scratch

ii.   Edit with AI

This option is used when you already have an image or design and want AI to improve or modify it.

1. Click Edit with AI to unlock editing tools.
2. Example features include: remove background, generative erase, frame images, upscale images, edit portions of photos or apply AI adjustments.

This mode focuses on enhancing existing visuals, not creating layouts from prompts.

Choose Edit with AI when:

- You already have an image
- You want to enhance or clean it
- You need AI-powered image editing
- You are not creating a layout from scratch

iii. Design from Scratch

This option is for full manual control.

1. Click Design from scratch.
2. After selecting a format, you are given a blank canvas where you can:
   » Choose a template to edit
   » Add text manually
   » Insert visuals
   » Adjust layout
   » Resize freely
   » Build the design yourself

II. WORKSPACE LAYOUT

1.   MAIN COMPONENTS OF THE WORKSPACE

Canvas Area: This is the main editing space where your design appears. All text, images, and elements are placed here. The canvas changes size depending on the format you selected (Poster, Flyer, Social post, etc.).

You can:

- Click directly on elements to edit them
- Drag items to reposition
- Resize objects by dragging corners
- Zoom in or out using the top controls

Left Editing Panel: The left panel changes based on what you select, but it is always the main control area when building a design. Common tools include:

- Edit: Used for adjusting objects already on the canvas.
- Text: Add new text boxes or headings.
- My media: Upload and reuse your own images and files.
- Visuals: Access icons, illustrations, and decorative graphics.
- Markup: Add manual drawing or emphasis lines.
- Layers: See every object stacked in your design and reorder them.Items are added using drag-and-drop.

Top Command Bar: At the top of the screen, you'll find essential controls such as Undo / Redo, Zoom controls, Copy the entire canva as an image or Export and share options.

2.   EDITING CONTROLS

When you click an object, formatting tools appear. For example:

- Text selections show font tools
- Images show size and adjustment options
- Groups show grouping controls

The interface changes based on what you select. If you don't see formatting tools:

- Make sure something is selected
- Click directly on the object itself
- Use the Layers panel to select hidden elements

III.   EDITING CONTENT AND OBJECTS

Microsoft Designer adjusts tools based on what you click. There is no fixed toolbar. Instead, the interface changes depending on whether you select text, images, or the canvas.

Text Editing

Text is fully editable and behaves like normal formatted content rather than a single image. When you click on text, the Text Editing Bar appears at the top of the screen. From here you can change font, adjust size, format text and adjust alignments, effects.

When editing text, focus on readability first. A design that looks decorative but cannot be read quickly fails its purpose. Adjust font size so it remains readable on both large and small screens. Avoid placing long paragraphs on a single design. Instead, break content into short lines or sections. Visual design favors clarity over volume.

Image Editing

When you click an image, the Image Editing Panel appears across the top. On the left panel, you can also:

- Edit background: remove, blur or replace background to a color
- Transform object: erase objects, move objects or cutout the objects. These option works well when you have multiple images to work in a design.
- Apply color filters
- Apply effects
- Enhance images: upscale, focus or apply color pop.

Images are not fixed. You can resize freely, reposition, replace or stack above or below text. If an image looks pixelated after resizing, replace it with a higher-resolution image.

IV.   LAYER MANAGEMENT

Designs often include overlapping objects such as text placed over images or shapes layered under buttons. Using the layer panel, you can:

- Select any item instantly to edit
- Reorder items by dragging
- Lock or unlock layers
- Add background layers

If something suddenly vanishes from view, it is usually hidden behind another object. Bring it forward until it becomes visible again.

Grouping is useful when moving multiple elements together. For example, group a title and background shape so they remain aligned when moved.

V.   EXPORTING DESIGNS

Microsoft Designer saves your work continuously while you design. You do not need to manually press Save.

When your design is finished, export it in the format that best fits its purpose. Designer allows export as:

- PNG – for high-quality visuals and transparency
- JPG – for smaller file sizes and online sharing
- PDF (if available) – for printing or document delivery

CHAPTER 2: REFINING DESIGNS, BRANDING, AND PUBLISHING

Once your design exists, you move out of creation mode and into refinement. This is where a design changes from "generated" into "intentional." This chapter focuses on:

- Improving overall quality
- Creating multiple versions
- Maintaining consistency
- Exporting safely

At this stage, the layout is no longer the priority. Clarity and presentation come first.

I.   IMPROVING AI-GENERATED DESIGNS

AI speeds up layout creation, but it does not understand purpose, emotion, or audience the way you do. Generated designs are drafts. They should always be reviewed and adjusted.

AI gives you speed. You provide judgment.

When reviewing your design, look carefully at:

- Meaning – Does the message say what you intend?
- Tone – Does the language feel right for the audience?
- Balance – Is one part of the design overwhelming the rest?
- Legibility – Can everything be read easily at a glance?
- Contrast – Do important elements stand out clearly?

Then ask yourself:

- Is the message instantly clear?
- Does this feel deliberate or accidental?
- Does anything look out of place or unnecessary?

Small adjustments often make the biggest difference. A new font, stronger color contrast, or simplified wording can completely change how professional a design feels. Smooth designs look planned, not assembled.

II.   REPLACING SUGGESTED IMAGES

Images influence how people react before they ever read your text. Designer may choose images automatically, but automated visuals rarely match your message perfectly. Suggested images often:

- Feel distant or generic
- Miss emotional context or don't reflect your style or tone

Images should never compete with your message. They should quietly support it.

III. CREATING DESIGN VARIATIONS

A design rarely exists in only one form. What works as a flyer may not work as a social post. What fits a poster may not fit a phone screen.

Instead of rebuilding the design from scratch, create variations.

Recommended Workflow

1. Duplicate the design page. Microsoft Designer allows to have different sizes in a project so all of your variations will be connected in a project.
2. Resize it for the new format.
3. Adjust layout spacing and text size as needed.

Always keep your original design untouched. Variations should be created from copies, not from the only version. This prevents accidental loss and makes it easy to compare versions later.

IV. BRANDING AND CONSISTENCY

Branding in Microsoft Designer isn't about fancy theory. It is about repetition. When your designs repeat visual patterns, they become recognizable. Consistency comes from:

*   Colors
*   Fonts
*   Image style
*   Layout structure
*   Tone of language

If these change randomly, the design feels scattered even if each individual design looks good.

1.   CHOOSING YOUR BRANDING BASICS

Before continuing, decide:

- One main color
- One secondary color
- One main font
- One optional accent font

Write these down and stick to them. The fewer decisions you make each time you design, the more consistent your work becomes.

2.   WORKING WITH LOGOS

If you use a logo, handle it carefully. Upload the logo once and reuse it across designs. Place it:

- In a consistent location
- At a readable size
- With enough empty space around it

Never stretch a logo to "fit." Resize it proportionally. A distorted logo weakens trust instantly.

3.   MAINTAINING TEXT TONE

Design includes language, not just visuals. A brand should feel familiar in both appearance and voice. Choose a tone and keep it stable:

- Informational
- Friendly
- Professional

Switching tone between designs creates confusion. A consistent voice builds recognition. If your audience knows what to expect, they trust your communication more easily.

V.   CREATING REUSABLE LAYOUTS

Microsoft Designer does not provide traditional saved templates the way Publisher did, but you can create your own reusable designs manually. When you find a layout that works well, treat it as a foundation rather than a one-time design.

How to Build Your Own Layout System

1. Create one clean, well-structured design.
2. Duplicate it.
3. Replace the content.
4. Keep the overall structure the same.

This creates a simple personal design system. Reusable layouts save time and help your work stay consistent. Instead of redesigning from scratch every time, you reuse a structure that already works. Over time, you will build a small collection of layouts you trust.

MASTERING MICROSOFT ONEDRIVE

YOUR GUIDE TO CLOUD STORAGE AND COLLABORATION

CHAPTER 1: GETTING STARTED

I. WHAT IS MICROSOFT ONEDRIVE?

Microsoft OneDrive is a powerful cloud storage platform that allows you to securely store, access, and share your files from virtually anywhere. Whether you're using a desktop, laptop, tablet, or smartphone, OneDrive ensures your important documents, photos, and videos are always within reach.

Key Benefits of OneDrive

- Anywhere Access: Your files travel with you, accessible on any device with an internet connection.
- Seamless Collaboration: Work with others in real time on shared documents.
- Automatic Sync: Keep your files updated across all your devices.
- Backup and Security: Protect your data with features like Personal Vault and file recovery.

II. ACCESSING ONEDRIVE: DESKTOP, MOBILE, AND WEB

Signing Into OneDrive on Desktop

1. Open the OneDrive App: On most Windows devices, OneDrive comes pre-installed. Search for "OneDrive" in the Start menu and open the app.
2. Enter Your Microsoft Account Details: Input your email address and password. Click "Sign In."
3. Set Up File Syncing: Select which folders to sync from your OneDrive account to your device.

Signing Into OneDrive on Mobile Devices

1. Download the OneDrive App: Open the Google Play Store or App Store and search for "OneDrive." Install the app.
2. Open the App: Launch OneDrive and sign in with your Microsoft account.
3. Grant Permissions: Allow the app to access your photos and files for seamless syncing.

Signing Into OneDrive on the Web

1. Visit the OneDrive Website: Open your browser and go to onedrive.live.com.
2. Log In with Your Microsoft Account: Enter your email and password, then click "Sign In."

III. EXPLORING THE ONEDRIVE INTERFACE

The Navigation Pane

The navigation pane is your primary tool for accessing different sections of OneDrive. Depending on the platform, it may include:

- Files: Displays all your stored files and folders.
- Recent: Shows files you've recently accessed or edited.
- Shared: Lists files and folders shared with you or by you.
- Recycle Bin: Holds deleted items for recovery.

- Personal Vault: A secure area for storing sensitive documents.

File View: the central area of the interface, where you can see and manage your files and folders.

- Sorting and Filtering: Organize files by name, date modified, size, or type.
- File Actions: Tick on the Selection area before a file to access options such as Open, Share, Download, and Delete.

Search Bar: located prominently at the top of the interface.

- Search Suggestions: Start typing, and OneDrive will suggest relevant files, folders, or keywords.
- Filters: Narrow your search by file type, modification date, or shared status.
- Advanced Search Tips: Use keywords like "type:PDF" for a specific format.

Toolbar: quick access to essential actions:

- Add new: Create new folders, documents, or notebooks directly in OneDrive.
- Filter by name or person; Find files easier by filtering.
- Settings: Customize your OneDrive experience, including notifications and storage details.

Desktop Integration

On desktop, OneDrive integrates seamlessly with your file explorer or Finder:

- OneDrive Folder: Appears as a folder in your file manager, allowing drag-and-drop file.
- Status Icons: green checkmark (file is synced), cloud icon (online-only) or red "X" (sync error).

IV. SYNCING DEVICES WITH ONEDRIVE FOR OFFLINE ACCESS

Syncing OneDrive on Desktop

1. Open OneDrive Settings:
   » On Windows, click the OneDrive cloud icon in the system tray (bottom-right corner).
   » On Mac, click the OneDrive icon in the menu bar.

2. Choose Folders to Sync: Go to the Account tab and click Choose Folders. Select the folders you want available offline.

3. Sync Location and Status:
   » By default, synced files are stored in the OneDrive folder in File Explorer (Windows) or Finder (Mac). You can change the location if needed.

» Synced files will show a green checkmark, while online-only files will display a cloud icon.

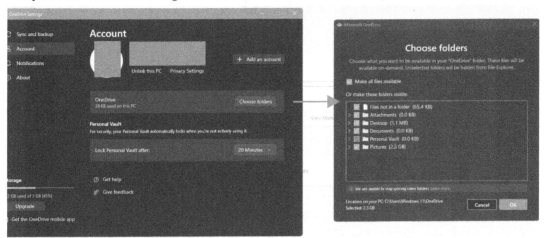

Syncing OneDrive on Mobile Devices

1. Enable Offline Access:

    » Open the OneDrive app and locate the file or folder you want to sync.

    » Tap the More Options (three dots) next to the file or folder and select Make Available Offline.

2. Access Synced Files: Files marked for offline use will be saved locally and accessible without an internet connection.

3. Manage Offline Files: Navigate to the Offline tab within the app to view all files currently downloaded to your device.

Managing Sync Settings

*   Files On-Demand (Windows and Mac):

    » This feature allows you to keep files online-only until you need them, saving storage space.

    » To enable, go to OneDrive Settings > Files On-Demand and check the box.

*   Pause Syncing:

    » If you're on a limited data connection or need to conserve resources, you can temporarily pause syncing from the OneDrive settings menu.

*   Resolve Sync Issues:

    » Look for red "X" icons indicating sync errors. These are often caused by file conflicts or insufficient space and can be resolved by checking your sync settings.

CHAPTER 2: MANAGING FILES & FOLDERS

I.   HOW TO CREATE A FOLDER ON ONEDRIVE

Organizing files is essential for keeping your OneDrive account tidy and easy to navigate. Creating folders helps you group related files together, making it simpler to locate, share, or manage your data.

Creating a Folder

1. Navigate to the Desired Location: go to the location where you want the new folder.
2. Create the Folder:
   » Click the Add New button (for web) or right-click inside the folder (for Desktop) or tap the + button (for Mobile) and select Folder from the dropdown menu.
   » Enter a name for the folder and click Create.
3. Sync Automatically: The folder will sync to your OneDrive account and be accessible on other devices.

Renaming or Moving Folders

- Renaming Folders: Right-click (or long-press on mobile) the folder, select Rename, and enter the new name.
- Moving Folders:
   » Drag and drop the folder to a new location (on desktop).
   » On the web or mobile app, select the folder, choose Move to, and pick the new location.

II.   HOW TO SORT OUT YOUR FILES

Sorting files helps you quickly find what you're looking for by organizing them based on different criteria.

On OneDrive Web:

1. Navigate to the Folder: Open the folder containing the files you want to sort.
2. Sort Files:
   » Click the Sort button (usually at the top of the file view).
   » Choose a sorting option such as Name, Date Modified, Size, or Type.

On Desktop (File Explorer or Finder):

1. Navigate to Your OneDrive Folder: Open File Explorer (Windows) or Finder (Mac).
2. Sort Files: Click the column headers (e.g., Name, Date Modified) to sort files accordingly.

On Mobile:

1. Open the OneDrive App: Navigate to the folder you want to sort.
2. Sort Options: Tap the Sort icon (usually three horizontal lines) and select your preferred sorting criteria.

III. VIEWING RECENT ACTIVITIES ON ONEDRIVE

Tracking recent activities on OneDrive helps you stay updated on file changes, uploads, and collaborations. Whether you're managing your files or working with a team, understanding what has changed recently ensures you're always in sync with the latest updates.

Viewing Recent Activities on OneDrive Web

1. Go to the Recent Tab:
   » In the navigation pane on the left, click on Recent.
   » This view displays a chronological list of files you've recently opened, edited, or accessed.

2. Check Activity Details:
   » Hover over a file to see additional details, such as the last modified time and who made changes (if shared).

Viewing Recent Activities on Desktop: Files you recently accessed may appear in the Quick Access section of File Explorer.

Viewing Recent Activities on Mobile Devices

1. Tap on Recent: Look for the Recent tab or icon at the bottom of the screen.
2. Review File Changes: View a list of recently accessed, edited, or uploaded files.

Using File History for Detailed Changes

For files stored in OneDrive, you can view version history to see detailed changes over time.

1. Access File Version History (Web):
   » Right-click on a file and select Version History to see past versions, including who made edits and when.

2. Restore Previous Versions:
   » From the version history view, you can restore an earlier version if needed.

261

CHAPTER 3:
SHARING AND COLLABORATION

I. FILE SHARING ON ONEDRIVE

OneDrive's sharing features make it simple to collaborate with others, whether you're working on a team project or sharing personal files. You can share files or folders securely with customizable permissions to ensure the right people have the access they need.

Sharing Files or Folders on OneDrive Web

1. Locate the File or Folder: Navigate to the file or folder you want to share.
2. Share the File or Folder: Click the Share button.
3. Set Permissions: Choose whether recipients can Edit or View Only.
4. Send the Link: Enter the email addresses of recipients or copy the link to share manually.

Sharing Files or Folders on Desktop

1. Open the OneDrive Folder: Locate the file or folder in File Explorer (Windows) or Finder (Mac).
2. Right-Click and Share: Right-click the item and select Share from the OneDrive context menu.
3. Set Sharing Options: Configure permissions, add recipients, and generate a sharing link directly through the dialog box.

Sharing Files or Folders on Mobile Devices

1. Open the OneDrive App: Navigate to the file or folder you want to share.
2. Tap the More Options Button: Tap the three dots next to the file or folder and select Share.
3. Choose Sharing Preferences: Configure permissions and either send the link via email or copy it for manual sharing.

Viewing Shared Files:

1. On OneDrive Web: Click on the Shared tab to view files shared with or by you.
2. On Desktop or Mobile: Look for the Shared section in the app or file manager.

Stopping Sharing or Changing Permissions:

1. Access Sharing Settings: Open the shared file or folder and click Manage Access.
2. Modify Permissions: Change permissions, stop sharing, or revoke access for specific individuals.

II.   REAL-TIME COLLABORATION ON OFFICE FILES

OneDrive's integration with Microsoft Office enables real-time collaboration on Word, Excel, and PowerPoint files. This feature allows multiple people to work on the same document simultaneously, whether for team projects, shared reports, or presentations.

Collaborating in Real Time on OneDrive Web

1.   Open the File in Office Online:
   »   Navigate to the file. Click the file to open it in the corresponding Office app.

2.   Share the File with Collaborators:
   »   Click the Share button in the top-right corner of the Office app.
   »   Enter email addresses, set permissions, and send the link.

3.   Collaborate Simultaneously:
   »   As others join the document, you'll see their names or placeholders (e.g., "Guest Contributor") and the sections they're editing.
   »   Changes are saved automatically, and edits are visible in real time.

Collaborating on the Desktop App

1.   Open the File from OneDrive: Navigate to your OneDrive folder in File Explorer (Windows) or Finder (Mac) and open the file.

2.   Enable Sharing:
   »   Click Share in the top-right corner of the Office app.
   »   Share the document by inviting collaborators via email or generating a link.

3.   Track Changes in Real Time:
   »   Changes made by others appear in the document with their names tagged to the edits.
   »   Use the Review tab to track changes or add comments for clarity.

Collaborating on Mobile Devices

1.   Open the File in the Office Mobile App: Locate the file, and open it in the Word, Excel, or PowerPoint app.
2.   Share the File: Use the Share option to invite collaborators or copy a link to share manually.
3.   Edit Together: Collaborators can make edits, with updates syncing in real time.

III.   MANAGING SHARED LIBRARIES AND TEAM WORKSPACES

What Are Shared Libraries?

Shared libraries are collaborative spaces where teams can store, access, and edit files together. These libraries are often connected to Microsoft Teams or SharePoint and are accessible directly through OneDrive.

Key Features:

- Centralized Storage: A single location for team files and folders.
- Shared Ownership: Files belong to the library, not individual members.
- Seamless Integration: Linked with Teams, SharePoint, and other Microsoft 365 apps.

Accessing Shared Libraries in OneDrive

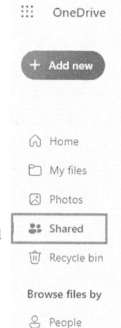

1. Navigate to Shared Libraries:
   » In the left navigation pane, click on Shared.
   » Select the library you want to access.
2. Access Files: Browse, upload, or edit files directly within the shared library.
3. On Desktop: Shared libraries may appear as separate folders in File Explorer (Windows) or Finder (Mac) if synced locally.

Creating a Shared Library

1. Use Microsoft Teams or SharePoint: Shared libraries are typically created when a new Microsoft Team or SharePoint site is set up.
2. Customize Library Settings: Adjust permissions, folder structure, and other settings based on your team's needs.

Managing Files in Shared Libraries

1. Organizing Files:
   » Use folders and subfolders to maintain structure.
   » Name files descriptively to make them easy to locate.
2. Setting Permissions:
   » Adjust Access Levels: Owners can grant edit or view-only permissions to specific team members.
   » Manage External Sharing: Limit access to external users if needed for sensitive projects.
3. Tracking Changes:
   » Version History: Review and restore previous versions of files to track edits or revert changes.
   » Activity Tracking: Use the Details pane to see recent activity on files.

IV. RECOVERING FILES WITH RECYCLE BIN AND VERSION HISTORY

Accidentally deleting files can be stressful, but OneDrive's Recycle Bin makes recovering them a breeze. This section explains how to restore deleted files, manage the Recycle Bin, and ensure important data is never lost.

Accessing the Recycle Bin

- On OneDrive Web:
   » Navigate to the Recycle Bin: In the left-hand navigation pane, click on Recycle Bin.
   » View Deleted Files: All recently deleted files and folders will be listed, along with deletion date.

- On Mobile Devices:
   » Open the OneDrive App: Tap the menu icon and select Recycle Bin from the list.

    » Review Deleted Files: Browse through recently deleted items for recovery.

- On Desktop:
  - » Files deleted locally from OneDrive folder will also appear in the web-based Recycle Bin.
  - » Check the desktop Recycle Bin if the file was removed directly from your computer.

Restoring Deleted Files

- On OneDrive Web:
  - » Select the File or Folder: Check the box next to the file(s) or folder(s) you want to restore.
  - » Click Restore: Press the Restore button at the top of the page. The items will return to their original locations.
- On Mobile: Select the File or Folder: Tap the item and choose Restore from the options.
- On Desktop: Recover Locally Deleted Files: Drag files from the desktop Recycle Bin back into your OneDrive folder.

Managing the Recycle Bin

- Storage Limits: The Recycle Bin can hold up to 10% of your total OneDrive storage space. Once it exceeds this limit, the oldest items are permanently deleted.
- Permanently Deleting Files: To free up storage, go to the Recycle Bin and select Delete Permanently for unwanted items.
- Retention Period: Deleted files remain in the Recycle Bin for up to 30 days (or longer, depending on your Microsoft 365 plan).

Preventing Accidental Deletions

- Use File Permissions: Limit editing or deletion access for shared files.
- Enable Version History: Restore earlier versions of files instead of deleting them entirely.
- Regular Backups: Sync important files with an external drive or backup service for added security.

Benefits of the Recycle Bin

- Data Recovery: Easily restore accidentally deleted files.
- User Control: Manage and organize deleted items without worrying about immediate loss.
- Safety Net: Protect against accidental deletions during team collaborations.

MASTERING MICROSOFT TO DO

ORGANIZE, TRACK, AND ACCOMPLISH MORE

CHAPTER 1: GETTING STARTED WITH MICROSOFT TO DO & TASKS

I.   INTRODUCTION TO MICROSOFT TO DO

Microsoft To Do is a digital task manager that helps you create, organize, and prioritize your tasks. It integrates with popular apps like Outlook, Teams, and Planner. This integration allows you to manage emails, appointments, and tasks in one place, providing a unified approach to productivity.

Microsoft To Do stands out because of its simplicity and integration capabilities. Here's why it's worth incorporating into your workflow:

1.   Ease of Use: The user-friendly interface makes it easy to create, manage, and organize tasks without a steep learning curve.

2.   Seamless Integration: To Do connects with Outlook and other Microsoft 365 apps, allowing you to manage tasks, flagged emails, and calendar events in one place.

3.   Flexibility: Whether you're using it for personal errands, professional projects, or team collaboration, To Do adapts to your needs.

4.   Accessibility: With desktop, mobile, and web versions, To Do ensures your tasks are always within reach.

II.   INSTALLING AND ACCESSING MICROSOFT TO DO

Microsoft To Do is available on desktop, mobile, and web, ensuring you can manage your tasks anytime, anywhere.

Desktop Application

1.   Open the Microsoft Store or Mac App Store on your computer.

2.   Search for Microsoft To Do in the search bar. Click Get to download and install the app.

3.   Once installed, open the app and sign in with your Microsoft account.

Mobile Application

1.   Open the App Store or Google Play Store on your device.

2.   Search for Microsoft To Do. Tap Get or Install to install the app.

3.   Open the app and sign in with your Microsoft account.

Web Application: Navigate to to-do.microsoft.com. Sign in with your Microsoft account to access your tasks.

III.   EXPLORING THE MICROSOFT TO DO INTERFACE

The Microsoft To Do interface is intuitive and user-friendly, designed to help you navigate and manage your tasks with ease. This section walks you through the key elements of the interface to ensure you're comfortable with its layout and features.

Navigation Bar

The navigation bar, located on the left side of the screen (desktop) or accessible via a menu (mobile), is your primary hub for switching between different sections of Microsoft To Do. Key components include:

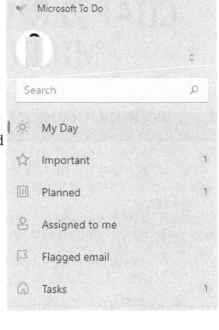

- My Day: A personalized space for planning daily tasks.
- Important: A smart list showing tasks marked as high priority.
- Planned: Tasks with assigned due dates appear here, organized by date.
- Assigned to You: Displays tasks that others have assigned to you (if using shared lists).
- Flagged Emails: Shows tasks created from flagged emails in Outlook.
- Task Lists: Custom lists you create to organize tasks by category or project.

Tips for Navigating Efficiently

- Use the Search Bar to quickly find tasks, lists, or notes.
- Rearrange lists by dragging and dropping them in the navigation bar.
- Pin important lists to the top for quick access.

IV.   CREATING TASKS

Task Creation

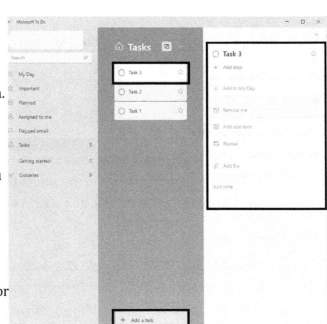

- Add new tasks using the + Add a Task button.
- Click on a task to expand it and see more options:
  » Due Dates: Set deadlines for each task.
  » Reminders: Add notifications to ensure you don't forget important tasks.
  » Priority: Mark tasks as important to highlight them in smart lists.

Attachments and Notes

- Attach files, documents, or images to tasks for easy reference.
- Add notes to tasks to provide more context or jot down ideas.

Completing Tasks

- Check the box next to a task to mark it as complete.
- Completed tasks are moved to a "Completed" section but remain accessible for review.

V.   ORGANIZING TASKS INTO LISTS

Organizing your tasks into lists is a key feature of Microsoft To Do, enabling you to categorize and manage tasks effectively. In this section, you'll learn how to create, rename, and delete lists, as well as how to organize tasks within them.

How to Create a New List

1. Click the + New List button (for desktop and web) or + Add List button(for Mobile).
2. Enter a name for your list and press Enter to save it.

Renaming a List

1. Select the list you want to rename.
2. Click or tap the list name to edit it. Enter the new name and press Enter or Done.

Deleting a List

1. Select the list you want to delete. Click or tap the three-dot menu (•••) in the top-right corner.
2. Choose Delete List from the dropdown.

Note: Deleting a list will remove all tasks within it. Be sure to move any important tasks before deleting.

Organizing Tasks Within Lists: Drag and drop tasks within a list to rearrange their order. Use this feature to prioritize tasks visually by placing the most important ones at the top.

Using My Day to Focus on Daily Priorities

"My Day" is a feature designed to help you concentrate on tasks you want to accomplish today. Tasks added to My Day are separate from your main lists but linked to them.

1. Go to the My Day section in the navigation bar.
2. Click + Add a Task to create a new task directly in My Day.
3. Use the Suggestions feature (lightbulb icon) to add tasks from your lists to My Day.
4. Suggestions are based on tasks with upcoming due dates or those marked as important.
5. At the end of each day, tasks in My Day are cleared but remain in their original lists. You can add them back to My Day the next day if needed.

VI.   ENHANCING TASKS WITH ATTACHMENTS, NOTES, AND RECURRING OPTIONS

1. ATTACHING FILES TO TASKS

Attachments are a great way to include supporting documents, images, or references directly within a task.

How to Attach a File

1. Select the task you want to enhance.
2. In the task details view, look for the Attach File option (paperclip icon).
3. Click or tap Attach File and choose the file from your device.
4. The file will be uploaded and linked to the task for easy access.

2. ADDING NOTES TO TASKS

Notes allow you to include important details, ideas, or instructions within a task.

1. Open the task you want to update.
2. In the task details view, locate the Add Note section.
3. Type your notes and click Save (if required).

3. SETTING UP RECURRING TASKS

Recurring tasks are ideal for activities you need to complete regularly, such as paying bills, attending weekly meetings, or daily reminders.

How to Create a Recurring Task

1. Create a new task or select an existing task.
2. In the task details view, find the Repeat option (circular arrow icon).
3. Choose the recurrence frequency:
   » Daily: For tasks that repeat every day.
   » Weekly: For tasks that occur once a week.
   » Monthly: For tasks that occur on a specific day each month.
   » Custom: Set a unique recurrence pattern, such as every 3 days or specific weekdays.
4. Save the settings to enable the recurrence.

Managing Recurring Tasks

- You can edit or disable a recurring task by selecting it and updating the Repeat settings.
- Completing a recurring task will automatically schedule the next instance.

CHAPTER 2: ADVANCED FEATURES AND INTEGRATIONS

I.   CUSTOMIZING LISTS WITH THEMES AND COLORS

Themes allow you to change the visual appearance of your lists, giving each list its unique style.

How to Change a List's Theme

1.   Select the list you want to customize.
2.   Click or tap the List options button (...) at the top of the list.
3.   Choose a theme from the available options: solid colors or images.

II.   ORGANIZING TASKS WITH TAGS AND CATEGORIES

What Are Tags and Categories?

- Tags: Custom labels you can add to tasks to group related items. For example, use tags like #urgent, #work, or #personal to categorize tasks across different lists.
- Categories: Predefined or custom labels integrated with Microsoft 365 apps (e.g., Outlook) to maintain consistency across tasks and emails.

How to Add a Tag to a Task

1.   Open the task you want to tag.
2.   In the Notes or Details section, type a hashtag followed by the tag name (e.g., #priority).
3.   Save the task.

Searching and Filtering by Tags

- Use the Search Bar in Microsoft To Do to locate tasks with specific tags.
- Type the tag (e.g., #urgent) to display all tasks associated, regardless of the list they belong to.

How to Apply Categories

1. Open the task and look for the Category option (available for tasks synced with Microsoft Outlook or other 365 apps).
2. Select a predefined category (e.g., "Red Category," "Project A") or create a new one.
3. Save the task to apply the category.

Viewing Tasks by Category

- Tasks assigned to categories can be viewed in both Microsoft To Do and integrated apps like Outlook.
- Use category filters to focus on specific tasks in your workflow.

Combining Tags and Categories for Maximum Efficiency

You can use tags and categories together to create a robust task organization system:

- Apply tags for specific attributes (e.g., #urgent, #lowpriority).
- Use categories to group tasks by broader themes or projects (e.g., "Marketing Campaign").

For example:

- A task could be tagged as #urgent and categorized under "Work." This allows you to search by urgency or view all work-related tasks.

III.   SEARCHING AND SORTING TASKS

How to Search for Tasks using the Search Bar

1. Locate the Search Bar at the top of the Microsoft To Do interface (desktop and web) or in the navigation menu (mobile).
2. Type keywords, tags, or task names into the search bar.
3. Press Enter (desktop) or tap the search icon (mobile) to view results.

What You Can Search For

- Task Titles: Find tasks by name or partial keywords.
- Tags: Search using hashtags (e.g., #urgent) to group related tasks.
- Notes: Locate tasks containing specific text in the notes section.
- Attachments: Search for tasks with attached files.

Tips for Effective Searching

- Use specific keywords to narrow down results.
- Combine multiple keywords (e.g., "report #urgent") for precise filtering.

Sorting Tasks

Sorting lets you arrange tasks within a list for better visibility.

1. Open the list you want to sort.

2. Select the Sort By option (usually found in the three-dot menu).
3. Choose a sorting method:
   » Alphabetical: Sort tasks by name.
   » Due Date: Arrange tasks from earliest to latest.
   » Priority: Group important tasks at the top.

Smart Lists for Automatic Organization

Microsoft To Do includes built-in smart lists to help you stay organized:

- Important: Displays all tasks marked as important.
- Planned: Groups tasks with assigned due dates.
- Assigned to You: Shows tasks assigned to you in shared lists.
- Flagged Emails: Automatically pulls in tasks created from flagged emails in Outlook.

Best Practices for Searching and Filtering

- Regularly Review Smart Lists: Use smart lists to monitor high-priority and time-sensitive tasks.
- Customize Filters: Adjust filters based on your current priorities to stay focused.
- Combine Tools: Use the search bar, filters, and sorting options together for maximum efficiency.

IV.   INTEGRATING MICROSOFT TO DO WITH OUTLOOK

One of Microsoft To Do's greatest strengths is its ability to integrate seamlessly with other applications, allowing you to manage tasks more efficiently within your existing workflow.

How To Do Works with Outlook

Microsoft To Do and Outlook Tasks are interconnected, enabling a unified experience for managing tasks.

1. Sync Tasks Automatically:

» Tasks created in Outlook's Tasks section are automatically synced to Microsoft To Do and vice versa.

2. Flag Emails:

» Flag an email in Outlook, and it appears in To Do under the Flagged Emails smart list.

Steps to Enable Integration

1. Ensure you're signed into both Outlook and Microsoft To Do with the same Microsoft account.

2. In Outlook, flag an email or create a task.

3. Open Microsoft To Do, and the flagged email or task will appear automatically.

V.   SHARING TASK LISTS FOR TEAM PROJECTS

Collaboration is a key strength of Microsoft To Do, making it easy to work with others on shared projects or goals. In this section, you'll learn how to share task lists, collaborate with others, and manage shared lists effectively.

Sharing Task Lists

1. Create or Open a List:

» Navigate to the list you want to share in the navigation bar.

2. Access the Share Option:

» Click or tap the Share button (person icon with a plus sign) in the top-right corner of the list.

3. Generate a Sharing Link:

» Microsoft To Do creates a unique link that others can use to join the shared list.

» Copy the link and share it via email, chat, or any preferred method.

4. Manage Permissions:

» Shared lists allow contributors to view, add, and complete tasks.

» If you want to stop sharing, revoke the link through the Manage Access option.

Collaborating on Shared Lists

- Adding Tasks Together

» All members with access to a shared list can add, edit, and complete tasks.

» Use subtasks to clarify individual responsibilities within a task.

- Assigning Tasks to Collaborators

» Open the shared list and select a task.

» In the task details, use the Assign To option to assign the task to a specific person.

» Assignees will receive a notification about their task.

- Tracking Progress

» Task updates, such as new additions or completions, are reflected in real-time for all collaborators.

» Use the Completed Tasks section to review what's been accomplished.

CONCLUSION

You've reached the end of the Microsoft Office 2026 Ultimate Guide. Throughout this guide, we've explored:

- Excel for analyzing and presenting data effectively with formulas, charts, and pivot tables.
- Word for crafting polished documents that communicate clearly.
- PowerPoint for creating engaging, dynamic presentations that captivate your audience.
- Outlook for managing communications and staying organized.
- Teams for connecting, meeting, and working together from anywhere.
- OneNote for capturing ideas and staying collaborative.
- Access for planning, designing, and managing robust databases that turn raw data into actionable insights.
- Designer for creating professional, visually appealing designs.
- OneDrive for secure, cloud-based storage and seamless file sharing.
- Microsoft To Do to prioritize tasks and manage your day efficiently.

Keep experimenting with what you've learned—practice new skills, explore additional advanced features, and personalize your workflow to match your unique productivity style. Stay curious, stay productive, and most importantly—keep learning.

ABOUT THE AUTHOR

Ethan Wells is a seasoned finance and accounting professional with over 14 years of experience in auditing, corporate finance, financial management, and strategic consulting. After building a strong foundation in global corporations, Ethan transitioned into a pivotal consulting role, helping startups and innovative ventures achieve sustainable growth and financial success.

Explore more titles in his Business Productivity Blueprint series to continue building your skills and boosting your productivity. From mastering Excel and Word to managing your business with QuickBooks and Office 365, there's a guide for every step of your journey.

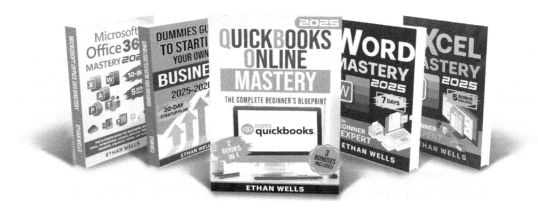

www.ingramcontent.com/pod-product-compliance
Lightning Source LLC
LaVergne TN
LVHW060121070326
832902LV00019B/3064